D1566541

The Embedded Self

*A Psychoanalytic Guide
to Family Therapy*

*In memory of my parents, Henrietta and Nathan Wirklich,
and my grandfather, Frank Sonnenblick*

The Embedded Self

*A Psychoanalytic Guide
to Family Therapy*

Mary-Joan Gerson

THE ANALYTIC PRESS

1996   Hillsdale, NJ   London

Published by
The Analytic Press, Inc.
Editorial offices:
101 West Street
Hillsdale, NJ 07642

Library of Congress Cataloging-in-Publication Data

Gerson, Mary-Joan.
The embedded self : a psychoanalytic guide to family therapy /
Mary-Joan Gerson.
      p.   cm.
  Includes bibliographical references and index.
   ISBN 0-88163-158-2
   1. Family psychotherapy.   2. Psychoanalysts.   I. Title.
RC488.5.G47   1996
616.89'156 – dc20   95-37630
                                                                          CIP

Printed in the United States of America
  10 9 8 7 6 5 4 3 2 1

Contents

	Preface	vii
1	Introduction: The Analyst and the Family	1
2	Theoretical Overview	5
3	An Orientation to Family Systems Theory	19
4	Theoretical Elaborations and Controversies	45
5	Nested Contexts	67
6	Family Patterning	87
7	Development from a Family Perspective	105
8	Diagnosis in Family Therapy	131
9	Interventions in Family Therapy	161
10	The Therapeutic Relationship	193
11	Playfulness, Authoritativeness, and Honesty	215
12	Referrals: Who? When? Where?	229
13	Epilogue	253
	References	257
	Index	267

Preface

If there is something we have learned in the last few decades in psycho-analysis it is how present we are, even when we feel we are most absent. The inflection in our voice, our posture as we sit, a spontaneous laugh—all inform our patients about the person they are working with. Writing a book for psychoanalysts tells an equally personal story.

My own interest in family therapy emerged early, in the collage of my own family life. A very late-born child, I had the vision of someone who does not fall neatly into place. Caught in oddly formed identifica-tions and alliances, I found myself seeing things from *all* perspectives. Aspects of my family experience convinced me of the impact of external circumstances (or context, as the family therapy movement would phrase it). I grew up (long before multiculturalism was the vogue) in the Lower East Side of Manhattan, a neighborhood in which every five blocks was staked out by a different European immigrant group; the appearance of the kids at school as well as the smell and look of their homes made it impossible for me to ignore the different cultures around me.

The clinical psychology program at New York University under the direction of Bernie Kalinkowitz (in the 1970s), where I earned my Ph.D., attracted some of the finest minds and hearts in psychoanalytic theory and practice as teachers and supervisors. However, as compel-ling as psychoanalytic theory was for me, I retained an interest in working with and within natural systems as a clinical complement to the therapeutically created system of the psychoanalytic dyad. No matter how subjectively focused I became or how interested I was in symbolic process and interiority, I think I always maintained the wide-angle perspective along with a zoom lens psychoanalytic focus. Thus, while I pursued psychoanalytic training in New York University's Post-doctoral Program in Psychotherapy and Psychoanalysis, where I paid little attention to family systemic thinking—other than as a by-product of my interpersonalist supervisors' characteristic interest in real events and cultural influences—I simultaneously pursued advanced family training: studying at Bronx State Hospital's family studies program for a year, teaching family therapy at the New School's clinical psychology program for three years, and consulting with senior clinicians in the New York area. When Salvador Minuchin came to New York to establish the Family Studies Institute, initiating a two-year program in family therapy supervision, I welcomed the chance to work with him.

There is a basic experiential difference between psychoanalytic treatment and family therapy. All clinical work calls on a triad of inclinations: empathy, imagination, and the ability to synthesize disparate data. However, when I work psychoanalytically, I become ensconced in a process that envelops both me and my patient. When I work with families and couples, I feel warmth and attachment but a somewhat greater sense of therapeutic separation, a recognition that the family shares a structure that only partially includes me. My family work is more focused, active, and playful.

There have—happily for psychoanalytic institutes and for families—always been levelers and sharpeners. This book represents the journey of a sharpener on the border of psychoanalysis and family systems theory and practice. I am well aware that there are other routes. But I do believe that psychoanalysis will best thrive if it, like a healthy family, maintains a boundary—though, preferably, a permeable one—with other forms of psychological treatment and other domains of investigation. Today there is a greater push for integration than ever before. The mental health community is exhausted by the onslaught of managed care; defining differences seems like a luxury when the dignity of clinical work is at stake. However, paradigms like psychoanalysis and family therapy can serve as figure and ground to each other, with each defined and refined by the other.

Acknowledging contribution to a completed book presents its own boundary problem. I feel indebted to so many people who have helped shape my clinical career: supervisors who challenged and believed in my work, colleagues who shared their own personal concerns and passions and thus enlivened mine, and students who ask the darndest questions. Here I will limit myself to the people who most directly affected my writing this particular book. First, I am indebted to the families who trusted me to work with them toward alleviating their distress and clarifying their dilemmas. In all cases, the demographic attributes of the families presented in this book have been changed to disguise their identities. More extensive case material has been included with the permission of the patients involved.

I want to acknowledge my very special mentor in family theory and therapy, a mentor whose artistry and brilliance as a family therapist remain enriching and inspiring to me: Salvador Minuchin. I thank the group I worked with most closely in the Family Studies supervisory program, colleagues who have always been supportive of my dual psychoanalytic and systemic focus: Linda Carter, Susan Friedberg, Ema Genijovich, Jonathan Lampert, and Ellen Landau. Constituting for me what Carl Whitaker called a necessary "cuddle group," they have substantially affected my thinking in family therapy.

I am deeply grateful to my colleagues at the New York University Postdoctoral Program in Psychotherapy and Psychoanalysis, particularly those of the Interpersonal–Humanistic Orientation, who have supported my interest in including family systems theory and therapy as a focus for exploration and integration into psychoanalytic scholarship: Ruth Lesser, who first helped me know myself as a clinician; Sabert Basescu, past coordinator of the Interpersonal–Humanistic Orientation, for first supporting my teaching a development course that included a systemic component; Al Atkins, present coordinator of that orientation, for his ongoing support of what has become the Project in Family Theory and Therapy at the Postdoctoral Program; and Barbara Waxenberg, who codirects the project with me. I am grateful for Edgar Levenson's supervisory mentorship, in particular for his unique and early interest in systemic thinking and his weaving of its concepts through a clinical perspective. The colleagues I have worked with in the Family Project—Phyllis Cohen, Susan Flinn, Sue Grand, Juanita Shell, Susan Shimmerlik, and Bobbye Troutt—have shared with me the pleasures and vicissitudes of wearing two clinical hats.

The development of my thinking has been enriched by my clinical psychology Ph.D. student supervisees at New York University and supported by the directors of the program, David Wolitzky in the past and Joan Welkowitz at present. Ruth Ochroch of New York University has been an inspiration to me, first as a rigorous and generous teacher and then as a colleague; she facilitated and supported the institution of the Committee on Psychoanalysis and Family Therapy of Division 39 (Psychoanalysis) of the American Psychological Association, of which I am currently chairperson.

I want to thank my colleagues who so generously gave of their time to read the manuscript for this book, question it, and improve it. My thanks to Patricia Minuchin for her very helpful reading of the chapters on family theory and on development. My deep gratitude to Virginia Kelley and Susan Bram who not only have incisive minds but can refashion a phrase for the better. My gratitude also goes to a budding psychological theorist and practitioner, my daughter, Jessica Gerson, who read and critiqued the book from the invaluable perspective of a

Ph.D. student. Elizabeth Nelson offered first-rate editorial assistance in the first phase of manuscript preparation. Fran Hitchcock offered her expert assistance in terms of both editorial comment and videotape transcribing in the second phase. It is with pleasure that I hereby publicly record my deepest appreciation for the erudition, wit, tact, and time-intensive dedication of John Kerr, my Analytic Press editor, who helped me know what I wanted to say and to whom I was saying it; I thank him for his support of this project and for enriching it with his own critical intelligence.

I want to express my appreciation to my husband, Charles Gerson, for believing in me so much and, true to his character, for backing up that belief with palpable support and at times personal sacrifice of pleasure and companionship. The family life we have created together, which includes our children, Daniel and Jessica, has been a source of profound meaning and sustenance for me and has fueled my ongoing interest in family functioning and relationships.

Above all, I would like to acknowledge Bernie Kalinkowitz, Ph.D., who was director of the clinical psychology program at New York University for 28 years and director of the Postdoctoral Program for 31 years. A major figure in the history of clinical psychology in this country, Bernie had a profound effect on generations of clinicians. From the time he interviewed me as a Ph.D. applicant to the period in which he encouraged me to initiate the Family Project at the New York University Postdoctoral Program, Bernie's message was consistently clear: listen to the beat of your own drummer and have the courage to act on your personal convictions. He was the father figure many of us looked for and found, and I am grateful that I knew him in my clinical lifetime.

chapter one

Introduction:
The Analyst and the Family

"My main goal is to get them into individual treatment."

"I started to see them as a couple; he was desperately trying to get through to her, and I wanted to help if I could."

"I've been seeing a family recently; the treatment is going really well, but I don't have a clear way to think about it."

"An individual patient of mine asked for the name of a couples therapist; although I think this will be helpful, I'm unsure how to deal with this other modality."

More and more psychoanalysts and psychoanalytically informed therapists see couples and families in their private practices and as part of their institutional responsibilities or become involved in this form of treatment by referring individuals to a couples or family therapist. Why is this so?

For one thing, patients are requesting it. It is probably not the case that intimate relationships are more difficult to establish during the final throes of the 20th century than they were during the last decade of the 19th century, when psychoanalysis emerged as a domain of inquiry and treatment. However, intimate relationships seem to be more difficult to *sustain* today—witness the soaring divorce rate of the past few decades. This is in large part because sweeping changes in social ideology (represented most forcibly in the feminist revolution) have deconstructed time-honored assumptions and expectations regarding family structure. These premises of traditional ideology regarding the family now lie about, like potsherds of a fractured vessel, requiring each couple and family to patch together for themselves an ideological framework for their lives that is both functional and serviceable. In a culture in which bonding with another person is an extremely difficult process they must construct a framework in which to address essential questions about interrelationships: What is "good enough" parenting? How can parents prepare children for a world that, in an age of information explosion, is relatively unpredictable? What is commitment in a postmodern culture? Does commitment still mean "forever" in any reasonable statistical or psychological sense? What can and should a couple pledge to each other? Is exclusivity possible in an age of distracted consumerism?

Such thorny dilemmas cause psychic discomfort and confusion for couples and families. Individuals are often largely oblivious to the overarching social context of their confusions, but they sense that the problems are not restricted to the sphere of their individual dynamics, either. Thus, couples and families often require a therapist to aid in the construction and testing of a fresh ideological framework in which to live. One of the most important and pressing reasons for psychoanalytically oriented therapists to explore family systems theory is that a study of it can enable them to feel more competent and creative in regard to clinical dilemmas in which, more and more, they will be asked to be involved.

In addition, it is increasingly the case that psychoanalysts who themselves do not wish to work directly with the "systemic others" in their patients' lives refer these individuals to couples and family therapists. The tracking of clinical data when a person is simultaneously in individual and family or couples therapy is complicated. For the referring individual therapist, an awareness of the theoretical underpinnings and forms of intervention used in the family or couples work can facilitate this tracking across multiple levels of clinical abstraction.

An awareness of family systems theory and therapy can both challenge and enrich psychoanalytic theory and practice. Families—their traumas and their struggles—are what psychoanalysts spend a great deal of their time hearing about. And yet *how* one hears this material is the question. How exactly does a vision of our patients' developmental experience inform our work? Does it alert us to transference–countertransference stumbling blocks? Corroborate our transference formulations? Let us know about significant others who have shaped the character of the person sitting (or lying) in our presence? Working with families sharpens these questions and also helps us formulate a series of responses to them. For the benefit of the reader who comes from a family therapy background, I add a note about current psychoanalytic theory: The field is a heterogeneous one, with a plurality of theories in evolution. Thus, the responses to the questions suggested above would offer an array of interesting possibilities rather than solutions to these integration puzzles.

To reap the heuristic benefits of family systems theory requires immersion in it, but this may be in the form of a refreshing dip or a full-fledged baptism. Chapter Two identifies the essential differences between the psychoanalytic and systems paradigms and attempts to capture the experience of the therapist crossing the divide. Chapter Three introduces the theoretical underpinnings of family therapy, which are elaborated in Chapter Four, as well as its principal theoretical innovators. Chapter Five identifies the principle of contextual influence, which lies at the heart of systems work, and Chapter Six elaborates the concept of pattern as clinical template. Chapters Seven and Eight discuss and compare concepts of development and diagnosis in the systems model and in the psychoanalytic model. The quality and quantity of family therapy interventions are described in Chapter Nine. Chapters Ten and Eleven detail the transformed nature of the treatment relationship for the psychoanalyst-as-family-therapist, and Chapter Twelve addresses the most common questions of the referral conundrum: who, when, and where.

One point of clarification: When I identify the reader as a psychoanalyst, I am including therapists who are psychodynamically oriented, that is, who work within what Gill (1994) identified as the "psychoanalytic situation." Several cautions may be in order before we begin. Our purpose is didactic-heuristic (getting acquainted), not a comparative evaluation. As a consequence, I will not generally be calling attention to the ways in which family work is limited. Similarly, I will not be emphasizing the ways in which the depth exploration of psychoanalysis may reasonably be preferred for a variety of reasons. Our first task is to understand one another, and both of these topics are for another book. Also not explored in this text are the points of convergence and divergence with group therapy. That, as well, could be the focus of another book.

I hope that this text will further spark the curiosity of the psychoanalytic reader who has already taken the initiative to begin learning about family systems theory and family therapy. How this appetite for new knowledge is satisfied—whether in a brief exposure to clinical readings or a full commitment to workshops and consultation—is a matter of personal choice and pacing. However, since it is hard to cross a bridge without a railing for guidance and support, it is hoped that this text will provide a sturdy yet flexible railing to assist those who are crossing into this new clinical territory.

chapter two

Theoretical Overview

The art of progress is to preserve order amid change and to preserve change amid order.

Alfred North Whitehead

"The map is not the territory." Korzibsky's (1954) pithy admonition is often quoted as an antidote to doctrinaire posturing, but from a contemporary constructivist point of view it is clear that we can see and know our territories only through maps. In fact, no territory has any meaningful existence without them.

There are competent reviews of basic theory regarding family therapy[1] that have been written for the beginning family therapist, but I believe they do not address the concerns of the psychoanalyst who wishes to absorb this material through a filter composed of familiar analytic concepts and concerns. Psychoanalysts and psychodynamically oriented individual therapists have well-defined maps for individuals. However, work with families requires a change to other maps, for it involves an experiential journey to another therapeutic realm. Psychoanalysts who embark on trying to educate themselves about family therapy soon find themselves on something like a transcultural journey.

Just as one struggles in a new culture to cope with unfamiliar forms of otherwise familiar categories of experience, as any traveler knows, so too does the psychoanalyst journeying into the culture of family therapy encounter unfamiliar rituals, artifacts, and linguistic customs. Take the matter of professional gatherings, for example. Family therapy conferences feature presentations on acting techniques and storytelling. The culturally mandated therapeutic stance is spontaneity, and it is *de rigueur* for presenters to "talk" their presentations informally. In contrast, psychoanalytic conferences are serious. Participants almost always read their papers, presenting their most polished formulations. In a manner isomorphic to their therapeutic efforts, they "interpret"

---

[1]Two useful books of this kind are by Goldenberg and Goldenberg (1991) and Nichols and Schwartz (1994).

5

their work to their colleagues. When psychoanalysts play, they play like serious children—mindfully and somewhat cautiously.

Every culture casts a hero. In psychoanalytic culture the ideal analyst, whether for a close-to-the-vest Freudian or a warm Winnicottian, is the patient's steadfast companion, a Virgil remaining at Dante's side however deep the descent. In testimony to this ideal are the myriad scholarly papers in psychoanalytic journals focused on "the impossible patient," a hyperbolic phrase invoking forbearance and commitment in the face of adversity. There are rarely such topic headings in the family therapy literature. The family therapist is not cast as an abiding companion but, rather, as a consulting architect of psychic life who is intent on designing new windows for light and ventilation. For the family therapist, the essential task is to open up possibilities. A fundamental assumption is that family energy is basically growth directed; that is, introduced to new structural possibilities by therapeutic intervention, the family will grow into this new structure, and systemic metamorphosis will occur.

Differences in cultural mores and rituals can engender a kind of stereotyping and xenophobia. Thus, family therapists sometimes view psychoanalysts as old-fashioned and stodgy. Their criticism is matched by analysts' suspicions that family approaches are mechanistic and slick. Sometimes fantasies of defection occur: one senior analyst confided to me the nagging suspicion that family therapists have more fun, and family therapists I know privately wonder, Are analysts actually deeper and wiser?

Psychoanalysts who journey into the territory of family therapy often feel tongue-tied and/or stymied by the new vocabulary. Terms like *homeostasis* are alien to them as a way of describing the clinical encounter. It may be helpful for them to remember that new orientations are often defined and legitimized as much by new terminology as by critical thinking. Sometimes the development of a new lexicon is as much a political maneuver as an intellectual necessity, and semantic distinctions that might not even be necessary become reified. Moreover, differences in the styles used to present clinical material to colleagues may be stranger and more alarming than the ideas they present. Clifford Geertz (1986) has persuaded us that the rhetoric of presentation is inseparable from the structures of meaning, but differences in presentation may inadvertently mask the commonality of shared values.

I recently suggested to the chairperson of a small psychoanalytic conference that the presentations be videotaped. Implicit in my suggestion, of course, was a guarantee that the materials would be carefully protected and that the papers would be prescreened for confidentiality.

However, she still seemed to be wary of my suggestion, as if I were suggesting we invade actual analytic sessions with video equipment. I realized, with a sense of irony, that the medium had unfortunately swamped the message.

Cultures are rooted in historical and social realities. The psychoanalytic movement was born in Europe, and its valuing of subjectivity is emblematic of the turn-of-the-century modernist movement. Modernists regarded the true life as one lived within individual subjectivity—a position that negated, or at best neglected, outward reality. Though varying in their view of outward reality as alien or chaotic, all modernists, T. S. Eliot and Henry James being among those who expressed this view most elegantly, valued inner subjectivity above all else. The true life was lived within. The prototypical modernist hero is Joyce's Stephen Daedalus in *Portrait of the Artist as a Young Man*, who is described by Ruland and Bradbury (1991) as "soar[ing] on imaginary wings into the unknown arts, breaking with home, family, Catholic religion and his Irish nation in the process" (p. 14).

Psychoanalysis as a clinical theory and praxis shares with modernism a profound commitment to expanding inner awareness and fostering clarity of self-definition. Utilizing the established parameters of clinical practice (e.g., neutrality in the analyst and commitment to the goal of free association on the part of the patient) as stable coordinates by which to remain oriented, the psychoanalyst ranges over an enormous expanse of conscious and unconscious material while crossing three time zones—the past, present, and future. Unconscious-to-conscious linkages are discovered through dreams, free associations, and—above all—through transference enactments. The patient's inner psychic life emerges as primary content, at first incoherently and in scattered formation. When a gestalt with shared meaning emerges as insight, an often stunning shift in the perception of self and other occurs. The analytic relationship offers an abstract but emotionally dense intimacy, and this structure allows for a drama of reenactment and rebirth.

Born in the second half of the 20th century, family therapy, in contrast, is a largely American therapeutic movement that draws its philosophical perspective from American pragmatism. R. Rorty (1989), a preeminent pragmatist, locates the essence of this philosophical perspective in a recognition of contingencies, that is, a recognition that *"everything—*our language, our conscience, our community [is] a product of time and chance" (p. 22). This pragmatic tradition, infused with constructs from the burgeoning fields of information theory and applied systems theory, lies at the heart of family systems theory. Its focus is on the how more than the why of relationships.

The ideology of family therapy closely follows the exigencies of family life. Family members live together and share a myriad of assumptions regarding their history and living arrangements, from the most ordinary culinary idiosyncrasies to the most arcane family secret. The family's shared database is so complex that it becomes organized in redundant loops of communication, both verbal and nonverbal. "Healthier" families are believed to be organized by somewhat more flexible loops of interaction whereas dysfunctional ones generally are rigidly bound by these loops, in unchanging and often outmoded repetitions. The family therapist locates the collective pulse—which is sometimes faint—at the heart of this dysfunctionally rigid binding and tries to revitalize the family. He or she does this by bringing systemic patterns into focus, often letting content drift where it may during the process.

The experience of therapy is necessarily kinesthetic and dramatic, for it must carry the family across what Minuchin and Fishman (1981) call the "threshold of redundancy." As the therapist attempts to redesign the family blueprint, he or she becomes engaged in a drama of enactment that allows for system expansion via the establishment of new loops of interaction. The drama is naturalistic, for the players play themselves, reflecting and reinventing a social system that has too often bred the contempt of familiarity.

The family therapy movement has been characterized by an orientation to fairly rapid and palpable change rather than to intensive exploration. Family therapists unabashedly look for and seek to catalyze palpable shifts in relationship loyalties and practices. They look for in-session evidence of at-home realities. To be sure, this proactive bias in favor of change is a cause for concern, and this concern has led to the development of an alternative position on intervention (which will be considered in Chapter Five). Nevertheless, family therapy praxis usually involves the use of active experiential techniques to encourage awareness.

Psychoanalysts often experience an uneasy sense of freedom when first working with couples and families from an explicit systems perspective, as though they have been illicitly untied from their respectable moorings. However, this freedom is generally accompanied by a more disquieting diminution of therapeutic centrality, as the analyst witnesses the unexpected power of healing and transformation that family members can offer each other. And it can be simultaneously exhilarating, humbling, and surprising to analysts to realize the impact of a systemic change on an individual family member.

This was the case with a couple I treated. They had been referred by the husband's individual therapist, who saw him twice weekly, because of persistent and unremitting marital discord. The therapist reported that the husband, feeling he could not "get through" to his wife, had defensively withdrawn from her. It quickly became clear that these two individuals were locked in mutually aversive perceptions of each other. The wife felt that her husband could not fulfill her emotional dreams, and he saw her as an unlovable shrew. The wife had a deep, impenetrable conviction that "true love" would carry her husband toward her, despite her intermittent humiliating and denigrating attacks. Her conflicts about being loved were a reflection of her developmental experience: Although she had been the favored, golden-haired child of her father throughout her childhood, she was nevertheless enraged at submitting to the hurdle jumping her father had required of her. Moreover, she had been forced to serve as a complicit witness to his cruel rejection of the less favored members of the family. The husband, considerably self-absorbed and emotionally unresponsive, had been neglected and exploited in his childhood. He was barely up to absorbing the indigestible mix of rage, need for tenderness, and sense of specialness that his wife communicated. Nevertheless, in the course of couples treatment he was enabled to continue to care about her and to better withstand her flash attacks. The change in him toward greater durability also engendered a powerful systemic shift in his wife. She began to acknowledge her role in making it impossible for him to love her as she wanted to be loved. Now this woman was not particularly psychologically minded, and she was wedded to a position of emotional denial of past traumas (she told her own story without personal involvement). Although she entered individual therapy (with a therapist I recommended) basically to placate her husband, she stayed only briefly. However, I was struck by how affected she was by her husband's efforts to reach her and by how open she rather suddenly became to new perceptions. Was it because he was a father, the father of their children, and the implications for her of change in him—toward greater tolerance—skidded across a transgenerational slope to her relationship with her own father? Was it because, in Winnicott's terms, she had the experience of sustaining her connection with an object (i.e., her husband) that had survived her most concerted attempts to destroy it, an experience made particularly powerful because the object was a real, not a transferential, other? Winnicott (1971) described a developmental relationship progression that begins with a simple recognition of objects as separate and external, progresses to a wish to destroy the object *because* it is external, and, finally, culminates in an exhilarating sense of the object's having survived the attempt to destroy it. He charmingly captured this last dynamic of "object usage" thus: " 'Hullo object!' 'I destroyed you.' 'I love you.' 'You have value for me because of your survival of my destruction of you' " (pp. 89–90). We are accustomed to thinking of these dynamics as crucial in infancy or in transference. Might they not be restorative in intimate relationships?

This experience also made me reflect on how I would have viewed this woman's husband if I had not worked with him but had known him only through his wife's report in individual therapy. I likely would have thought of him as depriving and selfish. The typically intense involvement of psychoanalysts in the inner world of their patients often (though inadvertently) leads them to view significant others as interfering with the patient's growth, restricting rather than facilitating characterologic change. What is often not sufficiently recognized by therapists is how the significant others in their patients' lives can provide healing and regeneration for the patient that are at times more comprehensive and more sustaining than what they themselves can offer.

It might be a relief to us to recognize this healing capacity. Willi (1987) noted how therapists' concentration on pathology often leads them to ignore the fact that a partnership that challenges an individual "to just the right degree" (p. 431), far from being restrictive, can actually provoke and shape personality development:

> In the interaction with others, we gain a deeper consciousness of self; we are shaped and modeled, our potential takes on form and becomes visible by our behavior and action. . . . I can realize myself only to the extent to which I can create an environment that is responsive to my self-realization. I depend on my partners for my self-realization. . . . This revolutionary aspect of applied systems theory has not been given much attention so far; possibly, it has even been repressed. It conflicted too strongly with the wave of belief in individual self-realization that culminated in the 1970s. It conflicts, too, with the different paradigms of the personality and the goal of psychotherapy used by some individually oriented therapists [pp. 434–435].

As individual therapists we sometimes become involved in awkward and partisan speculations about the dynamics of significant others (whom we have never seen). Our frustration arises from the fact that we are at times unable to do anything about these relationships—even in terms of evoking new insights in our own patients. In the worst-case scenario we may even resort to pathologizing our patient in relation to the other (e.g., "She's so fragile that I advised her on how to respond to the threatening note he sent") in order to deal with our own anxiety-ridden but empathic response to a patient's dilemma. Paradoxically, however, a full recognition of the phenomenon Willi described can release analysts from worrying about managing the marriages and other relationships of their patients.

The alternative to inquiring about absent family members is to include them, but this has its own problems. Inclusion of family members in a therapeutic session can mask basic paradigmatic assumptions about what their presence signifies. For example, child therapists, though working in terms of individual dynamics, will often see the whole family. From a systems perspective the child in this clinical context is viewed as the "identified patient" by the family, and the interview is likely to lock the child even more securely into the position of symptom bearer, as the clan of significant others gathers to catalog the child's difficulties.

The family therapist, on the other hand, views the child's symptoms as expressing something important about the family as a whole. In meeting with the whole family the therapist hopes to get a better grasp of the child's experience in the family and of his or her role in the family's redundant patterns of communication so that this information can be used to make sense of the child's symptoms.

In a similar vein, where appearance of inclusion does not signify a systemic perspective, analysts who work only with adults may feel quite comfortable opening their practice doors to couples for treatment. However, these analysts sometimes work within a formulation of reciprocal individual dynamics, not overarching systemic patterns.

The basic position of this book is that family systems and psychoanalytic perspectives can function as figure and ground to one another. Each perspective offers a different set of explanations and constructs on how relationship difficulties come to be, how they can be examined, and how they can be expanded and resolved. However, I think that one gestalt must dominate if we are to experience a necessary sense of coherence between what we are thinking and what we are saying and doing with patients. E. A. Levenson (1983) referred to this as the "frame" of psychotherapy, "the conceptual delineation of the constraints of patient–therapist interaction" (p. 56). He notes: "As Bateson pointed out, psychoanalysis is a game; it is structured *play;* it is not real life. Freud, too, referred to the transference as a 'playground.' Still, this is a point likely to offend anyone who equates play with not being serious or with triviality. No such pejoration is intended. Play is serious business; games can be played to the death" (p. 59). Bach (1985) noted that "psychoanalysis can take place only within an interpersonal and intrapsychic framework of a certain kind, with some 'rules of the game' delineated clearly by the analyst, others by the patient, and still other 'rules' or unacknowledged interactions which may be acknowledged and analyzed eventually" (p. 220).

Psychoanalytic therapy and family therapy, with their different rule
systems, are different games, in the Batesonian sense. In each, how we
act is informed by what we think and how we think is informed by how
we act. However, with both perspectives we are working in the realm of
intimate relationships, and there can be a useful interpenetration of
ideas from one to the other. Potentially, we can enrich our understanding of the operative rule system, and even perhaps amend it to our
taste, by borrowing from another perspective. We certainly can expand
our understanding of the developmental and motivational aspects of
the individuals we are working with regardless of the praxis frame that
organizes our relationship to them.

By way of illustration of how the ground of one paradigm can
backlight the figure of another, two possibilities come to mind, each
involving a psychoanalytic conceptualization as the figure, namely,
the concept of transference and Sullivan's concept of the personified self.

Transference, along with the concept of the unconscious, is a basic
cornerstone of the psychoanalytic model. Analysts are ever aware
that the task of elucidating unconscious meaning is enormously delicate; the organization of unconscious material emerges gradually as
if the invisible ink between the discontinuities of the patient's narrative is being put to candlelight. What we know about transference
we know dyadically, and the constructs we use to talk and think
about this phenomenon—for example, projective identification, parataxis, counterresistance—reflect that dyadic structure. But what happens to our familiar concept of transference when the relationship
system becomes triadic, quadratic, or an even higher order? Here is a
typical vignette:

A couples therapist receives a referral call from an analyst: "I've
seen the wife for two years, and she's made real progress. She is
less depressed and self-denying, and she's facing her rage at her depriving mother. As far as I can see, the husband is quite schizoid and
antagonistic, constantly berating her in an obsessive way for small
failures. I just hope you can get *him* into treatment. That's really why
I'm referring them."

As the hour approaches, the couples therapist sweeps her psyche
clean of obtrusive countertransferential debris that would impede a
therapeutic connection with the critical, angry spouse. However, the
woman who enters the office is noticeably withdrawn from her husband, locked into a kind of simmering resentment. She responds to her
husband's complaints about the relationship with a consistently opaque
self-justification. It quickly becomes apparent that her "antagonistic"

husband fails to win her attention without resorting to nit-picking and never really makes contact with her because she is so desperately self-righteous.

It is tempting for the couples therapist to conclude that the referring analyst is a muddled clinician. However, the analytically trained couples therapist is presented with an intriguing dilemma arising from this referral contretemps: How is it that a patient becomes so convincingly a certain kind of person within the analytic transference–countertransference matrix and yet appears quite otherwise within another intimate relationship system? More crucial still, what does it tell us about our concept of transference? Why is this woman different with her analyst than she is with her husband? One way to think about this is to question whether the transference data her analyst culls from treating her is essential. It might well be epiphenomenal, perhaps representing an accidental best fit with her analyst's characterological bent. In the latter case are we not thus challenged with the unnerving possibility that we ourselves are significant others to our patients, who might be organizing their analytic participation around their efforts to allay *our* anxiety (E. A. Levenson, 1992)? Following this unorthodox line of thinking, if the latter possibility is, in fact, an actuality, does it happen early on in analytic treatment or only later? Only in bad treatments or only in good treatments? Although we will return to these questions in Chapter Ten, suffice it to say here that the concept of transference in the individual therapeutic model can take on an interesting new look from the vantage point of family therapy.

When dealing with a couple's dynamics, it is arguably most useful for us to keep our favored construct of transference as background (this will be discussed in greater detail in Chapter Ten). Indeed, there are times when the individual transference of one family member may usefully come up for consideration within family treatment. However, it is really a different matter altogether to conceptualize the transference of a couple or a family. Can we (and should we) formulate a concept of shared, or collective, transference, that is, what a therapist represents to a couple or family?

Efforts have been made in this regard. David and Jill Scharff (1987) have developed a concept of the "contextual family transference." Since their ideas are covered more fully in Chapter Four, I will only point out here a paradox that besets even the most sophisticated attempts in this direction. In the presence of a significant other, patients are influenced in their perception of the therapist. An individual describing a mother or spouse *in the presence of* the mother or spouse is in a very different situation than when he or she is speaking to the therapist alone. There

will be differences not only in what is said but in how the listening of
the therapist is perceived. That is to say, the "shared transference"
necessarily involves a partial suppression of what we ordinarily think
of as transference. The original concept, our starting point, becomes
murkier. Ordinarily, our sense of well-being as we engage in psychoanalytic work depends largely on the sense of competence we derive
from organizing our data with respect to the trusted coordinates of
transference and countertransference. We can end by losing confidence
in our paradigmatic constructs if they become misshapen.

An altogether different figure–ground amalgamation emerges from a
view of the self within interpersonal psychoanalytic theory. A minor
concept in Freud's original schema (where it took the status of a clinical,
as opposed to a metapsychological, construct), the construct of self
became the focal point of Kohut's revision of classical theory, his now
fully elaborated self psychology. Today we psychoanalysts are actively
struggling with notions regarding the essence, experience, and muta-
bility of what we call the self. These issues in relation to systems theory
will be discussed more fully in later chapters. For illustration here,
however, one particular concept of the self within the psychoanalytic
canon, Sullivan's notion of the "personified self," is offered as a particularly promising link between the two theories.

The personified self was introduced by Sullivan (1950) in his paper
"The Illusion of Personal Individuality," where he argued that our
"illusion" of uniqueness is precisely what prevents us from curing
ourselves of our neuroses. Sullivan believed that "anxiety is what
keeps us from noticing things which would lead us to correct our
faults" (p. 216) and that we manage our anxiety by dint of our security operations and by constructing a powerful defined and bounded
"self." According to Sullivan, this mythologized self plows through
life on the tracks of selective inattention and never veers off its overlearned and overly restricted course. In effect, the self, misguided
by anxiety and in the service of supposed self-preservation, deemphas-
izes and at times ignores the role and importance of others in shaping us
as individuals.

Sullivan emphasized his belief that there is significant "interpenetration" between the self and others, whether the self chooses to acknowledge this or not. This is not to say that he eschewed subjectivity or the
concept of an inner life. Rather, according to Sullivan (1950), inner
psychological life is importantly populated and shaped by others:

> For all I know every human being has as many personalities as he has
> interpersonal relations; and as a great many of our interpersonal relations

are actual operations with imaginary people—that is, in no-sense-mate-rially-embodied people—and as they may have the same or greater validity and importance in life as have our operations with many materially-embodied people like the clerks in the corner store, you can see that even though "the illusion of personal individuality" sounds quite lunatic when first heard, there is at least food for thought in it [p. 221].

The personified self is created precisely to offset the anxiety of inter-penetration by others. However, in one's intimate relationships, whether in friendship, marriage, or psychoanalysis, there is a possibility for wholesome interpenetration and expansion.

This personified self can be brought into focus in both psychoanalytic treatment and in family treatment, though the process is slightly differ-ent in each. When the frame is analytic, personification is addressed as a transference phenomenon. The psychoanalyst may wonder, for ex-ample, how a notion of specialness is rendering the patient impervious to engagement and interpretation. When the frame is systems therapy, the focus is on how the patient's sense of uniqueness and specialness inhibits him or her from listening to or collaborating with a significant other. In fact, one of the interesting aspects of couples therapy is the powerful effect of shifts in the personification of the significant other, which not only affect relationship functioning but self-awareness and self-experience as well. People who suddenly change their working definitions of the other feel radically different themselves. If simply *seeing* the other differently makes one feel like a new person (a common experiential aspect of family treatment), this phenomenon raises in-triguing questions about the assumptions of the psychoanalytic one-person (drive-based) and even two-person (internalization-based) psy-chologies: If the patient–therapist relationship is a transference con-struction (as assumed by classical Freudians) or based on projection and introjection (as assumed by object relationists), why should seeing the significant other differently, in fairly short order, cause a radical shift in internal dynamics and object relations? Arguably, the Sulliva-nian notion of the personified self, backlit by systems theory, can account for a significant proportion of variance in the change in peo-ple's perceptions of self and other, a change so often witnessed by family therapists. Both schools of thought, Sullivan's and systems theory, assume that one's understanding and experience of oneself is inextricably linked to one's experience of systemic others.

Of course, there are many more ways to link the systemic and psychoanalytic paradigms. Certain concepts are related, such as splitting and triangulation. One could choose to think of intrapsychic dynamics as foundation and family dynamics as supporting infrastructure. Alternatively, we can think heuristically of clinical problems as existing on multiple levels of organization. The intellectual flexibility to be gained by being exposed to both paradigms cannot but enrich our lives and work. But before we lose ourselves in abstract formulations, let us try to be candid. The level on which we intervene during therapy can reflect many factors, including our version of what is truth, what we think is the most effective approach to change, and even how we make our living.

At whichever level we choose to intervene, it seems to me essential that we do make a choice in terms of our clinical practice. I take this position as a normative one, and yet in many ways it seems out of step with today's professional climate of compromise and theoretical assimilation and with the sociopolitical climate advocating unbridled celebration of diversity. But I believe that a secure paradigm frame serves as an indispensable life raft to the therapist navigating new clinical waters. It nurtures a sense of competence because it clarifies intentions as well as responsibilities toward patients. The clinical enterprise is sufficiently fraught with ambiguity because of the complexity of the data we deal with, largely resisting orderly categorization. We can at least try to keep our paradigms in order. It is simply too much to try both to grasp the complex individual world of a person in marital distress and to manage the marital crisis itself.

My own experience is that therapists who feel grounded in a paradigm take flight most creatively and gracefully. We are today perhaps too much aware of the importance of constructivist admonitions, that is, that there is nothing out there for us to discover *de novo*. Although such perspectival openness may have its own value in making us more flexible—as people and as therapists, it is not without its own anxieties. If in struggling with a particular clinical dilemma we keep shifting theoretical figure and ground in our thinking about our work, we may become uncertain about why our technique has moved a patient in a certain direction—with no small consequences for our ability to learn from experience. In serendipitous instances, perhaps we may learn important things about ourselves as therapists or about our patients as persons. However, often we simply feel increasingly anxious and less focused without a clear theoretical perspective underlying our participation.

The issue, ultimately, is not simply one of personal flexibility and openness. Psychoanalysts have certainly moved beyond the strictures of rigid technique that characterized the early professionalization of our praxis. However, we know that everything we express to patients, including warmth and flexibility, is apprehended by them as part of a specific relationship with specific parameters. Therapists are really most comfortable when their capacity for concern can be translated into a praxis in which they have "good faith," in Sartre's words. Havens (1986) closes his text *Making Contact* with the following impassioned statement:

> Caring is the term most often used for clinical concern, but the word passion better transmits the deep-running sense of interest and often outrage that must infuse difficult and persistent clinical efforts. . . . As with the great stresses that engineers must mobilize and control, effective clinical behavior needs to render the presence of passion largely invisible, like the still structure of a bridge. . . . Even more important, the energy of concern needs to be conserved for effective action; it cannot afford to waste itself in empty display. It is by its results that therapeutic passion is best known [p. 182].

chapter three

An Orientation to
Family Systems Theory

A clash of doctrines is not a disaster; it is an opportunity.
Alfred North Whitehead

The family therapy movement, like all therapeutic innovations, reflects intellectual currents located in social and economic realities of a particular time. Its zeitgeist may have been best expressed in popular culture by the Beatles, who sang about "getting by with a little help from their friends." They were slyly suggesting pharmacological assistance, but their refrain also applied to the optimism and communal ideology characteristic of that time.

The two decades following World War II were marked in America by an unparalleled rise in economic prosperity. One need not be a Marxist scholar to appreciate the link between prosperity and optimism. This was a time of pragmatic optimism, and it was in this era that the discipline of family therapy flourished, paralleling the heyday of the community psychology movement. We Americans were unusually confident that we could solve all our collective social problems; as other parts of the world began to recover from the tragic global war that had decimated central Europe, we initiated our "war on poverty."

There were multiple therapeutic currents that fed into the headwaters of the family therapy movement. The need to treat World War II combat casualties with limited staff gave rise to the concept of milieu treatment, based on the theory that analogues of individual dynamics could be tracked externally. Essentially, it was believed that what was inside the heads of ward patients became inextricably linked to what was outside in their hospital environment. In their landmark text *The Mental Hospital* Stanton and Schwartz (1954) provided illustrative examples of how tensions among nursing staff members are reflected in exacerbated psychotic symptomatology among resident patients. In parallel fashion the burgeoning group therapy movement proposed that it is the experience of altruism, rather than of uncovering the past or receiving an interpretation, that is restorative. As Yalom (1975) noted, "When patients look back over the course of [group] therapy, they invariably credit other members as having been important in their improvement; if not for deliberate support and advice, then at least for having been there and permitting the patient to learn about himself from their relationship" (p. 13).

The birth of the therapeutic movements of community psychology and family therapy both benefited from the optimism of an America living very well. With the gross national product rising with each postwar year, it was easy to be democratic. Social theorists and therapists felt that the information proliferating within the social sciences could and should be applied to a wide range of social and psychological difficulties. Americans felt their culture should embody the democratic ideals of community and shared opportunity; as increasing affluence facilitated a deemphasis on privilege and status, it seemed that all could live comfortably, even if some lived luxuriously. A belief in the community as curative became the prevailing ideology of the era, and eventually the psychiatric hospitals were emptied out. The community psychology and family therapy movements developed within this context and shared the following touchstones: (1) an emphasis on health and strength as opposed to pathology; (2) an implicit assumption that normal development is wholesome or at least benign (as opposed to the bleaker Freudian preoccupation with darker, self-destructing passions); (3) an emphasis on the embeddedness of the individual in social systems (a perspective now generally referred to as ecological); and (4) a commitment to the demystification of professional personnel, including therapists.

The last created shifts in professional identity, both personal and institutional. (The family therapist Carl Whitaker, a psychiatrist, asked families to bring in the grandparents because they had accrued wisdom he sorely needed.) In similar fashion but at the level of the larger professional system, an unparalleled shake-up—or, rather, shakedown—in traditional hierarchies occurred among the social workers, psychologists, nurse practitioners, and psychiatrists at family therapy training sites.

It is quite interesting to contrast this shift away from elitism with the psychoanalytic ethos of that era. Psychoanalysis arrived a second time on American shores in the 1930s, revitalized by refugees from Nazi-dominated Europe, and achieved a dominance in the psychiatric domain during the 1940s and 1950s. To Jacoby (1983), the "Americanization" of psychoanalysis entailed an essential repression of its more radical theoretical essence. The American emphasis on professional-ization—abetted by the absorption of psychoanalytic treatment into a medical domain—"deeply penetrated the institutional, intellectual, and finally human bases of psychoanalysis" (p. 17). There are intriguing complexities embedded in this transformation, which we will not pursue here, but it is clear that the excitement about the yield of psychoanalytic treatment was itself part of the current of therapeutic optimism that nurtured the development of other therapeutic approaches. On the other hand, the professionally predominant position that psychoanalysts assumed within the mental health field was at the same time one of the spurs to a head-on challenge by the new generation of systems theorists.

THEORETICAL UNDERPINNINGS OF FAMILY THERAPY

Before turning to a discussion of each of the key theorists in the field of family therapy, a brief discussion of shared ideology is in order. The presuppositions of family therapy four decades ago may now function more mythically than operationally. However, just as creation myths continue to shape the structure of a culture, even long after it has been considerably transformed, the ideological keystones of the family therapy movement continue to shape professional discourse in ways large and small.

The theoretical underpinning for all family theories is general systems theory, which developed simultaneously in a variety of fields during the 1950s. In medical science, for instance, although the discovery and identification of bacterial agents were major milestones, it became clear that the action of microorganisms did not account for all the variance in disease contagion. Some people seemed genuinely invulnerable to the supposed linear effect of the identified organism on the resultant disease state. A heuristic model was needed that would describe the interrelationship of host and invader and differentiate among host environments on a qualitative basis.

Describing such a systemic relationship required bold theoretical brush strokes to capture the back-and-forth pattern of interrelationship. It necessitated investigation of the context in which interactions occurred and forced inquiry into the relationship between constituent parts of the system as well as the relationship of parts to the whole. The biologist von Bertalanffy (1968) was struck by this important but previously unrecognized interrelationship between host and invading organism in the development of illness and was the first to make the critical categorical distinction between "open" (essentially living) and "closed" (essentially inorganic) systems.[1, 2]

The most therapeutically relevant implication of this difference is that closed systems, like minerals or mountains, are governed by the law of entropy. Because their closed systemic pores ensure insularity, closed systems deteriorate into undifferentiated chaos. Open systems, organic in nature, progress negentropically; that is, they move toward a higher and higher degree of complexity because information is exchanged with the external environment in such a way as to maintain "a steady state," or equilibrium. The final states of open systems are characterized by *equifinality*; that is, within the same basic parameters different means lead to the same ends. Clearly, adopting the perspective that families, like other systems, are "open" has substantial implications for defining both the means and ends in therapeutic interaction.

For example, suppose that Johnny has become aggressive and is routinely beating up other children in the neighborhood. This "end"—the presenting problem of lack of impulse control—likely has a variety of causal "means." Intrapsychically, it may well be that Johnny identifies with his father's lack of impulse control. However, if we assume that the family is an open system, we know that Johnny's behavior serves in some way to maintain the status quo within his family, and we can guess that control of aggression is a problem for this family as a whole. Seeing the symptom in this way allows us flexibility in treating it. We may choose the "level of abstraction" upon which we will conceptualize our intervention (e.g., the level of the individual, the family, or the community), recognizing that change at any level will affect how aggression is displayed and controlled in the family. From this vantage point, it is not necessary to struggle through Johnny's internalizations and work individually and interpretively (although we could). Instead, we might ask the father to systematically regulate his son's aggression, perhaps with a behavioral reward system. If the family's systemic difficulties with aggression reappear in the marital subsystem (where it

[1]Although the pioneering family therapist Murray Bowen singularly claimed that he had never read general systems theory when he developed his own theory, von Bertalanffy's ideas permeated the air of family thinking during the 1950s and Bowen's theory, in turn, arose out of and became part of that theoretical ecosystem.

[2]Perhaps it is not incidental but crucial to recognize that von Bertalanffy, who had established himself professionally in Vienna as a professor of biology, emigrated to Canada in 1949—and thus was familiar with crossing cultural as well as intellectual and theoretical boundaries. He went on to found the Society for the Advancement of General Systems Theory and had been nominated for a Nobel Prize at the time of his death in 1971.

perhaps originated), we would then focus our work on the couple's relationship. Alternatively, our view of both the aggression and the potential control of it within the system might shift following an observation that Johnny is the "aggression warrior" in a sibling subsystem that is otherwise meek and overly identified with the mother. Or perhaps it is the case that Johnny would like to be more like his gentle mother but is actively discouraged by his father, who is angry with his wife but cannot express this directly.

This general theoretical framework will be elaborated further in later chapters. For the moment, note two of the tenets that have become basic to family therapy theory: First, a system is more than a grouping of parts; it is organized in such a way that a change in any part of the system affects all its parts. Second, causality is not linear (if a, then b) but circular. Causality can be extended infinitely, and there are, concomitantly, infinite points of entry.

The main link between systems theory and family therapy is not the work of von Bertalanffy or any of the other general systems theorists but that of the English anthropologist Gregory Bateson. Bateson is truly of mythic stature in family therapy. The appearance or citation of Bateson's name in association with a statement, as G. D. Erickson (1988) noted wryly, confers immediate legitimacy in the family therapy literature. One of the preeminent minds of this century, Bateson studied Balinese culture with his wife, Margaret Mead, and then became engrossed in the new cybernetic model. This model developed out of a series of conferences in the 1940s sponsored by the Josiah Macy Foundation, which brought together engineers, mathematicians, and social scientists. The outgrowth of this groundbreaking interdisciplinary meeting of minds was the study of the regulation and control of communication, in computer systems and human beings alike. The emergent area of study was dubbed *cybernetics* by mathematician Norbert Weiner (1948), building on the Greek word for "steersman," to reflect the concept of information systems (including human information systems) being guided by means of feedback mechanisms.

In a case of science imitating life, Bateson wedded the ideas captured in this new model with anthropological constructs to produce a new theory: "cybernetic epistemology." A core construct of this epistemology is that information is "a difference that makes a difference" (1972, p. 381), that is, perceptions are shaped by the relationship between two phenomena, not their separate essences. He evolved a comprehensive new look at communication, concerning himself particularly with the pragmatics of speech acts, that is, with what speech acts, in their syntax and semantics, accomplish interpersonally. His most daring application of this perspective was in his research on schizophrenic communication, which he viewed as part of a systemic process of communicational mystification and paralysis, the famous "double-bind" theory. According to this formulation, two levels of communication are rendered together in an impossible contradiction. For example, his mother urges Jimmy to "Come hug Mommy" (verbal) and simultaneously extends to him a pair of stiff, uninviting arms (nonverbal). There is an additional, tertiary, command in this double-bind situation – "You cannot leave this field of interaction" – that reveals the dependency of the vulnerable child. A pileup of double-bind communication makes for "madness" or "badness" in children (Watzlawick, Beavin, and Jackson, 1967) and certainly disallows rational and coherent responsiveness.

Systems theory provided a fertile medium for the growth of family theory. Its legacy to *clinical* family therapy, however, has been a set of dilemmas not unlike those that psychoanalytic practitioners inherited with the metapsychology of their founding father. Holt (1985) included among the latter the reification of concepts, the faulty translation of concepts from other scientific areas, and the failure to "take clear and consistent stands on basic philosophical issues, for example . . . the nature of reality" (p. 291). There are similar problems in translating into the reality of clinical interaction the abstractions of Von Bertalanffy's systems concepts and, even more so, the constructs of Bateson's cybernetics. S. Minuchin (1985) captured the divide this way:

> The world of systems thinking is a world of ideas. Ideas are organized at different levels. They can be reversible. Wrapped in language, they can be manipulated without breaking. They can deal with ideal types; they can conflict and cancel without bloodshed. They exist on infinite axes of time and space. Humans do not [pp. 8–9].

Regarding Bateson, Minuchin added, "Bateson's thinking . . . doesn't give enough significance to the family as a complex system with subsystems with different agendas, and somehow makes the individual disappear" (p. 9).

CLINICAL THEORISTS

Although I will return to more general considerations of systems thinking in the next chapter, let us now consider how the abstract principles of systemic organization and communication were translated into specific theories.

Family therapy has four founding fathers: Salvador Minuchin, Murray Bowen, Carl Whitaker, and Jay Haley. These four theorists function as the institutional cornerstones of the family therapy movement. Because of their energy, enthusiasm, and exposure in the first two decades of the family therapy movement, they have achieved a pervasive influence on subsequent generations of family therapists. And though their professional offspring quibble with them and challenge them, their imprimatur remains in place.

There is also a founding mother: Virginia Satir. Even the briefest history of family therapy theory reveals a polemic that arose in the last decade and is only now beginning to recede. Feminist family therapists (Goldner, 1985; Goodrich et al., 1988; Luepnitz, 1988; Walters et al., 1988; Hare-Mustin, 1989) charge that the theory of systemic family therapy, developed by men, is patriarchal. Not only does it privilege males, it has grossly ignored the importance of nurturance in both families and family therapy. Nurturance is "a matter so taboo under patriarchy that it must always be distinguished as 'unconditional positive regard' or 'positive countertransference' or 'multidirectional partiality' " (Luepnitz, 1988, p. 52). Virginia Satir (1967, 1972) was alone among the pioneers of family therapy in being comfortable addressing the importance of nurturance. Beyond that, she is widely recognized as having helped shape the concepts of family rules and family roles. However, she did not construct a distinguishing orientation of her own that can be easily encapsulated; rather, true to her therapeutic beliefs, she seeded and nurtured the work of many of her (male) colleagues, particularly those she worked most closely with at the Mental Research Institute (MRI) in Palo Alto in the 1960s. Satir subsequently focused her interest on the human potential movement in the late 1960s and left the MRI to become director of training at Esalen in the late 1960s—just when the major presentations of the new systems paradigm were being organized.

Each of the approaches developed by Bowen, Whitaker, Minuchin, and Haley is now associated with a major orientation in family therapy, though the connection with the paterfamilial name persists. Bowen's work can be subsumed under the rubric *extended family systems theory* and Whitaker's under *experiential family therapy* (Nichols, 1984), but their singular influence dominates these orientations, much as Kohut's dominates self psychology. Minuchin's work, *structural family therapy,* is largely his construction. *Strategic family therapy* has been developed most actively and probably most substantially by Jay Haley. The four founding fathers occupy a bifurcated territory. Minuchin (1989) refers to the West and East Coast "divisions" of family therapy. The East Coast group—including Bowen, Minuchin, and Whitaker—began their careers with traditional psychodynamically rooted clinical training, which lends their clinical formulations a certain familiarity for psychoanalysts. The West Coast group—including Haley (originally a library scientist), John Weakland (a chemical engineer with cultural anthropology training), and Don Jackson (a psychiatrist)—initially gathered around Bateson, as members of the Palo Alto group, to study communication in animals and humans. This group clearly was dominated by nonclinicians, and their formulations about family interaction are generally experienced by psychodynamically oriented clinicians as strange and provocative (the psychoanalytic reader often has difficulty reading concern and commitment between the lines of models based on game theory and cybernetics).

All four founding fathers share a common point of origin inasmuch as the focus of the early work in family therapy was on severe pathologies. Bowen, Haley, and Whitaker studied schizophrenia; Minuchin, juvenile delinquency. The seemingly intractable nature of these clinical problems added a note of daring and perhaps even machismo to their ventures.

These four theorists, along with Satir, have, of course, worked in collaboration with others, who in turn have enriched, expanded, and redirected their ideas. Fresh advances were often made by women, who have provided an alternative perspective on the inevitably patriarchal assumptions embedded within the theories of the founding fathers. For instance, Haley is perhaps the most cogent and witty spokesperson for the highly directive strategic family therapy. Yet it is on the porch of that strategic edifice that Cloe Madanes (1981, 1984) developed her playful strategic approach, which involves inviting people to pretend to have their symptoms, thereby upsetting the inured power relationships around "sick" and "well" behavior. Another leading spokeswoman for the strategic approach is Mara Selvini Palazzoli. She and her Milan group have evolved a technique based on circular questioning rather than on directing. The essence of this approach is to inquire in a manner that promotes a cognitive-experiential sense that all relationships in the family are connected and that unidirectional causality is an illusion.

Let us begin a delineation of these four foundation perspectives in family therapy with a case example. However elegantly we clothe our theories, we all stand naked in the clinical moment. In fact, our moment of truth occurs when we try to resolve the human dilemmas presented to us, an effort that leads us to greet—and sometimes welcome—even the strangest of bedfellows.

CASE EXAMPLE: THE GIBSONS

Sally and Bob arrive at a therapist's office with two children in tow. The guidance counselor at their son's school has urged them to consult a psychotherapist. John, ten years old, is angry and withdrawn. He has never performed well at school, has been thoroughly evaluated more than once, and has been diagnosed as having a mild learning disorder. A course of Ritalin yielded equivocal results and was discontinued. John's objectionable behavior in the past involved some petty stealing and chronic lying. Lately, he strikes everyone as simply being miserably unhappy and sullen; he is socially isolated, and his academic work is considered unacceptable by his classroom teacher.

His eight-year-old sister, Meg, is slightly combative. She seems unsympathetic to her brother and detached from her parents. Nevertheless, she is the apple of her parents' eye because academically and socially she is a much closer fulfillment of their expectations.

Sally Gibson is an emotionally sympathetic mother who forgives and forgets the lapses of her children, partly, it seems, because she feels uncomfortable about the amount of time she spends away from them. She seems dedicated to offering compensatory "quality" nurturance for what she considers "quantity" neglect. She provides ready emotional explanations for John's difficulties, focusing often on her own failure to shield him from such traumas as her resuming full-time work.

Sally hints at, but does not directly ask for, more emotional involvement on the part of her husband, Bob, who is formal, reserved, and quite detached. He says that he cares a great deal about his family but appears to feel both helpless about and removed from his son's difficulties. He finds it hard to understand John's lack of self-discipline and perseverance. Sally and Bob have been married for ten years and spend most of their time together planning their schedules around parenting responsibilities.

John has spent considerable time in individual therapy, which has involved his parents in generally frustrating and gloomy parent guidance sessions. It is something of a therapeutic event to have this foursome convened together in a therapist's office. However, before applying our family therapy lens, it would be interesting to speculate about the clinical prognosis for these individuals in the absence of family therapy. One possible scenario follows (although the reader is encouraged to develop others):

John *might* find another individual therapist who would form a uniquely strong alliance with him, but John's record of failure (and thus his suspicion of individual therapy) militates against this possibility.

Meg would drift through latency. Increasingly perceiving pressure to compensate for her brother's emotional waywardness, she would feel angrier and angrier. She would also feel guiltier and guiltier about eclipsing him. Sally would seek individual therapy because of increasing dysphoria regarding John's development, but she would have enormous difficulty working through her maternal guilt, particularly if John becomes increasingly troubled. Bob would remain ostensibly outside the loop, detached but lonely.

What can family therapy offer them? Let's take a walking tour of each of the four theories, emphasizing points of uniqueness rather than areas of commonality, a tour highlighted by a brief dramatization of the response to the Gibsons of a family therapist from each of the four foundation perspectives.

The Orientation of Murray Bowen

Of the four foundation theories, Bowen's (1978) often seems most inviting to psychoanalysts. The cornerstones of his theory are the constructs of triangles, anxiety contagion, differentiation of self, and multigenerational transmission processes, constructs that at first glance have a familiar ring to them. However, although some of the conceptual formulations of Bowen's theory are resonant with analytic concerns, there are also striking differences between his theory and psychodynamic theory. And when his theory is translated into practice, these differences sharpen. Most significantly, Bowen disavowed the existence of the unconscious. He declared transference artifactual, elicited by analytic set and expectation. However, what can be inviting for psychoanalysts about Bowen's theory is that his theoretical corpus and his suggested approaches to treatment emphasize freeing oneself from family-of-origin relationship positions that are repetitively and compulsively restricting. Unlike other family therapists, Bowen usually focuses on the "then" rather than the "here and now."

Bowen and his followers have developed the use of the genogram to map multigenerational family structure. The genogram is generally a spatial representation of three generations, organized around demographic data (i.e., births and deaths, work commitments). Alternatively, a genogram can be problem focused and involve a transgenerational scanning of emotional themes (such as over-closeness between mother and son or deception). When it is centered on a theme of deception, for example, the therapist investigates the presence of secrets or lies in relationships within each generation as well as in those between generations.

I recently taught genogram construction to a first-year class of family therapists. What impressed me on this occasion was the reaction of a student who was initially, and intelligently, skeptical about so diagrammatic an approach to personal history. She nonetheless reported that creating the genogram was a powerful experience for her because it invited her to reflect anew on the meaning of her parents' divorce, despite the fact that this event has been harvested repeatedly in her own analytic sessions. It was striking that the offering of this information about her family—even in the context of a self-conscious simulation with a fellow student—had this much impact on her even though she had already focused on it in individual therapy. It leads me to speculate that family data may be encoded in some inchoate, not exactly unconscious form, and that its recall is uniquely facilitated by a schematic, diagrammatic instrument.

When and where did Bowen develop his theory? Bowen developed his family-of-origin theory in the 1950s when he was granted enough funds by the National Institute of Mental Health to house entire families on research wards. He was most struck by triangulation processes. In his view, dyads are inherently unstable as relationship units because of the anxiety generated about both separateness and merging. The a priori assumption of Bowen's theory is that anxiety is an automatic response of the human organism to threat and that it is passed from one individual to another in subtle and multiple ways. Bowen believed that disruptive anxiety could be reduced by involving a third party and that when the seas of anxiety were calmed, the two-person craft could set sail once more.

Bowen shares with psychoanalysts a disinclination to differentiate pathological from normal processes and structures. He views dynamics on a continuum. Dyadic anxiety is, in his opinion, a norm. However, he posits that it is less well functioning units that are most likely to rope in a third party, whose function resembles that of the intermittently summoned but always available extra in stage productions. When the anxiety abates, the third person once again becomes peripheral. Anxiety is most disabling to dyads whose members have the least differentiation from one another. Differentiation of self is characterized by the ability to control anxiety by distinguishing thought from feeling. The differentiated person takes a moment to assess the danger and thus reduces the contagious emotional response to it.

The Bowenian family therapist remains central during therapy sessions, discouraging "reactivity" or emotional responsiveness between family members. Most importantly, the therapist resists being triangulated by the couple—that is, drawn into an unholy alliance with one of its members or serving as a temporary mediator or judge—and urges the couple to own their wishes and needs by making "I-statements" rather than accusations to each other. The most important goal of Bowenian therapy is increased differentiation of self.

In passing, some criticisms may be noted. There is a rather assumptive quality to Bowen's constructs and clinical descriptions, such as his asserted link between cognition and differentiation. This formulation, which credits cognition at the expense of affect, fails to account for current psychological research and theoretical findings regarding the inseparability of these functions. Additionally, it smacks of traditional male gender bias in its evaluation of affect and responsiveness. Finally, there is the emphasis, unique to Bowenian family therapy, on working with one person in the family—presumably the most differentiated person—around explorations of his or her family of origin, with the expectation that other family members will in due course rise to that person's enhanced developmental level. Some of this work grew out of the treatment of families with an alcoholic member, and in that context it made clinical sense to work with whatever strengths were available. However, many family therapists—certainly those of other orientations—are wary of working with only part of the relationship system.

Bowen's Approach to the Gibsons

What would be Bowen's approach to the Gibsons? For family therapists working within the Bowenian orientation children are most often viewed as stabilizers in their parents' anxiety field. Thus, before long, the Bowenian therapist would dismiss the children, and the parents would then begin the long journey toward defining and articulating their differentiated selfhood. The therapist would invite Bob and Sally to listen attentively to each other's I-statements about responsibility and nurturance. Bob might be encouraged to say, for example, "I know how to support my children and wife financially; it's the only way I've learned" or "I'm haunted by the guilt of not being more available to Meg and John." By the same token, requests of the other would be discouraged. Sally would be discouraged from demanding or beseeching Bob for more emotional involvement ("Never pursue a distancer" is an axiom of Bowenian family therapy). She would be encouraged instead to calmly state her preference for increased involvement and intimacy and to reveal the steps she planned to take to achieve it.

Sally and Bob would be encouraged both to reflect on their families of origin and to consider disengaging from the triangles that ensnare them therein. How would this be accomplished? Sally and Bob would be urged to return to their families of origin to locate the zones of anxiety between themselves and other family members that had been covered over through the actions of another person, a third party who served as mediator or even scapegoat for the anxious dyad. It is expected that they can now deal with the anxiety directly. As they investigate family-of-origin relationships, Sally would be encouraged both to find the source of her high-intensity nurturing and to desist from it. Bob would seek the roots of his disengagement and sense of paternal impotence. The focus would be on each spouse individually, though in the presence of the other. In the final phase of therapy, disentanglement from family-of-origin triangles would be formalized by "coaching," that is, planned investigative sojourns to family-of-origin sites. Together the couple would meet with their Bowenian "coach," perhaps on a monthly basis to review their impressions and, one hopes, their de-triangulation.

The Orientation of Salvador Minuchin: Structural Family Therapy

Salvador Minuchin was fully trained in interpersonal psychoanalysis at the William Alanson White Institute in New York. However, though psychoanalytic treatment informed his development of the structural model, particularly in his emphasis on the wedding of participation to observation, Minuchin's early work with delinquent youth took him on a very different therapeutic journey (Minuchin and Nichols, 1993). Minuchin had been trained in child psychiatry before his training at the White Institute, and his first position after graduating from White was at Wiltwick School for Boys during the 1960s. The families of the children housed there were overburdened and overstressed by psychological and economic hardships (Minuchin et al., 1967). Minuchin found it impossible to explore anything at all in the chaotic and anxiety-packed parent–child meetings he was conducting, and he was compelled to find a creative way to encourage self-reflection. Moreover, self-observation had to be concretized and dramatized for an underclass population strained to the psychic limit by the struggle for mere survival. (Indeed, the psychic fluidity required to move to and fro from self to object—the assumed sine qua non of psychoanalytic work—is achieved with difficulty by many patients less stressed than Minuchin's original population.) Minuchin hit on an ingenious solution: he began to use a one-way mirror with family members. He asked one "subsystem" of the family (i.e., the children or the parents) to go behind the mirror and observe and comment on the other.

In general, family confusion and anxiety was contained when Minuchin met with subsystems of the family, and a narrower interactional

field allowed him to work with strong affects and resulted in his patients' having a greater focus and a reduced tendency to externalize.
Once he was working with subsystems, Minuchin became aware of the
nested systems of unspoken rules and the webs of alliances that supported these subsystems and of the armamentarium of behaviors the
subsystems could use to erect walls and establish boundaries to protect
themselves from outside influences. Thus, the basic approach of structural family therapy was conceived, with the therapist's first job being to
construct a map of family structure, considered in all its operative
subsystems, around a particular presenting problem.

Minuchin's clinical approach has sometimes been viewed as an oppressive strong-arming of patients into changing their customary and
reflexive relational approaches. In fact, the directorial, challenging role
he has taken in family sessions was in the service of battling redundancy, or what L. Hoffman (1981) calls the "cross-joined" density of
family patterns. Minuchin believes that his therapeutic interventions—
for example, his stereotypical invitation to people to change seats and
experience new cues of proximity and distance or his request that
fathers as tall as basketball players stand next to tyrannical eight-year-
olds for "sizing"—provide the experiential intensity required to expand
awareness. What has been underemphasized in Minuchin's work is his
exquisite skill at bonding with the family, often by speaking to family
members in their own language and idiom. He identifies this necessary
process in therapy as "joining" with the family.

Characteristic of his work from the beginning—and this is the essence
of the participant-observational stance, even as it was first introduced
by Sullivan—is Minuchin's own willingness to move in and out of the
family drama. The therapist is enjoined to enter the system and to
experience its pain and test its flexibility. Minuchin's theory developed
organically as he repeatedly experimented with entering and leaving
the proscenium on which family interaction takes place and became
more and more persuaded of the usefulness of a dramaturgical model.
Over time, he has evolved an advanced therapeutic approach that uses
metaphoric concepts such as intensity, punctuation, and enactment
(Minuchin and Fishman, 1981).

An inveterate iconoclast fond of sphinx-like communications, Minuchin now disclaims his belief in "structural family therapy." This
recantation is rather like disowning a wayward child, although here the
waywardness largely has been the fault of bad companions rather than
poor parenting. Much more committed to experience and poetics than
to technique, Minuchin was somewhat dismayed by the often random
translation of his theory into diagrams and charts of family structures.

Still the therapeutic iconoclast, he now emphasizes his therapeutic stance of "challenging the family's reality."

Minuchin's Approach to the Gibsons

Minuchin's original schema of structural family therapy prescribed a very useful mapping of family structure, one that characterized the quality and organization of the sibling, parental, and grandparental generations (one certainly wonders about the latter in the case of the Gibsons). Topographical features to be mapped include coalitions (clearly, mom and the kids) and boundaries sustained or invaded (stealing is an overly obvious boundary-invading behavior, but what does it represent more subtly in a given family's organization?).

During the course of treatment Minuchin (1974) would hope to redraw a family's map experientially, with the therapist being in the position of a director who is both active and immersed in the action. With the Gibsons perhaps therapy would begin with an enactment, a heightened and dramatic exemplar, of how John's sullenness depletes the family's emotional resources. Minuchin might first encourage John to rage at his parents, sister, teachers, and athletic coaches (and anyone else available) for his mistreatment and might then have John and his parents note the strewn emotional battlefield they are left occupying. "On whom would John plant the flag of victory?" Minuchin might ask. The enactment would then continue with a second act: a new dramatic denouement in which John would be helped to recede in emotional valence, perhaps by sharing a bit of playful and ordinary brattiness with his sister. In this way, John and his sister would be linked in an ordinary and expectable sibling interaction. Perhaps Bob might help Sally feel less responsible for John's difficulties, deepening their parental collaboration. In fact, the enactment might well conclude with the parents finding a moment of rare but welcome pleasure with their wayward son.

The Orientation of Carl Whitaker: Existential Family Therapy

Carl Whitaker is an original. Stylistically folksy and homespun, Whitaker is determined to speak, as he puts it, from his human rather than his clinical sensibility. He is as likely to ask any or all family members about the previous night's dream as he is to disclose his own dream fragments, and with the same insouciance (Neill and Kniskern, 1982). As a young therapist, Whitaker asked for grandparental visits so that he could have some "wise" people on hand; as an old man he asks parents to "remind" him how to raise kids. Skipping over some of the more difficult conundrums inherent in our current philosophical per-spective, Whitaker has a ten-point list of rules for beginning therapists (Guerin, 1978), including: "Guard your impotence as one of your most valuable weapons" and "Build long-term relations so you can be free to hate safely."

Whitaker's approach to therapy focuses on highlighting the most essential and existential aspects of human experience and advocates the use of creative absurdity:

> The use of the absurd may be a fragment . . . or it may become an ongoing process. When it is such, it resembles the leaning tower of Pisa. The patient comes in offering an absurdity, and the therapist accepts the absurdity, builds upon it, escalates it until the tower has become so high and so tilted that it crashes to the ground [1975, p. 6].

Thus, Whitaker, arm in arm with family members, enters into realms of experience sometimes avoided by other family therapists. His funda-mental belief is that bringing the irrational and the seemingly indigest-ible into awareness will liberate the family to find new solutions and new forms of support. In a remarkable videotaped demonstration interview of a family with a hospitalized preadolescent suicidal son, he brings to life the image of the entire family performing a dirge-like symphony of death—feared, longed for, and persecutory—in which each family member is a musician and the son is no longer a solo performer. In the video Whitaker absurdly claims that all death is a form of suicide and asks the sensible and sober father in the family why his own father, who died as a result of cardiac arrest, might have killed himself. He proceeds to tell an anecdote about a returned war veteran who had to give up his work as a door-to-door salesman because he was terrified of an impulse to garrote women who refused his wares. By the end of the session both therapist and family (now embracing the identi-fied patient) are absorbed and tethered together in the human dramas of death and survival.

Whitaker's hope is that by allowing himself to respond honestly and vitally to a family he will awaken hope and slough off some of the encrusted expectations and projections. With his response including everything from wrestling with latency-age toughs to confabulating with demented grandmas, his work is a crucial antidote to some of the carefully planned and engineered intervention strategies in family therapy. His de-emphasis on purposeful change makes him an impor-tant compass for psychoanalysts entering the family praxis arena. In fact, a key concept of Whitaker's theory is the necessity to dip into primary process; his idea of a healthy family is one that allows its members to do so. From a family therapy training perspective, his ideas are usually offered as a ballast to more conventionally codified schemas of interventions and techniques.

Whitaker's Approach to the Gibsons

Obviously, it is difficult to imagine Whitaker's response to the Gibsons, save that one can be sure it would be unexpected. Perhaps Whitaker would play with the parents around their humorless response to the behavior of their children, in effect rooting around for projected wishes and disclaimed potentialities. Perhaps he would ask "Where did John learn to be a crook?" or, in an attempt to discover what the parents have "stolen" from each other, "Any other crooks in the family?"

Whitaker might wonder whether John is trying to breathe life into his enervated and depressed parents. Is he trying to provide for Dad the mischievous childhood he never dared claim for himself? Is he trying to help Mom become the good-enough mother she always wished she had? "Hard work, that," Whitaker might comment, and then he would perhaps proceed to reminisce about his own boyhood projects, projects that, he might note, led him into a career in psychiatry and family therapy—at which point he might stop to warn John to be careful!

Whatever else, the interview would be emotionally intense—for Whitaker and for the family. Richard Simon (1985a) quotes Milton Miller, who worked with Whitaker in the early Wisconsin Medical School years:

> "It's always safest in a human encounter if nothing happens," says Milton Miller. "But with Whitaker there are few non-events. People may love him or hate him, but something happens. He's unwilling to pretend to go through the motions. It is as if he lives by the principle that the perfunctory kiss is the worst perversion" [p. 32].

The Orientation of Jay Haley: Strategic Family Therapy

Haley (1976, 1980), who has most comprehensively delineated the strategic approach in family therapy, was one of the original members of the Palo Alto Mental Research Institute during the 1950s, the think tank under whose aegis strategic family therapy was first developed. He, John Weakland, Don Jackson, Virginia Satir, and, later, Paul Watzlawick attempted to map the patterns of communication—at multiple and often confused levels—that determine dysfunctional relationship systems. Among the array of theoretical models upon which this group drew to capture the vicissitudes of communication, models unfamiliar to most psychoanalytic thinkers, are the following: game theory, group theory of mathematics, cybernetics, and Russell and Whitehead's (1910–1913) logical typing. The lattermost model in particular yielded a bumper crop of paradoxical interventions. Essentially noting that a member cannot be itself and also a class of members, this group adopted the command "Be spontaneous" as their standard. Note that if one is to obey the injunction as an injunction, spontaneity cannot be a member of a class of behaviors so ordered—that is, if I obey your injunction to act spontaneously, I'm not being spontaneous because that class of behaviors cannot be ordered. However, if I cannot be spontaneous, I've abrogated my relationship to you, which was based on an agreement to comply with your commands. Thus, I'd better consider being spontaneous again. And so it goes, in a mad circular illogical chase. This kind of logical instability seemed characteristic of communication patterns in schizophrenic families and provided a point of departure for working with that clinical group. The MRI group also discovered, however, that deliberate logical ill-typing was an effective means of destabilizing rigidly organized families, for whom prescribing the symptom was ultimately liberating. Essentially, prescribing a symptom to a patient locks the patient in a therapeutic double bind. The patient is told to change by remaining the same. The involuntary (the symptom) becomes voluntary; resistance and rebellion become cure.

Strategic family therapy has been given the worst press in the psychoanalytic community. Its very name is anathema. How dare a therapist have a strategy when the essence of therapy, if it is at all humanistic, is the enhancement of the client's *self*-expression and *self*-determination? In fact, those in the strategic group have coveted their *enfant terrible* status; it abets, as they are only too aware, their overall strategy of shaking and moving the mental health community. Their theory and work are inherently and deliberately exclusive of analytic theory.[3] They may not be opposed to the idea of the unconscious, but they are not interested in it either.

Strategic family therapists prefer to greet the mysteries of self-destructiveness and self-deception from the perspective of "second-order change," which is a change of set. Second-order change, when it occurs naturally or is deliberately induced, changes the system itself.

---

[3]Haley considers Dr. Milton Erickson, with whom he studied hypnosis in the 1950s, a key influence and mentor in terms of the development of his strategic technique (see Erickson, 1973).

First-order change is change within a system (usually the attempted solution becomes, recursively, part of the problem). Watzlawick, Weakland, and Fisch (1974) capture the quintessential difference between the two in the example of a nightmare: Changing its imagery to make a nightmare somewhat less terrifying is a first-order change; a second-order change is waking up. As long as the dreamer stays in the dream, he or she cannot "solve" its preconditions. Second-order change can appear absurd and foolishly simpleminded, partly because it overturns so much laborious, nose-to-the-grindstone, first-order kind of thinking. In fact, Watzlawick, Weakland, and Fisch (1974) warn that because it "is always in the nature of a discontinuity or a logical jump, we may expect the practical manifestations of second-order change to appear as illogical and paradoxical" (p. 12). There is tremendous emphasis in the strategic approach on evaluating ongoing ideologies and assumptions about change and on then changing them. Thus, it is understood that mothers who exquisitely query their school-phobic children about their daily terrors will, if the central dynamic is separation anxiety, confirm their fears that their mother needs access to their every worry and preoccupation. To be sure, creatively arriving at something else that might be truly helpful for a mother to do—something that takes her, her child's, her husband's, and perhaps her other children's character into account—is not a simple task. Therein resides the artistry of the strategic family therapists. Although they think very carefully and thoroughly about family relationships, they work counter to subjectively experienced rationales, and thus they appear dispassionate and Machiavellian to the psychoanalyst. In what might be an alternative strategic approach to a case of school phobia, a mother would be advised to encourage her child to talk to older siblings about his or her anxiety. The mother could thus remain active (she probably feels she has to be), but the child would be freed of her overwrought interest and could then reconnect with the siblings, who almost certainly would be more relaxed about his or her difficulties at school.

A more psychoanalytically palatable arm of strategic therapy has been the circular questioning approach of the Milan school. Psychoanalysts by training and Marxists by ideology, Selvini Palazzoli and her associates (1978) worked intensely in a therapeutic collective to develop an approach to severe family dysfunction. Many of their clients were poor southern Italian families who could make the train trek into Milan only once per month. Thus, the group evolved a highly structured session that lasted several hours and culminated in either a formal written statement (a strategic positive description of the dysfunctional behavior) or a ritual prescription, read aloud as if a papal bull were

emanating from behind the one-way mirror. On the basis of information garnered in the intake phone call, the group formulated hypotheses about the family's dynamics; these hypotheses were tested in the
session by means of an inquiry approach. The style of questioning was
conceived of as circular, that is, as derived from a Batesonian emphasis
on information emerging from difference and difference signifying
relationship. Circular questions generally involve locating events in the
family on a spatial or temporal continuum; rank-ordering family members in terms of a specific characteristic; questioning the effect on a third
person of an interaction between two members; and inviting one family
member to comment on the relationship between two other family
members. The Milan team believed that through circular questioning a
family could be induced to think in a circular, interdependent manner.
The work done during the first segment of the session (i.e., the garnering of information through circular questioning) is considered critical to
the formulation and tailoring of the final prescription.[4] Thus, when the
Gibsons are interviewed, the following circular questions might be
posed: "Was Mom more or less worried about John after she started her
new job?"; "When Dad and John are arguing, what happens to Meg?"

Haley's Approach to the Gibsons

What would Haley's approach to the Gibsons be? It would center on
the symptomatic presentation; strategic family therapists emphasize a
focus on the symptom as requisite to respecting the family's reality,
their psychological suffering, and consumer rights. Indeed, strategic
interventions always employ the symptom as a central organizer and
principal metaphor. This approach both treats the symptom with respect (for, after all, it truly has become a central organizer for this family
system) and brings it clearly into focus so that (to use a surgical metaphor) it can be cleanly excised.

Haley's work with the Gibsons would be clearly delineated in stages
or sequences. John's sullen withdrawal would be dealt with first, via
hierarchical bolstering of parental authority by means of two prescribed
subsequences: (1) a schedule of increased contact between father and
son in an effort to dissolve overly close mother–son involvement, and
(2) increased parental collaboration around clear and consistent expectations for John's behavior.

If this direct approach failed, paradoxical injunctions would be de-
vised and delivered. That is, John might be encouraged to remain

[4]An interesting presentation of circular questioning focused on imagined future-
oriented possibilities for the family is found in Penn (1985).

difficult to prevent Mom from unleashing her frustration toward un-available Dad. Or John might be advised that his sullen behavior is actually helpful to his mother and that since she clearly wants to excel as a mother, he has to provide her with his bad moods and angry outbursts—in fact, perhaps he might work harder at it—so that she can "solve" them. (One could not responsibly advise a *truly* depressed youngster in this fashion, but John is sullen, not seriously depressed.)

Although the marital affective imbalance would be kept in mind while addressing John's difficulties, Haley would cordon off marital difficulties during the first stage of therapy and would focus exclusively on the presenting symptom, John's bad behavior.

COCONSTRUCTIVISTS RESPOND

There has always been an anchor trailing the schooners of Minuchin, Bowen, Haley, and Whitaker (though this is probably less true for the latter). That anchor has been the concern about the directive and regulatory quality inherent in many family therapeutic interventions. The concern has congealed during the last five years in the form of an alternative orientation to praxis within the family therapy movement— the narrative approach. A word of caution may be in order here. A psychodynamic theorist entering the family realm needs first to acquire a working sense of the four basic perspectives as background to grasp the thrust of the narrative position in the family therapy movement, because the narrative perspective was originally and essentially a reac-tion and corrective to the more directive and intentional approaches. In that respect, the cornerstone positions (family-of-origin, structural, experiential, strategic), which offer a sharp contrast to psychoanalytic practice, if not theory, inform the theorizing of the narrative school. However, the underlying essence of the systems perspective can be lost in an immersion in narrative work, which seems quite natural to psychodynamic theorists, who are trained in the domains of inquiry, subjectivity, and the give-and-take between therapist and client but who lack a working sense of how systems function.

The key figures in this narrative movement are Harlene Anderson and Harold Goolishian (1988, 1990) at the Galveston Family Institute in Texas and Michael White and David Epston at the Dulwich Center in Adelaide, Australia. Their work is refreshing and inviting. Essentially encouraging therapists to think of their work as conversation and to eschew what they consider to be rhetorical positions of influence and persuasion (which have been carefully crafted as technique in the family realm), the narrative school seeks a democratization of therapy. Practitioners in this school move considerably beyond an analytic coconstruction of narrative, an approach posited by Schafer (1992). However, at times it seems that their approach gives insufficient credence to the knotty therapeutic dilemma of maintaining a balance between reassuring expertise and empathic immersion, a dilemma all therapists face. Anderson and Goolishian (1990) describe their proposal:

> Therapist and client come together in dialogue and neither maintains an independent meaning structure that works only in an interactive [i.e., turn-taking] fashion. In effect they generate a dialogically *shared domain* of meaning that belongs *to* the moment and *in* (and only in) the therapeutic conversation [p. 162].

Most widely influential within the narrative movement is the work of Michael White and David Epston, who sit—somewhat comfortably—on the conversation–intervention border. Although they work within the narrative form and want to see something shift in the family's experience, they believe that "re-storying" is the genre within which to work. Using the whole cloth of Jerome Bruner's (1986) concepts—the narrative authoring of lives and the "relative indeterminacy of a text"—White and Epston "re-story" with clients to create new versions, second chapters, and spicy epilogues, which then, they assume, become the performative texts of living. A favorite technique is "externalization," whereby members of a family are first encouraged to tell their ordinary narrative about their principal difficulty (essentially to tell a story of distress and conflict) and White and Epston then ply them with a steady stream of questions in an effort to characterize the problem as *external* to the persons who suffer it. Epston (1994) states: "I am like a butterfly catcher, waiting for the metaphor to rise up so I can net it and then display it to the clients" (p. 35). In telling how the problem has affected their life and vice versa, family members become witness to their self-persecution via the problem, an experience generally outside what White and Epston consider the "dominant story" of subjective distress. These therapists look for "unique outcomes" or "moments when the problem is subverted, critiqued or protested" and invite family members to consider themselves rather like psychological warriors who defeat or circumvent a long-standing source of distress (p. 32). Epston characterizes as dialogic the letters he writes to clients after each session, letters in which he shares his reactions and asks for input. However, those who observe and appreciate the work of White and Epston find resonances of hypnotic induction in their work and are impressed with the unmistakable and central authority they wield in session (O'Hanlon, 1994; Waters, 1994).

It is as if the narrative tradition that is emerging pervasively but cautiously in the psychoanalytic paradigm were suddenly magnified to the fifth power within the field of family therapy. Theory and practice within the field of family therapy does, indeed, tend to move in fast-forward because the threshold for instigating therapeutic change is steeper. I believe that there is much to learn from the narrative attempts within family therapy. Most essential to that learning are the implications of a shared versus individually scripted narrative. Do patients bring to psychoanalysts an individual life story or a family tall tale? When psychoanalysts coconstruct a new narrative with their patients, what happens to the larger text of the family narrative? As more and more psychoanalysts move back and forth between these paradigms, we will begin to have answers to such questions.

PSYCHOANALYTICALLY ORIENTED FAMILY THERAPISTS

There is a group of psychoanalytically oriented family therapists who have produced a small but important body of literature. Several different psychoanalytic orientations are represented by theorists interested in integrating systems theory with their own. These integrative efforts can only be reviewed in synopsis form here, though they warrant more careful analysis.

For the most part, the psychoanalytic paradigm has remained figure and the systems literature has retained the background position in this literature. In contrast, my intention here is toward greater volatility, toward opening up the possibility of syntheses weighted in either paradigmatic direction. I hope to provide readers with greater familiarity with basic family systems theory in order to enhance their understanding of the scholarly contributions of these adventuresome psychoanalytic family theorists. Robin Skynner (1976) has developed a model of family development relevant to classical theory in which he diagnoses *family* problems psychosexually (e.g., as anal level versus oedipal). Forrest (1978), Siegel (1987), and Gerson (1993) have developed links to the interpersonal model, notably around such concepts as the personified self, selective inattention, and consensual validation. If, as Sullivan believed, we heal ourselves by courageously checking out our sense of reality with another, then this process can involve a significant other besides the analyst. To date there has yet been noticeably little developed within the self-psychological model, though one attempt to link self psychology and systems theory has yielded some interesting possibilities: Brighton-Cleghorn (1987), drawing on self psychology and Winnicottian theory, has speculated about the child serving as self-object for the entire family as a collective unit.

It is the object relations theorists who have been most active in forging links to systems theory. Of this group, Boszormenyi-Nagy (1987) has produced the most comprehensive body of work, representing his attempt to flesh out systemic concepts with object relations processes and dynamics. Notable among these is his concept of invisible loyalties, which is based on the notion of a ledger of unsettled accounts from past family experience (with entries determined by whether or not there has been "fairness in what has been given relative to what has been received"). Stierlin (1977), who stressed that we transfer unbalanced columns into later intimate relationships, has identified a particular transgenerational phenomenon, which he calls the "family delegation process." Offspring are sent out into the world on elastic psychological leashes to find a solution for their parents' long-standing conflicts at the same time that they are enjoined, irreconcilably, to keep their parents company in their misery.

The Scharffs have attempted a major integration of the systems and object relations perspectives. Ecumenism is an explicit issue for the Scharffs, who lament the fact that therapists have had to choose between family systems and psychodynamic work because of a supposed theoretical or clinical incompatibility between these approaches. They have produced a substantial body of writing representing thoughtful applications of the object relations perspective for different modalities and settings, such as sex and group therapy and school consultation. The Scharff family therapy is atypical in that it is longer (two years on average), nondirective, and reliant on interpretation as intervention. Scharff and Scharff (1987) apply fundamental psychoanalytic clinical constructs—transference, countertransference, and working through—to family work (none of these have found a ready home in the family systems literature). Valuing the emergence of affect, they "aim for derepression, for the emergence of unconscious motivating forces and the elucidation of repressed relationships" (p. 10). A very interesting distinction they develop is between the "focused transferences" of individuals to each other as well as to the therapist (the latter being our common definition of transference) and the "contextual transference" that the whole family develops toward the family therapist. The contextual transference derives from a range of personal experiences, including "the mother's holding of the baby" and "the previous generation and its holding of the current family" (p. 68). This form of transference thus entails projection onto the therapist of the family's experience of "shared holding," with its own particular signature deficit, such as a shared experience of mutual deprivation. According to the Scharff perspective, family members oscillate between focused and contextual transferences. This, of course, necessitates that the family therapist track the fluctuations between the two kinds of transference, though the contextual transference is considered more important. The Scharffs work with individual maps of family structure that reflect the internal object relations drama of each family member. Their work is enormously complex and rich. However, as I have indicated elsewhere (Gerson, 1988), I think that in their effort to keep psychoanalytic concepts both primary and untransmuted, they unduly stretch these constructs at the same time that they lose the heuristic value of an organizing systemic frame. Letting systems concepts carry the weight of the family's process is a more parsimonious solution, I think.[5]

[5]Since this text is an attempt to present the model of family systems theory in introductory form for psychoanalysts, I have chosen to use a minimalist form of presentation, neglecting to describe some theorists who made significant conceptual contributions to the literature. Of particular interest to psychoanalysts, though not covered in the text, are the writings of Nathan Ackerman, which document his shift from a psychodynamic to a systems paradigm, and those of Theodore Lidz (1976), whose particular focus, highly informed by psychoanalytic thinking, was on schizophrenia and family relationships.

chapter four

Theoretical Elaborations and Controversies

Rosencrantz: Consistency is all I ask.
Guildenstern: Give us this day our daily mask.
Tom Stoppard

Our walk through systems theory may have been a bit too rapid for the psychoanalytic reader, who is more likely than not to want to stop to examine some of the theoretical guideposts. Therefore, to supplement the necessarily impressionistic look at the major theorists in the preceding chapters I will map out here some of the underlying theoretical issues that provide the common ground of family therapy theory, as well as some of the criticisms leveled at the family systems model from within the field of family therapy. These conceptual struggles can be compared to controversies within psychoanalysis, though there is a notable difference in the intensity of disputation. I will then examine some of the basic similarities and differences between family therapy and psychoanalytic thinking, especially as they bear on that most profound of all issues – the question of the self.

CONCEPTUAL STRUGGLES

Let us begin with disputation. Theorists of family therapy rarely lock conceptual horns. One could say that the four basic orientations have existed essentially as fiefdoms, respectfully acknowledging each other's presence but attending primarily to internal affairs. Minuchin (1985) is the one exception to the rule; he talks about "hearing the voices" of his colleagues as he works: "I am pleased to acknowledge that when I say to a man 'When did you divorce your wife and marry your office?' it is Carl's [Whitaker's] voice speaking. He might not recognize it in my accent, but it is there, as are all the others" (p. 20). On a nuts-and-bolts training level, professionals who study family therapy are, in most cases, presented with one fundamental orientation, but eventually they feel comfortable weaving in techniques and interventions from other orientations. The large areas of commonality make this relatively easy.

Conflicts in the psychoanalytic domain have historically been livelier and more heated, as in the critique by object relational and interpersonal theorists of the classical drive model, which they consider too biologically rooted and teleological. But psychoanalysts have become much more catholic of late. In fact the relational model has emerged as an attempt to provide an overarching structure for semiautonomous psychoanalytic orientations, rather like the unification of nation-states in the late 19th century. The effort is welcome because theoretical differences had become paramount, obscuring the similarities between psychoanalytic perspectives. Moreover, there exists a general admission among psychoanalytic clinicians that work with certain patients necessitates a certain stretching of our favored technical, if not theoretical, stances and that someone else's theory sometimes has a place in this stretching. Nevertheless, a measure of the passion in psychoanalytic theory building still derives from exegetic disputes. Many classical theorists still continue to regard object relational analysts and interpersonalists as perhaps too softhearted (if not softheaded) and therefore reluctant to face the Armageddon of unbridled instinct expression. Interpersonal analysts still define themselves as rebelliously relinquishing deterministic biological models. The debates may have become decidedly more good-natured but they remain grist for the conceptual mill and psychoanalysis, like Talmudic study, is all the richer for it.

By comparison, discussions in family therapy are pacific. This is not to say that there is a complete absence of intellectual debate within family therapy, but thus far it has been contained within what Auerswald calls a "both-and" frame. The commitment to pluralism derives in part from the post-Newtonian scientific ethos, in which one grows up knowing that light is somehow both particle and wave, and from a postmodern discomfort with grand and inclusive explanations for the way that people or nature behaves. Then, too, the commitment to pluralism benefits from the fact that all of family systems theory was born of Bateson and Von Bertalanffy and that all family therapy orientations have evolved during one scientific era.

Psychoanalytic theory developed segmentally, over several eras and under the aegis of different paradigms. As E. A. Levenson (1972) points out, a paradigm shift occurred within psychoanalytic theory when the shift was made from Freud's Newtonian model (person as machine) to Sullivan's informational model (person as communicator). The battle to reframe 19th-century classical theory in a post-Newtonian language and then to locate interpersonal theory in its multiple 1940s sociological and scientific paradigms—and bring it all together—has been hard fought. In family therapy the suborientations evolved in the same era, creating an ecumenical spirit. Ecumenism also emanates from the basic pragmatic orientation of family therapy. An instrumental stance toward change, oriented to shifting redundant patterns, honors efficiency and parsimony. This stance invites playful self-conscious debate, not the impassioned arguments generated within psychoanalytic theory.

There are those who view a pragmatic stance as the most enlightened philosophical position. Thus, Minuchin, seemingly almost amused by the acerbic interventions generated by the cybernetic model, nonetheless hospitably integrates them into his more personally intense and engaged work with families. Within a both-and frame, therapists typically choose those segments of the available spectrum of theory and technique that fit best with their own basic way of being and working.

INTERDISCIPLINARY CONTRIBUTIONS

Far from being a closed and completed model, family therapy theory is constantly stretched by new ideas, often from other disciplines, particularly the sciences. In fact, reading the leading family therapy journals can be a bit like sitting in on a "science for lit majors" seminar. In recent years family therapy theory has been considerably perturbed by ideas from biology, chemistry, and physics.

Auerswald (1987) has commented on the use of models from physics to provide a scientific rationale for family interventions:

> [Planck and Einstein] stepped through the cracks in the Cartesian/ Newtonian view of physical reality and laid the groundwork for a new view of reality . . . [and] this transformation in physics became an important metaphor. [Family therapists] were looking for methods of intervening that could create transformations to improve the lives of people. . . . For ourselves, we wanted to validate ourselves as scientists, not as mystics. And here was an event shape that satisfied both these criteria. It was rooted in science, and it contained a large-scale transform [p. 322].

This science is often called "new science" because the formerly predominant Western epistemology, which demanded that a paradigm be either true or untrue, has yielded under the influence of Planck and Einstein to a new epistemology, which demands a "both-and rather than an either-or perspective" (p. 323). Truth can no longer be *the* truth;

truth can only be heuristic. And within this overall framing, many models have proven heuristic. A profile of "new science" perspectives that have influenced family theorizing follows.

Chaos Theory

Chaos theory is not really about chaos. It is about the implicate order of our very complex systems. Where a system is multiply integrated, such that each of its parts is capable of influencing others of its parts (e.g., a network of home computers), small, essentially random perturbations within it can give rise to large-scale events.

> Traditionally, when physicists saw complex results, they looked for complex causes. When they saw a random relationship between what goes into a system and what comes out, they assumed that they would have to build randomness into any realistic theory, by artificially adding noise or error. The modern study of chaos began with the creeping realization in the 1960s that quite simple mathematical equations could model systems every bit as violent as a waterfall [Gleick, 1987, p. 8].

Modern physics has made important contributions to family therapy, particularly with regard to a tenet of chaos theory, namely, that very small initial differences can result in wide variations in a process. The essence of chaos theory is that complex systems are sensitive to initial conditions. Thus, when a bowling ball is launched, microscopic differences in how it is thrown lead to a gratifying strike or to a disappointing gutter ball. One can depend on *some* effect because of a general tendency of a complex system to generate order out of chaos because of deeply encoded structures of order.

The focus on intended or specific results is illusory. Chaos theory encompasses why, for instance, it is impossible to reproduce a Stradivarius violin or cello in spite of the best mathematical analyses of acoustics, chemical analysis of varnishes, and the finest of archaeological investigations into the techniques of Stradivari's workshop:

> Cellos . . . are nonlinear systems; their behavior cannot be predicted precisely in the conventional sense. . . . Every component of a cello—back, belly, ribs, sound post, varnish, and the rest—reacts differently when agitated by different amounts of energy . . . a small change in the input of energy to a component can trigger a major change in what the component does. . . . The sensitive dependence on initial conditions that characterizes a cello's nonlinear performance means that even very slight differences between the observed, measured value and the actual one out there in the body of the cello can throw off the results in a direction that

cannot be anticipated. Because all measurements are only as exact as the tool used to make them, errors are inevitable, and those errors have, so far, been enough to prevent anyone from imitating Stradivari [Levenson, 1994, pp. 373–374].

How does chaos theory inform family therapy? This lively development in new science leads us to keep our faith in disrupting redundancy while realistically tolerating uncertainty. If we invite the Gibson family, our case example, to return for one more—and this time an even more speculative—visit, we might note the following. If we are successful at linking John more securely to his sibling, thus extricating him from his triangulated position with regard to his parents, we might see a quite unanticipated kaleidoscopic rippling through the family network triggered by this specific subsystemic shift. For example, if Sally became unburdened from maternal guilt, she might go on to challenge her own parents for their parental behavior, and in turn they might (in a burst of retirement energy) allow themselves some marital pleasure after a long dry season of mutual avoidance!

Order out of Fluctuation

A new science analogue for clinical narratives with highly pragmatic value has been found in the work on systems theory by Ilya Prigogine, a French chemist. Working with the concept of open systems—that is, systems "partially open to the inflow of energy (information) and/or matter"—Prigogine showed that "the ensuing instabilities do not lead to random behavior . . . ; instead, they tend to drive the system to a new dynamic regime which corresponds to a new state of complexity. In such a transition, the system acquires . . . new possibilities for action" (Jantsch, 1975, p. 37). Prigogine's work offers systemic theory a welcome metaphoric complement to cybernetic redundancy. From this complementary perspective, the occurrence of instabilities inherent in an open system are not system threatening; rather, they make the system flexible and able to adapt.

Minuchin and Fishman (1981) have stated the implications for family therapy:

The family, a living system, exchanges information and energy with the outside. Fluctuation, either internal or external, is normally followed by a response that returns the system to its steady state. But when the fluctuation amplifies, the family may enter a crisis in which transformation results in a different level of functioning that makes coping possible [pp. 21–22].

Only at certain times does a family experience periods of disequilib-
rium. These arise from either individual family members or from
changes in the family context and throw a family into a period of
fluctuation. The result can be a jump to a new and more complex stage,
in which new tasks and skills are developed. Thus, for example, the
Gibsons may never have entered therapy if Bob Gibson had lost his job.
Economically threatening though it might have been, the increase in his
at-home presence—and the release of Sally's concern about being too
involved in her work, which would then have been necessary—might
have shifted the family into a generative stage of fluctuation. Actually,
families frequently enter therapy at the cusp of reorganization, that is,
during and as a direct result of such periods of change. It then becomes
the therapeutic goal to help them make the necessary adaptations to
move to the higher level of complexity, adaptations that will allow them
to respond to their new internal and external circumstances.

Autopoesis

The concept of autopoesis, or self-organization, suggested by Humberto Maturana, a Chilean biologist working in collaboration with
Francisco J. Varela, a cognitive scientist, has aroused considerable interest in the field of family therapy. Maturana's ground-breaking study at
M.I.T., which was titled "What the Frog's Eye Tells the Frog's Brain,"
provided conclusive evidence that each structure in the frog's brain had
a "mind of its own" and that what the frog sees has more to do with
those structures than with what stands in its path of vision. In other
words, Maturana and Varela suggest that the nervous system is self-
enclosed (autopoesis literally means "self-authorship"). Systems are
composed of components; each component is maintained through a
process of "structural coupling" or congruent functioning in relation to
other components. How does change in any system come about? More
to the point, how can the concept of autopoesis be applied to systemic
change in families? Maturana's answer to this question is as follows:

> If you want the family to disintegrate so that its components stop their
> complaint, you must interact with them through some other dimensions
> than those which will confirm it. These other dimensions you have to
> discover through your interactions with the members of the family.
> If you look at what Minuchin does or other successful family therapists
> do, you will discover that they do exactly that. Their interventions trigger
> changes in the components which result in the disintegration of a system
> and the appearance of another because the components cannot reenact
> their original behavior [Simon, 1985b, p. 42].

One can infer a position on intersubjectivity from the work of Maturana and Varela that closely resembles the position of the constructivists, who emphasize that there is no "real world" independent of human mentation (i.e., we create the world we know). If the observer (therapist) and family members are a closed system with no demonstrable connection to an "out there" that is demonstrably really there, then all therapy is a form of conversation between people and conversations "have no other 'reality' than that bestowed by mutual consent" (L. Hoffman, 1990, p. 4). More than anything else, the influence of this biological perspective has been to support a critique of the therapist as "expert" or as active change agent.

The fascination of Maturana's ideas for some family therapists has been harshly questioned by others on theoretical grounds. The constraint imposed on meticulously planned strategies has been welcomed by some therapists, but that has been balanced by the skepticism of others toward the globalizing scientific models invoked. S. Minuchin (1985) asks: "How do we understand the complexity of the human systems by confining our focus merely to its neurobiology? How can this isolationist view encompass the family as a social group existing in its historical and cultural environment?" (p. 19). Similarly, some critics have been wary of a model that describes the variegation in human relationships in terms of random biological "perturbations," thereby erasing what is recognized as the cultural and social commonality binding all human discourse.

> There is nothing for the therapist who operates solely within these models to mentally see, hear or touch but the content and arrangement of the words the family uses while in the therapist's office. . . . There is no reverse, no threads, and nowhere to follow them. Yet it is on the other side of this one-dimensional film of words that what is real for the family actually occurs [Fish, 1993, p. 228].

Describing people with the language and concepts of mathematics, chemistry, and biology has its obvious dangers. Nevertheless, models inescapably inform our clinical experience—for good and ill. Certainly within psychoanalysis we have experienced the limiting effects of our founder's hydraulic and evolutionary models. Perhaps family theorists should be as wary of the limiting factors in the current favored ecological or narrative models. What we really seek in borrowing models from science or literature is both an enrichment of our thinking and facilitation of flexibility. Within family therapy, the models from the new science have suggested fresh opportunities within the prevailing instrumental stance toward change.

CRITIQUES OF THE SYSTEMS MODEL

The systems model has been comprehensively examined in family therapy theory, particularly in regard to the ways it is applied in practice.

Larger Systems

One critique of the systems paradigm is directed at the boundary of
what is commonly defined as a family system. The systemic metaphor
derived from Von Bertalanffy's basic model can be read like a set of
nested Russian dolls, that is, with each seemingly encapsulated figure
fitting neatly into another, each just a little bit larger—at least if one
assumes that the dolls all hierarchically interact with each other. So
how can it be correct to pinpoint any one of those dolls as the proper
unit for intervention? The larger-system perspective in family work is
most associated with the work of Evan Imber-Black (1991), who pointed
out that determining what the meaningful system is can be a major
therapeutic challenge. Not only may different system definitions define
different loci of problems, but systems designed to alleviate one problem may exacerbate another.

For instance, a substance abuse program might perpetuate family
problems by replicating patterns of family interaction and thus contributing to a macrosystem that becomes less and less capable of change.
For example, a mother abusing drugs might be disempowered by both
her children—who no longer listen to anything she says—and by her
own mother, who has since become their primary caretaker. A reha-
bilitation program that insists that the mother remove herself from
family and community while she deals with her drug problem in a drug
treatment unit might well reinforce the mother's disempowerment. If
the mother recovers, she will return to a family in which she has no
maternal status, her quondam extrusion by the family having been
ratified by the experts.

Imber-Black encourages therapists, particularly those who work with
multiproblem families, to keep their eye on the larger mental health
systems they are part of. Virtually every mental health professional at one
time or another has found himself or herself in a duel with other therapists, be they psychoanalytic, familial, remedial, or medical. Sometimes
this reflects self-protective or defensive action taken by the therapist,
sometimes it is a respite from the therapist's own sense of impotence,
and sometimes it is a result of the systemic landscape. The clearest
example of the influence of larger systems for the couples therapist arises
in working with divorcing spouses. Any attempt to invite understanding

or regard for the departing spouse, a stance that can enhance parental cooperation and self-acceptance, is usually linked by the other spouse to anxiety-ridden visions of a diminished financial share. Working behind the scenes may be the most relentless of puppeteers, adversarial lawyers defending these clients, as they have been trained to do. In many cases it is hubris for a therapist to believe that psychological peace making is possible before the material spoils are divided.

The Problem of Power

Another critique of how the basic systemic paradigm is applied to therapeutic work attacks strategic interventions as inappropriately manipulative and directive, an arrogant use of power within the therapeutic system. Lynn Hoffman (1985), among others, has labeled highly strategic interventions as belonging to a first-order cybernetic realm, in which the emphasis is on feedback mechanisms that maintain the family's homeostasis. She posits that a first-order cybernetic view is based on an illusion of objectivity in which the observer is believed to remain outside that which is observed. She argues on behalf of a second-order cybernetic view, where "the observer is included in the total arc" (in family therapy terms this is called "therapist-plus-system"). "Thinking back, it seems clear that the cold-war years set a pattern that was informed by a fascination with control" (p. 382), she charges. Hoffman believes that second-order cybernetics, the broadened view of therapist-plus-system, does not lend itself to "concerns of purpose, power and control." A therapist, as part of a system, by definition cannot "control it from the outside or program it." In other words, you "cannot influence *people*—you only influence their *context*—maybe the only part of which you can control is yourself" (p. 393).

Hoffman is a proponent of social constructionism, a perspective that advocates recognizing that "the terms in which the world is understood are social artifacts, products of historically situated interchanges among people."[1] In Hoffman's view, recent "advances in cybernetic biology

---

[1] It might be useful to distinguish here between constructivism and social constructionism. Constructivism originates in the philosophical tradition of Berkeley, Kant, and Cassirer and posits that the world we know is created by the structures of our mind and our language. Particularly associated with I. Z. Hoffman (1991) in the psychoanalytic literature, constructivism's central tenet is that both participants in the analytic relationship perceive and influence each other's behavior and intention through reciprocal and unconscious processes.

Social constructionism, emerging from the philosophical tradition of Spinoza, Kant, and Nietzsche, arose principally as a challenge to positivist-empiricist

and cognition," particularly the work of Maturana and Varela, have provided a "substrate of scientific research that the social construction theories of American social psychology did not have" (p. 391). Fore-warned is forearmed for Hoffman, who underlines the danger that the therapist, as a closed observing system, may "forget about the assump-tion of fallibility built into the fact that we are all observing systems, and that there is a Heisenberg Uncertainty Principle of Human Relations to which we cannot not subscribe" (Hoffman, 1985, p. 391).

The foregoing dispute may well be a bit rarefied for the psychoanalyst entering this paradigm—or, indeed, for anyone else who has to live in the day-to-day linear world. Nor has the position of Hoffman and others escaped criticism in the family literature:

> Do we ourselves create the realities that we think we discover? Can we influence people at all? Worse, isn't it impossible *not* to influence them, usually in unintended and even unhelpful ways? How do we know we are not simply agents of social control rather than healers or teachers? . . . Constructivists did not invent these questions. The concept of personal and cultural relativism is no more critical to an effective therapist than it is to a good teacher, scholar, minister or anybody else in a position of moral, intellectual or psychological authority. Indeed the idea that all truth is relative, that there is no way of escaping the closed perceptual limitations of the individual mind, has haunted thinkers throughout re-corded human history. Why, then, are these questions, long embedded in the Western philosophical tradition, suddenly so important to family therapists? [Minuchin, 1991, p. 48].

However, the more clinically pressing and pragmatic question con-cerns therapeutic stance and intention. Should family therapists be proactive, slaying the dragons of redundancy, or should they retreat to the position of cultivated collaboration? The debate, like the proverbial snake of knowledge, twists around itself. There is no doubt that the social constructionist influence in family systems has been salutary in its recognition that

> what is taken to be a psychological process at the very outset becomes a derivative of social interchange. The explanatory locus of human action

domination of contemporary scientific thought. The essential tenet of social con-structionism is that we organize our knowledge of the world in terms of culturally derived, historically located categories of experience and that these categories are constantly being reshaped and renegotiated in social interaction. D. B. Stern (1994) cogently summarizes the difference between constructivism and social construc-tionism in relation to clinical process by saying, "The culture makes the words and grammar; the dyad makes the message" (p. 294).

shifts from the interior region of the mind to the processes and structure of human interaction. The question "why" is answered not with a psychological state or process but with consideration of persons in relationship [Gergen, 1985, p. 271].

There is also no doubt that the social constructionist perspective has supplemented a somewhat limited examination of the influence of the therapeutic presence on the observation of family process and reporting of family data. However, the emphasis of the social constructionist movement on challenging the position of therapist as both expert and authoritative presence in the session is somewhat excessive. I think that family therapists, however much they may at moments sound like scions of family wisdom in suggesting interventions, do not really believe they know what is right, in terms of value choices, for families. Though there has not been quite enough attention paid to subcultural issues in the family therapy literature, culture and class have been important variables in systemic work from the beginning. The call to conscience of the social constuctionists seems a bit like preaching to the converted. This is not to say that their critique of the proclivity for high-intensity intervention, rather than just inquiry, is not well worth hearing. However, the essence of what the family therapist offers is a way for the family to hear itself differently. Expertise lies in recognizing constriction and redundancy and structural imbalances. What we do when we intervene as family therapists is to unhinge family neurosis, which is an overlearned but currently nonuseful way of living and being. We are challenging a shared and narrow reality and listening for the response. If we are trying to provide a new experience for—or with—a family, we can identify our effort, but we cannot predict its reception.

It is in its utter preempting of any illusion of linear predictability, in therapy as elsewhere, that chaos theory becomes useful. An example is the case of the Reillys, a vivid young Irish couple attending graduate school in New York. Though very much in love, they reported a rocky first year of marriage, in part because they were in full revolt against the Catholic patriarchy in which they had both been reared. Against the teachings of the Church, they had engaged in mutual masturbation and premarital intercourse, and both felt guilty (Mary especially, because she was usually the initiator). They were also having problems negotiating a lifestyle consistent with the feminism they both believed in strongly. Of course Jim was to take a turn at the laundromat: That was fair as well as correct. But when? And why couldn't he fold sheets the "right" way?

This couple was intelligent, articulate, and seemingly so happy together that the therapist was initially bewildered by their seeking therapy. It seemed that Mary had discovered that Jim sometimes rented pornographic videotapes when she was out of town. This had sent their relationship into a tailspin. Mary could not stop talking about it. She cried, she was panicky, she was resentful. But she also bought Jim the *Sports Illustrated* swimsuit issue, so he could look at photos of beautiful women; at the same time, she told him that she hated thinking of him as a man who would look at a woman simply as a body. She wanted to talk about the incident again and again. Jim was caught between wanting to talk about it—if that was what she needed—and resentment over her keeping at an incident over what was by now a period of months.

Exploring their relationship in therapy revealed a pattern. Typically, Mary was the initiator. She set the agenda for discussing problems, she initiated lovemaking, and she had taken charge of enriching the couple's sex life through her explorations of sexual fantasies. But the object of all of this was to keep Jim happy, to keep him devoted to her. Intent on his pleasure, she faked orgasms.

The therapist did what family therapists typically do. She chose a point of entry (one of probably dozens of possibilities) and made a linear intervention, hoping to disrupt the redundancy (the repetitive interaction sequences) characterizing the couple's life together. Targeting Jim and Mary's mix of feminism and Catholic guilt, she pointed out that Mary was enacting the role of the traditional Catholic wife, not only subordinating her needs to Jim's but also suffering like a guilty Eve, punishing herself for being the seducer in the relationship. The therapist's intervention was to suggest to Jim that he, as a good feminist man, should share the blame and the punishment for sex in their relationship. "I'd like you to try to expand your roles," the therapist told the couple. "We'll shift the focus. Jim, I want you to be the seducer for the next week, conversationally as well as sexually. Maybe part of the reason Mary is insecure is that she's been the caretaker of the relationship so long she doesn't know if you'll take care of it or drop it. Mary, try to trust Jim. He's going to take care of the relationship in the ways that are important to you, emotionally, sexually, *and* spiritually. He will take responsibility for discussing feelings and initiating sex. Okay?"

"I hope I don't fall on my face," Jim said.

"I have perfect confidence in you," the therapist assured him.

Jim took his assignment seriously. He took increasing responsibility for initiating sex and paying attention to the details of the relationship. In a session a month later Mary remarked to him, "I still find your sexuality and your arousal ninety-nine percent of my arousal. Maybe that's why it was so threatening that you could satisfy yourself without me." Upon hearing this Jim said, "I guess the question is how do we overcome that. How do we get a more healthy approach?"

"Women are socialized to be objects," the therapist pointed out. "And taught that their sexuality should be dependent on men's. It's a psychological and cultural reality, but you two can challenge it." The therapist helped the couple begin to discuss how to communicate more honestly, in sexual and other matters, but urged Jim to continue initiating sex for the time being.

As this role reversal continued, Mary found it easier to trust Jim's commitment, but she still used the subject of pornography as the measure of his willingness to confront important issues in the relationship. The therapist therefore instructed Jim to stop Mary whenever she brought up the topic of pornography and told Mary to watch for the verbal and nonverbal cues Jim used to express his love for her. As this shift occurred, the couple began to see the event as an incident that had occurred in the context of underlying tensions. The importance of the incident receded, and ultimately Mary was able to express her sexual desire on her own terms.

Thus, the redundancy of guilt, inhibition, and accusation was interrupted. The point of entry was quite specific, namely, the feminist implications of the couple's religiosity as it affected their sexual relationship. However, the spin-off from disrupting their accustomed beliefs in one area generalized to broad sectors of their perceptions of self and other—the kind of unexpected reorganization that chaos theory posits. Note that the language we use in the therapy process does not encompass our full understanding of a case. How much can we understand complex systems, anyway? The therapist in this case used feminist thought strategically, and the result of the role reversal was a liberated husband cherishing a self-image that included a sense of his free will, and strength and a wife freed from having to live via a false and guilty self.

The theoretical disputes that swirl about the practice of family therapy notwithstanding, it remains a praxis largely focused on changing, or at least opening up, consensually defined problems in living. Its interventions, however, remain characteristically experimental and playful. Minuchin, in particular, has exhorted family therapists to help families change, proudly, as an existential commitment. He argues that Bateson's emphasis on the "life of the mind," if taken too much to heart by clinicians, leads them toward a position of interpersonal indifference.

Up until this point, we have been discussing current debates in family therapy theory. Now I would like to shift and talk briefly about recent changes in analytic theory and practice, for here, I think, is an area where a comparison is heuristic. Two psychoanalytic issues in particular warrant this comparison: therapeutic neutrality and the immediacy versus redundancy of experience.

PSYCHOANALYTIC ENGAGEMENT

A New Perspective: Neutrality

Psychoanalysts work with an ambiguous commitment to change. We know that Freud had a more hands-on, extra-analytic involvement with his patients than any analyst would today. Yet the methodology of psychoanalysis became sanitized over time. Cloaked in American medical respectability, the parameters of psychoanalytic engagement became highly prescribed and constrained during the middle decades of the psychoanalytic century. Analysts locked themselves into an ideal position of neutrality, which was impossible to sustain and thus confusing to both therapist and patient. Neutrality has been considerably reexamined in the analytic literature. Greenberg (1986) posits a contemporary definition of neutrality as "the goal of establishing an optimal tension between the patient's tendency to see the analyst as an old object and his capacity to experience him as a new one" (p. 97), thus distinguishing this therapeutic intention from the misguided techniques that have become associated with this construct, such as inactivity and nonresponsiveness. Moreover, it has now become generally more acceptable, through the influence particularly of self psychology and object relations theory, to show caring to patients, not just imply it. But for psychoanalysts to let patients know specifically how they might want them to change is still off-limits. This is the strength of the model. In fact, wanting a patient to change is a clear signal of countertransference problems for most analysts. Psychoanalysts are expert guides in a journey of self-examination; they do not focus on problem solution. The assumption of the psychoanalytic approach, which bears fruit in most analyses, is that self-examination leads naturally to changes in how life is lived. The opposite assumption underlies family therapy: An approach to resolving systemic dysfunction and entanglements leads naturally to renewed self-interest.

I think the deliberateness of intervention shaping in family therapy can actually, paradoxically, assist the development of analytic neutrality, as well as the measured and reflective absorption in a patient's subjective world. In deciding which approach would best capture a family's jangled relationship system, family therapists shuttle through a multiplicity of possibilities, and their perspective on the relationship system actually becomes denser and more open-ended.

To illustrate, let us look at a case example of a young man who believes that he will never be attracted to his wife, that married life will always be a tedious, passionless compromise. She tolerates his talking about her as a boring fixture in his life. Moreover, he is a severe worrier, and she spends many long nights reassuring him that his work and his health are not endangered. However, she regards him as psychologically crippled for needing this care. What are their family histories? Each reports a key narrative element: He feels that he had to submit to the capricious tyranny of his mother most of his life. She bitterly describes witnessing her mother's callous dismissal of her father's serious psychological difficulties.

In order to disrupt their interlocking behavior, expand their relationship, and (it is hoped) include an erotic element in it, what should the family therapist be thinking about? That the interpersonal dynamics of caregiving are substitutive and compensatory for the lack of satisfying sex? That these dynamics, now in place, virtually preclude passion and sexuality? That marriage necessarily invokes in the husband the sense of oppression he felt in his family of origin, a feeling that now preempts sexual desire? That the husband may be looking to his wife for the mothering he never received? That through her compulsive attentiveness to her husband, the wife is determined to erase the painful memory of her mother's callousness toward her father, perhaps in this way competing with her mother or keeping out of awareness the fact that her mother was depriving to her as well as to her father?

Having to choose one focus, or at least a first focus, for change, highlights for the therapist the perhaps all too familiar principle of multiple determination. We know from psychoanalysis that many dynamic factors coalesce in forming any particular dysfunction. However, in our psychoanalytic work, multiple determination functions implicitly as backdrop, providing the basis for our following patients down divergent paths of association and motivation. In family therapy, we deliberately access as many possible causal pathways as we can from the beginning and self-consciously choose one entrance point for intervention. In fact, psychoanalysts who become immersed in family therapy often report that they come more naturally and palpably to assume a skeptical stance toward specific dynamic hypotheses in their psychoanalytic work!

Immediacy Versus Redundancy

What can feel impossible in psychoanalytic treatment is to keep the therapeutic faith—however merited—in transference exploration as the royal road to change when working with patients in severe distress. A woman with whom I work struggles to free herself from the inner voice of her mother. It is a critical, demeaning voice; nothing about her is ever good enough—not her walk, her weight, her worth. Accordingly, continual self-improvement has been her only hope, and she lives a life of itemizing, profiling, and measuring herself and everybody else. We have spent some time exploring the pain, emptiness, and anger of her daily experience, past and present, but she seemingly cannot get inside a self that could cancel the incessant measuring and quantifying process. She insists that I, qua therapist, am prohibited from judging her. Thus, the treatment remains more outside than inside the core of her constricting developmental experience.

I feel a nameless tension with this patient more often than not, as though I am being diminished, but I cannot figure out how. In one session she reports jealously observing the result of one of her mother's creative activities, a newly decorated room. She admits once again to feeling inferior, attests once again to her mother's creative talent. However, this time she admits, a bit sheepishly, that she tried to memorize the room's contents so that she could copy the results. She thus openly shows how much she covets her mother's talent. It occurs to me that her ever-present critical inner voice might well mask her intense envy of and competition with others. If she is so lowly and so despicable, how could she presume to envy talent or success? And how could her mother be envious of her? What was a dramatic shift in the therapy was the movement from one-down inferiority to sideways envy vis-à-vis her relationship to her mother. This shift then affected her transference relationship to me, invoking a more complex and painstaking transference exploration. But when the dynamic shifted, it moved with it her deep attachment to me (now both threatened and enlivened by competition) as well as a whole assemblage of fantasies and relationship systems she had previously delineated in the therapy.

Family therapists try to evoke this kind of thematic discontinuity (in this case, inferiority to envy) directly and fairly rapidly. Whenever they hear a familiar frame for family difficulties, they set it at an empathic distance, giving it a new perspective. If dad is chronically depressed, he has probably gotten a lion's share of compassion for his condition. Why not ask instead if his depression might not be conveniently taking the spotlight off the son who has just dropped out of college?

A family I consulted with had rejected its daughter-in-law for a series of minor slights. She had become a virtual pariah, bearing the scarlet letter of disloyalty. I met with the husband and his parents. It seemed to me that by focusing on the daughter-in-law's "sinfulness," the husband's family of origin could remain distracted from its internal disappointments and failures. Now it was assumed within this nuclear family that mother was responsible for the edict of banishment. She seemed to relate to this assumption somewhat ambivalently, that is, with a warrior's pride mingled with an uneasy sense of loss. When I met with the daughter-in-law and husband alone, they were indeed convinced it was the mother-in-law's singular irrationality and cruelty that had led to the estrangement. Quite discontinuously I asked the husband about the wounds his father had inflicted. "Weren't these wounds that left no visible mark the most insidious kind?" I asked. I entered into a fairly directed inquiry with him about paternal exploitation, which had been illustrated in a family session in which his father had encouraged him to ridicule and disparage his mother. Didn't this serve, I asked him, to assuage his father's guilt and culpability about neglecting his wife? Was it fair for his father to ask him to bail him out in this way?

The son was provoked to anger by my theory. How dare I upset the applecart of his mother blaming? Wasn't she the one who behaved outrageously and irrationally in the family? He left the room demanding that I reconsider my perspective. There was a lot at stake in the son's reconsidering his unholy alliance with his father. If he reconsidered and faulted his father's behavior, he might withdraw from the intense blaming–defense circle he was locked into with his mother. If he withdrew, the ways in which he was inappropriately overinvolved with her (openly noted but minimized in the family in the face of the current mother–son dissension) would be more salient. His wife could then attend to how tight the mother–son bond was and to why her husband had, in fact, participated in her banishment.

In family therapy one abandons the notion of dynamic truth but assumes instead a commitment to expansion and liberation from repetition. From this perspective the time-honored analytic commitment to working through becomes more subject to scrutiny. Working through can be viewed as the necessarily painstaking and delicate refiguring of what was second nature and second skin.

Or, in some instances working through can serve, unfortunately, as a safe arena for redundancy. In this worst-case scenario of psychoanalytic praxis, exploration becomes a striking illustration of first-order change, change that stays within the old set and old gestalt, partly because the solution becomes another facet of the problem. If, for example, one were working with the husband in the aforementioned clinical vignette, an intensive historical and transferential focus on his undifferentiated relationship with his mother (if it consumed all his therapeutic space and time) might simply underline and reinforce, rather than expand, the symbiosis. Similarly, if in the case of the envy-prone woman the transference got stuck on the guilt evoked by acquisitiveness and expropriation, there would be no real expansion of self even though self-criticalness might expand; the patient's sense of self would remain organized around self-rejection. Working with discontinuity intentionally and playfully in family systems work keeps open the possibility of second-order change, of awakening from the nightmare rather than developing alternative dream imagery.

THE NATURE OF THE SELF

A most important distinction between psychoanalysts and family therapists lies in family therapists' radically different conception of the self. According to Bruner (1990):

> As a *qualia* of "direct" human experience, Self has a peculiarly tortured history. Some of the theoretical trouble it has generated, I suspect, can be attributed to the "essentialism" that has marked the quest for its elucidation, as if Self were a substance or an essence that preexisted our effort to describe it, as if all one had to do was to inspect it in order to discover its nature. . . . Psychoanalysis, of course, was a principal essentialist sinner: Its topography of ego, superego, and id was the real thing, and the method of psychoanalysis was the electron microscope that laid it bare [pp. 99–100].

For Bruner, the intellectual history of the past 50 years, which he summarizes in terms of "the rise of antirealism in modern physics, of skeptical perspectivalism in modern philosophy, of constructivism in the social sciences" (p. 100) has led inevitably to a new conception of self. Bruner anoints the contemporary self "distributive," a "product of the situations in which it operates" (p. 109). This new self is remarkably more other-oriented than we psychoanalysts have been comfortable with in our own theory building.

In the development of psychoanalytic theory there has been little attention, with the exception of the work of Sullivan, to the distributive self. The self has remained relatively encapsulated in our theories. The vision of a Winnicottian "true self" buried under the dross of other-directedness sustains many practitioners today, despite long stretches during which little evidence of it can be discerned. Self psychologists pursue the cohesiveness of the self as a therapeutic milestone, and relational theorists have recognized the privacy of the self, unavailable to exploration, even within the intersubjective field of psychoanalysis. (Both Sullivan and Winnicott identified a sector of self that remains private and unprocessed in social discourse, though not necessarily dissociated [D. N. Stern, 1985].)

Recently, however, there has been a dawning of the theory of the distributed self in psychoanalysis. Mitchell (1993) has eloquently posited a dialectic between the "multiple, discontinuous" self and the "singular, integral" self, explaining that "because we learn to become a person through interactions with different others and through different kinds of interactions with the same other, our experience of self is discontinuous, composed of different configurations, different selves with different others" (p. 104). Harris (1994) trenchantly remarked that "we may talk postmodern but we practice in the enlightenment model, thinking of the separate autonomous self whose boundedness and efforts at coherence must be respected" (p. 4). How far will psychoanalysts go in balancing the dialectic between the discontinuous and the continuous in the phenomenology of selfhood? Harris (1994) cautions us to remember that "alienation, the loss of agency, the ruptures in self are lived in agony" (p. 6). According to Mitchell:

> One of the great benefits of the analytic process is that the more the analysand can tolerate experiencing multiple versions of himself, the stronger, more resilient, and more durable he experiences himself to be. Conversely, the more the analysand can find continuities across his various experiences, the more he can tolerate the identity diffusion entailed by containing multiple versions of self. The analyst helps to enable him to find and recognize himself when he is experiencing and behaving "out of character" [1993, p. 116].

Beyond psychoanalysis, those who become interested in contextualizing or distributing the self in general psychological theory seem to feel most comfortable doing so in the narrative domain. This work draws on the conceptual work of William James (1890), particularly his distinction between "I" as subject of action and "me" as object of reflection. In addition, they are informed by linguist Bakhtin's (1981)[2] notion of a polyphonic novel, in which multiple subjective voices are simultaneously given credence.

However, in the texts of many of these theorists, one witnesses the return of the repressed—autonomous selfhood. Thus, after an effective proposal of a model for a reworked dialogical self-concept, although Hermans, Kempen, and Van Loon (1992) conclude that "the self is not only 'here' but also 'there,' and because of the power of imagination the person can act as if he or she were the other," they then continue as follows:

> This is not to be equated with taking the role of the other (Mead, 1934), as this expression implies that the self takes the actual perspective of the other, outside the self. Rather *I* construe another person or being as a position that *I* can occupy and a position that creates an alternative perspective on the world and myself [p. 29].

In other words, even dialogists retrench to a notion of the self that is separated and encapsulated.

Family systems theory, in contrast, more explicitly challenges our Western notions of encapsulation and autonomy in proposing that we are organized by external others and not simply by internal versions of these others. The shaping by significant others, moreover, becomes overdetermined and redundant, an etching of self burned in acid on a template. Crucially at stake is acknowledging (1) the extent to which what we are is determined by whom we are with, not in internal dialogue but in actual "external" relationship, and (2) that the influence of significant others in intimate relationships has a unique kind of power over us. By this reasoning, whom we marry shapes the very essence of our psyches as much as any principle of dynamic motivation for mate selection. The implications for psychoanalytic treatment are unsettling: a patient could assume a very different gestalt of selfhood each time he or she enters into a new relationship, right before our psychoanalytic eyes! Moreover, it would mean facing foursquare the fact that the our patients respond to our personality and our characterological needs and that no amount of supervision or personal psy-

---

[2]Mikhail Bakhtin was a 20th-century philosopher and literary theorist who shifted attention away from an abstract conceptualization of language to a study of language in social contexts. He viewed language as "dialogic," or oriented toward the speaker and embedded in relationship.

choanalysis in the world can prevent the vagaries of psychoanalytic coupling. In this way, countertransference influence can be viewed as a dimension of self-to-self-creation and re-creation and not unresolved transference neurosis. It ultimately means rethinking what psycho-analytic participation and process are all about.

chapter five

Nested Contexts

Only the shallow know themselves.
Oscar Wilde

The analyst creates or cocreates a context with the patient. In contrast, the family therapist discovers a context in which the family is embedded; it is there, it is real, and it is consequential. What influences relationship patterns in the family goes beyond anyone's individual psychic reality and includes not just relationships but cultural and subcultural values and economic and social vicissitudes. What are the consequences of this difference in contextualization? There is a big difference in what the therapist attends to and takes seriously. The analyst invites the patient to become immersed in subjectivity, to become acquainted with previously unacknowledged fantasies and wishes, to question the very tenets of civilized life. The family therapist focuses on a full awareness of forces that exist consensually in the culture, forces that shape subjectivity. For the family therapist, a similar relationship complaint has an altogether different meaning when expressed by a recently emigrated Dominican and by a third-generation WASP. Above all, the working premise of analysis is that you can write a new version of your biography; the family therapist, however, is aware that you cannot change the world you inhabit in the same way.

There is a lot of scholarly focus today on the degree to which the self can be regarded as decontextualized. In the postmodern world the sense of self is saturated, as Gergen (1991) has illustrated. The relatively coherent and unified sense of self inherent in a traditional culture has given way before the electronic era, in which relationship connections have increased exponentially as people half a world apart are seconds away by phone, fax, and electronic mail. We can rewind message tapes and hear an intimate other's voice even long after a relationship has ended. The analytic relationship is, by design, decontextualized, for the analytic context is in fact created *de novo*; its ingredients do include the specific sociological and psychological characteristics of patient and therapist, but these become ingredients that mix in a unique dyadic blend.

The paradigmatic context of the analytic relationship is the transference–countertransference matrix, the analytic "playground" in which memory, affect, and association comingle. The denser this field of examination, the richer the data. Although only classical analysts consider it essential that a full-blown oedipal neurosis hatch, all psychoanalysts know that the more embroiled the patient becomes with them and the more preoccupying the analytic relationship, the greater the possibility for personal transformation.

Ironically, however, as the analytic process intensifies, the patient–therapist relationship actually becomes increasingly decontextualized. It becomes more impassioned, certainly, but the power of the psychoanalytic experience lies in its having no real-life contingencies or consequences. Weighted with meanings accrued from comparisons and imaginings of significant others, the analyst becomes a fire-breathing effigy, the taming of which releases the patient to new experience and new explorations.

However, in our everyday lives we can tolerate just so much decentering, and the current emphasis in many scholarly disciplines on historicism and contextualism has probably been spurred by our need for a psychological anchor. It is this anchoring that family therapy provides.

The family therapist is ever cognizant of being an outsider to the powerful internal circular loops that organize the family's relationship experience. For the family therapist, context is the gestalt of real relationships between family members who share a myriad of binding, multiply layered day-to-day experiences. Individuality is always viewed and constrained and shaped by relationships. Second, the family therapist perceives the family as "held" by the culture; ethnic, religious, and socioeconomic factors are woven into the tapestry of family life. These two domains of context—of specific relationship and culture at large—are not truly distinct, for cultural expectations become part of the fabric of any particular family's configuration. However, for purposes of illustration, context as interpersonal reciprocity and context as cultural template will be discussed separately. The implications of these two different understandings of context will be discussed.

THE CONTEXT OF RELATIONSHIP

The family therapist is necessarily struck by the fact that members of a family or couple provide context for each other. The most important contribution that the family therapist can make is to highlight this sector of influence. Although it involves a loss of pride to face it squarely, we are all restricted in achieving our potential by the context of our family relationships, both past and present (in fact, family therapists would argue that it is unwise to emphasize past versus present restrictions).

Caroline reports inhibiting anxiety about her partner's, Sue's, bullying tactics and persuades Sue that the ghost of her oppressive and traumatizing father stalks their intimate relationship. As their couples therapist, I am struck by Sue's considerable sensitivity (albeit strong-mindedness). However, I am also impressed by how constricted Sue's expression of her sensitivity is. Sue seems to believe, simply because she is so terrified of it, that she may really be a bully deep down, just like her dad. She inhibits her emotional expression towards Caroline, including, at times, her anger.

It is the welding of the Caroline's concerns about anger to Sue's traumatic history, not a latent identification with Sue's abusive father, that is the central problem. Adding fuel to the fire, Sue is (predictably) plagued by angry fantasies, which currently may function as her only form of retaliation and defense. Sue seems to be struggling too much with her identification with her father in her individual therapy and too little with her capacities for concern and empathy.

It is an expansion of the individual historical narrative in the direction of considering Sue's family of origin as a system that liberates her. When I inquire about how her mother attended to her father's tumultuous distress, Sue is shocked to realize that her mother ignored it. Sue had never before considered her mother's participation in or influence on the level of household anxiety. This awareness brings into relief Caroline's participation in Sue's self-doubts and muffled sensitivity.

Sue's own therapist had not dealt with the problem of her suppressed sensitivity because she simply did not have the opportunity to hear about it or witness it. The more she talked with her therapist about her aggressive fantasies, the more convincing she became as a perpetrator within the transference–countertransference matrix. Within the psychoanalytic paradigm, personal history illuminates and clarifies the transference. Within the family paradigm, personal history becomes a language with which to shape and organize the significant other.

There are many ways to think about how family members organize each other's feelings and behavior. Jackson (1965a) was one of the first to point out that we need a language that makes it possible to think about interaction. He delineated the idea of "family rules," that is, the redundancies or "typical and repetitive patterns of interaction which characterize the family as a supraindividual entity" (p. 590). Jackson's (1965b) further differentiation of family rules from family roles and values is particularly germane when discussing the importance of the larger cultural context. It is the family rule, a powerfully binding agreement on the cusp between dissociation and awareness, that best captures systemic context. However, a focus on the idiosyncratic rules of a specific family system cannot help but take into account the larger cultural context within which this system has developed. Rules define a particular family's balance of power whereas values and roles are culturally derived. For example, in Western culture, independence of offspring is often equated with financial independence as a role attribution. However, how financial independence is represented in any particular family can reflect an idiosyncratic rule. Thus, a father can indicate seniority to young adult offspring by advocating the "value of money" principle, but he might be less interested in fostering their independence than in advertising his own financial success. The operating family rule is "Father has *innate* superiority."

Marriage for Jackson is a rule-governed system (not altogether conscious) in which "each party must receive something for what he gives and which, consequently, defines the rights and duties of the parties in the bargain" (p. 591). Jackson explicitly discussed the resulting rule system in terms of a *quid pro quo*. What maintains the rule system if it is highly idiosyncratic in the way the ledger gets balanced? Building on the work of Bateson (1956), who had been the first to propose that communication is bimodally distributed into report and command functions, Jackson (1965b) elucidated the importance of communication as the "gluing medium" of the infrastructure of rules within a family:

> *Every message (communication bit) has both a content (report) and a relationship (command) aspect; the former conveys information about facts, opinions, feelings, experiences, etc., and the latter defines the nature of the relationship between the communicants. . . .* In every communication, then, the participants offer to each other definitions of their relationship, or more forcefully stated, each seeks to determine the nature of the relationship [p. 118].[1]

For example, a young woman tells her boyfriend, "You never say what you mean!" What does he hear? On the report level he hears that

---

[1]Jackson apologizes for his language in defining report and command, that is, he is forced, linguistically, to differentiate or "abstract" the individual from the "individual-in-this-relationship-with-this-other," and thus to violate in deed (though not in intent) a contextual system credo. Most of us are less constrained than Jackson in using the notion of "individual." I prefer Bruner's (1986) notion of the individual self, namely, that it is the self that "gets us about the business of daily life."

he is neither honest nor forthright nor courageous; the content of the message is a moral critique. On the command level the communication is even more alarming. Is she informing him that she can read his mind? Does she believe that she knows him better than he knows himself? Is she suggesting that she ought to manage his self-improvement?

What is essential here is that although both report and command derive from individual sectors of personality or character, they become highly redundant. Repeated over time, they coalesce as a family rule. The young man cannot reveal himself with dignity to his lover; for him, self-revelation is now tantamount to transfer of self-ownership. It becomes a rule for this couple that the young man withholds the truth from the woman and she must pursue him for it. If they could, hypothetically, jointly identify their bind, they could release it. However, one of them would have to initiate this transformative discussion. Probably, the other would instantaneously assume the familiar rule-bound position, and they would be off on their usual course.

What one sees particularly clearly in working with couples is the way the rules carve out the territories of competency. For example, he will let her intrude on his space and shut him out of a close relationship with his daughter if she will let him be the professionally superior partner. Once this pact is operative, each partner's sense of self and worth depends on the other's staying in position and delivering what Sullivan called a set of "reflected appraisals." Thus the circle is never broken.

A true appreciation of interpersonal reciprocity indicates both the virtues and the limitations of the object relations perspective. Fairbairnian models are extraordinarily useful in understanding what goes on in an individual's head and also offer an interesting hypothesis for understanding the tenacity of many relationships in the face of misery. It may well be that we project onto others unacceptable aspects of ourselves and are both repelled and pleasured in remaining connected to them. We may even dread losing these partners because they so crucially embody self-experience for us. According to Dicks (1967), who first introduced object relations theory to systemic thinkers:

> By protecting the image of the partner (for example as a "drunk" or as "sexually inadequate" or "slovenly," and so forth) they are in the other secretly cherishing the rejected, bad libidinal ego with its resentments and demands while *within* the dyadic system they can persecute it in an interpersonal framework [pp. 122–123].

But object relations, principally Fairbairnian models, do not adequately capture real relationship patterns between significant others. If I am a woman who must deny my neediness and project it outward, it matters a great deal whether I project this need onto a partner who is dominating or onto one who is humiliating. Even the concept of projective identification is too linear (i.e., she does, then he does in turn) and by itself too reductionistic to account for the multiplicity of variables that are called into play and then jelled by a relationship system.[2]

What becomes quite clear in a family therapy session is the sheer power of attribution. I worked with a family in which the father was given to angry outbursts and occasional grabbing of children's arms for emphasis. His seriously disturbed mother had been prone to truly irrational outbursts (e.g., refusals to communicate for weeks on end). His young daughters could stop him dead in his tracks and preempt any exercise of legitimate parental authority by describing his most recent outburst in detail. These critiques would invariably end in his agreeing that he had been wrong, for he felt ashamed and frightened of his identification with his mother. Moreover, his daughters had a clear and open alliance with his wife concerning his irascibility, although the nature and quality of his rage toward his wife had an altogether different history and complexion. His wife never directly faulted him for outbursts, but she supported her daughters' critiques. The problem was that the repeated experience of having their father submit to their embarrassing reproofs prevented the daughters from taking his rules and guidelines seriously; the children felt they had the final word on their father's behavior. As a consequence of this generation-inappropriate reversal, they would do something utterly unacceptable, and the same cycle would repeat.

The point is that there is a significant difference between a haunting resemblance to a parent, whether fantasized or real, and a transactional acting out of that resemblance. Note that in the terms I delineated in the previous chapter concerning Sullivan's personified self this father did have an overly restricted sense of himself. I witnessed his caring behavior toward his daughters and his capacity for self-reflection, but his daughters preserved an image of him as irrationally undependable—and in doing so imprinted their perception on him. He took it to heart because of his painful experiences with his mother. This image was not etched in him or in them; it was a cocreated unlimited edition of a family etching.

---

[2]A working definition of projective identification is provided by Ogden (1979). It involves a threefold process including: Step 1, the fantasy of projecting part of oneself on another, the self-fragment then controlling the recipient from within; Step 2, pressure on the recipient to think, act, and feel congruent with the projection; and Step 3, the reinternalization of the projection after it has been absorbed and processed by the recipient.

One sees the transactional negotiation of internal scripts regularly in family work. For example, a young woman had been traumatized in childhood by a family pattern of nondisclosure, particularly regarding the unusual circumstances of her parents' divorce and, later, her brother's sudden death when she was an adolescent. Her partner had been terrified of his mother's black moods and sudden rages and had developed a noncommittal pattern of reticence and withdrawal. In terms of object relations, one could say that the young man's secrecy maintained a projected characteristic that the young woman first became acquainted with in her family of origin. From an interpersonal perspective, one could say that vagueness is the emotional environment the woman was damned to feel most comfortable in, the one her security operations could most readily equilibrate, that she simply might not feel at ease with a forthright, self-disclosing mate. Likewise, a reciprocal set of interpersonal dynamic needs could be postulated for the man, that is, for someone who was always off-kilter, anxious, and potentially explosive. One could further think of this mutual reciprocity in terms of opportunity, in terms of a dissociated search for a second chance to resolve genetic trauma. This formulation would bring to the systemic relationship precisely that property hypothesized as central to the analytic relationship by Weiss and Sampson (1994), namely, the powerful wish to disprove pathogenic beliefs acquired in childhood. According to Weiss and Sampson, if the analyst does not act as the patient's worse beliefs predict, the patient "may feel relieved and take a small step toward disproving the beliefs. He may also feel less endangered by the mental contents warded off in obedience to the beliefs and therefore may permit himself both to experience these contents and to act upon them" (p. 238). In a more somber vein, one could view the mutual attraction of this couple in terms of a relationship-based repetition compulsion. But no matter how we formulate it in terms of individual dynamics, the ensuing jointly constructed relationship system causes one sector of each person's dynamics to jell, rendering it potentially impermeable to revision even through self-awareness of contradictory tendencies.

Minuchin and Fishman (1981) designate the process of cocreation "complementarity" and stated:

> One of the therapeutic goals in family therapy is to help family members experience their belonging to an entity that is larger than the individual self. . . . If the family members can achieve a way of framing their experience so that it spans longer periods of time, they will perceive reality in a new way. The patterns of the whole organism will achieve salience, and the freedom of the parts will be recognized as interdependent [p. 193].

In addition to complementarity, there are contexts of shared mythology. The mythology need not be consciously salient; sometimes a family provides a shared context that is limiting or debilitating but selectively and collectively ignored. Then, too, the mythology may be highly salient—and yet equally debilitating. A couple I treated spent most of their time talking to each other in terms of position papers. The wife ardently defended feminism while the husband took the role of an apologist for psychoanalytic self-examination. Both felt hurt and unrecognized. Their arguments had taken on a passion and meaning beyond the ideas. When I pointed out that their marriage was 80 percent ideology—or, rather, ideological warfare—they were astonished. This complicity had never occurred to them. Ideology had become the air they breathed, oxygen-depleted though it was.

There are a few notable resonances to complementarity in current psychoanalytic theorizing. Benjamin (1988) creatively delineated the psychical wish to be recognized by the other and tracked the vicissitudes of this wish from a gender perspective. Beebe and Lachmann (1991) traced the dyadic cuing of mother and infant in the affective domain and suggested implications for the transference relationship. Sandler (1976) stressed the "role-responsiveness" that patients have encoded and subsequently unpack in psychoanalysis. And from an interpersonal perspective:

> Sullivan made it clear that the illusory other is part of a dyad made up as much of my version of myself as it is of my version of the other person. This "self-other" envelope seems to reduce my anxiety by providing a framework of expectations within which I can be comfortable. . . . The difference between sickness (rigidity) and health (flexibility) is whether or not my version of you can be readily enriched and modified by our interaction. My openness to new data requires a healthy degree of self-confidence because it necessarily requires that I modify my version of me as well [Dyrud, 1990, pp. 337–338].

All these different analytic perspectives can potentially enrich the abstract descriptions of transactional rules and mutual influence given by systems theory. Each, moreover, recognizes circularity as an inexorable process. However, none of these analytic schema allows for more than a dyadic encoding of relationship, and each is focused on a fairly limited range of developmental or relational characteristics.

Transgenerational Exploration

Both psychoanalysts and family therapists recognize that individuals are subject to powerful and often veiled influences by family members of preceding generations. In psychoanalytic treatment we are always dealing with identifications with and representations of parents. But identification is a slippery concept. I think that in some way we never really have an imprint of our parents, precisely because they are so much a function of our evolving image of ourselves. In fact, too clear a maternal representation is probably the choicest correlate of an overly refined personified self. "I am just like my mother, too solicitous of others" can be the complaint of a person who, to others, may seem altogether too ready to exact a pound of flesh for every good deed rendered.

Family therapists work both explicitly and literally with the transgenerational players in the system. The Bowenian school of family therapy relies on coaching, that is, encouraging family members to make I-statements in previously tangled and blame-ridden triangles and dispatching them to find out facts about shadowy relatives so that new relationship positions can be taken. Salvador Minuchin advocates inviting members of the extended family directly into the session, at least with therapies that have come to feel stuck. In an extension of a communications model, new information can be a hedge against redundancy and entropy. James Framo (1976) and Carl Whitaker (1976a) are two family therapists who regularly invite extended family members to sessions. Whitaker's comments on his own work cast an interesting light on some of our psychoanalytic assumptions about therapeutic change:

> Interaction within the three-generation group may neatly define and lubricate the interface between the generations. The therapist can easily stimulate them to talk about the good old days which allows the grandchildren to picture family rituals and enjoy biographical tidbits. Each generation group may come to admit that it is only possible to belong to one's own generation, so that role expectations are eased, and new roles are developed. The interface between the sexes—flirtation between grandma and grandson, between grandfather and granddaughter—may often serve to relieve much oedipal guilt in the nuclear family, and turn love and sexuality into an integrated, rather than a dissociated recreation [p. 191].

Whitaker added that as a result of such actual transgenerational interaction, "covertly, and at times overtly, the individual sees himself twenty-five years ago and twenty-five years from now, and this sense of projected time redefines the present in right-brain wholeness in a way not possible by an episode of therapeutic working-through" (p. 191).

Whitaker's approach offers a view of dynamics as an open and flexible system of interpersonal meanings. I worked with a couple who

bitterly complained about the wife's parents' upper-middle-class refusal to accept the husband's blue-collar status. However, the wife
functioned as a double agent in this system, a tormenting position but
one she felt bound to take. She was outraged both at her snobbish,
rejecting mother and at her underperforming husband. Her mother
seemed at first to be functioning as an easy vehicle for triangulating the
disappointment the couple felt in their marriage. However, try as I
might to reframe mother's behavior as somewhat positive (i.e., concerned, available, passionate), I could not realign the triangle. I finally
proposed inviting the wife's parents to a session. The young couple
consented, though with trepidation about the possibility of the mother
"losing it." This session revealed something remarkable: Dad, who had
been portrayed as a ineffectual and beleaguered peacemaker, emerged
as a key protagonist. He confessed to adoring his daughter. Mom
admitted past resentment and feelings of betrayal about the depth and
strength of this attachment, which was not so readily available to her.
The whole gestalt of perceptions shifted kaleidoscopically. Mom's
snobbishness was desperate, daughter was not really so bereft of affection, and young husband was presented with the timeless challenge of
claiming her for his own.

A case I supervised involved a highly intelligent but erratic and very
active (possibly hyperactive) eight-year-old boy. Working with Jared
and his mother, the therapist found that the boy was deeply attached to
his grandmother, Cecilia, who had cared for him during the week from
infancy until he was three and a half and who still babysat and took care
of him during school vacations. The child's mother, Veronica, frequently referred to Cecilia in a way that indicated that she was clearly
still dependent on her mother's approval (e.g., "My mother probably
wouldn't tell you so, but I think . . ."), somewhat to the detriment of
her own maternal self-regard. The therapist finally asked Cecilia to
come to a session with Veronica, to act as a family expert.

In the process of drawing a genogram with the assembled group, it
became clear that in this large, multigenerational child-valuing family,
multiple parenting was the norm. Cecilia had been parented by many
relatives both before and after the early death of her own mother in North
Carolina. "Whoever could, helped out," she explained. "That's just the
way it was." Veronica had embarked on single parenthood ("The one
thing I always wanted to do, since I had sense, was to be a parent," she
said) with the understanding that Cecilia, recently retired, would take
care of the infant. Yet by virtue of this arrangement Veronica felt she had
missed part of the experience of being a parent. Cecilia, meanwhile, felt
that she was now being excluded from the rearing of a child who was like

her own. Each woman felt undervalued by the other. And Jared was being pulled by two mothers. The grandmother relentlessly patholo-gized: "Is Jared hyperactive? Should he be on medication? Does he, possibly, have Tourette's syndrome?" The mother was as relentless in normalizing: "He's getting better at this. We're working on that."

It was clear that there were many strengths in the relationship. They argued, but the women were quite comfortable with each other, joining readily in pleasurable strategy sessions about the best ways to raise a child and agreeing on how much better it worked to reward than punish. The therapist complimented Cecilia on her success as a parent, as demonstrated in Veronica and her siblings, and in her care for Jared. Then she suggested that Cecilia could relax and simply enjoy being a grandmother because, thanks to her success as a parent, Jared had a very competent mother in Veronica.

"I always felt in my mother's shadow," Veronica said. "I'd like to hear, just once, that she thinks I am a good parent." Turning to Cecilia, the therapist asked,

"Can you say that?" It was a bit of a struggle, but Cecilia managed. Veronica, clearly gratified, responded with a strong statement about her own efforts and competence as a parent. It was clear that being in her mother's shadow would no longer be quite the problem for Veronica that it had been.

THE FAMILY IN CULTURAL CONTEXT

Beyond relationship or transgenerational contextualization, families are contextualized in culture, in all its contradictions and discontin-uities. In essence, family therapists attempt to facilitate as broad an exploration of the larger context of life as possible, rather than focus only on an exploration of the treatment relationship. This is not to deny the recent surge of attention to sociocultural and nonfantasized influences in psychoanalytic treatment, for example, the feminist revisionist challenge; the burgeoning interest in the trauma of early abuse; and, of course, the gauntlet Masson (1984) cast at the very development of psychoanalytic epistemology. However, it is an alto-gether different level of treatment abstraction to be dealing with a group of people who share a natural, culturally legitimate structure (however dysfunctional its particular version) as opposed to working purely within the transference on the issues informed by these structures. The very institution of family is created by culture, and it does not arrive excised from that culture at the therapist's door.

For example, I have worked with two different couples who both initiated couples therapy because of indecision about continuing their relationship. In each case the wife became pregnant early on in the treatment, and both couples then decided to carry the pregnancy to term. In individual treatment pregnancy would of course be considered important, but the pregnancy would be explored dynamically and symbolically. From the perspective of couples treatment, however, the lives of the two sets of partners were assuming totally different complexions. Both couples were taking on new culturally designated functions, with multiple resonances across both their kinship network and their separate and collective identity issues. In each case, moreover, pregnancy was a catalyst for important systemic shifts within the couple, and these shifts took place within a cultural context that defined the new roles being assumed on top of the preexisting role of spouse.

Similarly, parenthood involves confronting consensually defined role expectations of the particular culture, however much these may be flouted by individual parents. Moreover, individuals construe prevailing role definitions in their own unique way. An analytic patient of mine, highly ambivalent about becoming a father, bemusedly imagined himself joining the long "tired march" of fathers and toddlers, lugging bottles, diapers, toy trucks, and so on. His litany emerged from his own free association. In a consultation I did several years ago I encouraged a middle-aged father to talk to his very rebellious son, Carlo, about fatherhood. This was encouraged during a focused "live supervision" session with both therapist and family present. The set goal of the exercise was to emphasize the tangible difference in experience, exposure, and responsibility between 50-year-old men with dependents and their rebellious (and, in this case, self-destructive) sons.

Carlo was a delight, sensitive and intelligent. "My mother's job is to remind me of appointments," he explained, "My job is to forget them." Yet he was in full adolescent revolt against his mother: "My mother is always in my way!" Then he added, "And for some reason, I'm always in hers!"

"I was annoyed with my mother when I was seventeen," the father said gently. "Not before, and never after, but when I was seventeen, my mother annoyed me."

Carlo tried to enlist his father. "She's so disrespectful!" he complained. "She throws tantrum fits! Well, I do, too, but I'm seventeen and she's forty-something! The things she calls you! You've got this incredible patience. But she outright insults you. I get very angry, and I just say hit her! That would stop her."

"Youth is all for quick solutions," the father said, turning to the therapist. "Mostly violent. But from an adult point of view . . ." He looked at his son.

"Can you talk to Carlo about that?" the therapist asked.

The father turned to his son and said, "If I reacted to your mother the way you suggest, there would be no marriage." Carlo froze, studying the floor. "It's a long-term commitment." The father was not preaching, just explaining. "You can't understand, but we can talk about it. You should be mature when you go into marriage and stay mature through the marriage and not treat it as a game."

I complimented the father on his ability to explain all this to his son, pointing out that it is part of the job of fatherhood to explain a man's relationship to a woman. The father nodded, accepting this. "I was seventeen," he went on. "Now I'm fifty, and a father, and someday I hope I'll be a grandfather." Carlo looked up, startled, his eyes quite literally opened. Why? The father's litany concerned the role of father-hood, like my analytic patient's, but this father's musings were in-tended for his *son's* edification. The conversation transcended both their individual personalities and located them both in the same cultural meaning system.

In family therapy, in general, one participates in a balancing of roles, particularly spousal and parental, which are often interesting foils to each other. I once invited a woman to talk about her husband as a father. Up to this point in the session, she had been attacking him, as usual, and describing him as an utterly insensitive bully. She had just re-minded me that he was verbally abusive and had once threatened her physically. The husband was sullen and withdrawn until I turned the subject to their children. He sat up—apparently, this was an area of shared responsibility—and described how he and his wife had agreed, from the moment of deciding to have a child, that it was important to give children a routine, some predictability. "It gives them a sense of security," I prompted. He agreed eagerly, elaborating on the point. "I've heard a lot of good things," I concluded after a few moments. To the husband I said, "You're very loving. You show a lot of affection and caring, a lot of patience, which young children certainly require."

"I'm very grateful to have him," the wife interpolated softly.

"You have a lot of natural ability with children," I continued, compli-menting him.

"He really does," the wife agreed.

"Not everyone can do it. You know the idea that you still have the child in you and the ability to express him? Not everyone can do that. It's very special."

"When I play with the children, I'm very serious," the husband contributed happily. "I'm dead serious."

"You mean you're . . ."

"He's a kid," the wife laughed affectionately. Clearly, she was hearing herself render an image of this insensitive husband as a tender father. He heard it, too. The gestalt of abusiveness and tenderness subsequently shifted for both of them. Not many interventions can be so seemingly magical as this one turned out to be, of course, but the point is that the cultural weight ascribed to each side of the parent–spouse balance makes potential shifts like this a real possibility in family work.

Cultural configurations are generally in low profile in the psychoanalytic literature. The specifics of religion, social class, and ethnic origin are often invisible within the largely culture-free theories of dynamics, development, and diagnosis, which are determinedly universalized in classical analytic theory. They are recognized somewhat more frequently in the interpersonal literature and are noted in Kohut's elaboration of self psychology (especially in his later writings, Kohut, 1977, emphasized the vicissitudes of particular cultural constellations, e.g., the relationship of absentee parenthood to narcissistic pathology in children).

Family therapists more readily relate treatment issues to cultural belief systems. McGoldrick (1981), for example, discussed the tendency of Irish-Americans to socialize their children with a deep sense of original sin and pointed out that exploratory probes aimed at uncovering erotic or aggressive feelings in members of this culture only increase their anxiety and suffering. By contrast, interventions that are playful and humorous tap a different, but equally strong, cultural bent and therefore are often highly helpful with them. In a suggestion she called "ritualizing the badness" McGoldrick once asked a young Irish-American man to let himself feel intense guilt for at least one-half hour each day, before he began his academic work. His problem was procrastination, as well as total inhibition in talking about his experience to his wife. These problems drove his guilt, which in turn fueled his procrastination and his inhibition. McGoldrick's intervention was straightforwardly paradoxical: if the young man found himself feeling guilty once his work began, he was to ruminate for another 15 minutes before resuming. According to McGoldrick, this intervention is culturally syntonic with the Church's teaching about examining one's conscience. So was the client's diligence in following it. After one week he said he hoped he would not have to repeat this process, since he was running out of issues to be guilty about. His procrastination had abated significantly.

NARRATIVE DISTINCTIONS

In keeping with its historical origins in modernism, psychoanalysis is predicated on the idea that the patient comes to refashion a narrative that might be more deeply reflective of a uniquely individual inner world. Both the patient's complaint and the remedy that will eventually be fashioned partake of this sense of personal inwardness. In contrast to the psychoanalytic perspective, the family therapist's view is that the problems presented for resolution significantly and directly reflect cultural or subcultural influences, a view that, accordingly, results in a different perspective on character and identity. Not only is circumstance accorded more weight, but the notion of selfhood is correspondingly amended, and this changes the kind of therapeutic narrative that is possible or desirable.

> Character is an extraordinarily elusive literary idea. Perhaps it is elusive for reasons beyond the literary. For even in "real life," it is always a moot question whether the actions of persons should be attributed to circumstances or to their "enduring dispositions" — their character [Bruner, 1986, p. 37].

Solomon Asch demonstrated that what we call character is not a bundle of autonomous traits. It is an organized conception. He demonstrated, for instance, that intelligence is interpreted very differently depending on whether the intelligent person is seen as cold or warm. In a cold person, intelligence is negative, as in the word *crafty*; in a warm person, intelligence is taken to mean wisdom. Citing Asch's famous experiments, Bruner (1986) has made it clear that character is always understood as a gestalt, not merely a list of traits, and that the choice of one gestalt rather than another has real consequences for how we deal with others.

According to Bruner, character, setting, and action are integrated in the nature of narrative thought. Indeed, it is only with difficulty that we can conceive of them in isolation. Drawing on the work of Amelie Rorty, Bruner has argued that people are represented in literature in a multitude of distinctly different forms: as character, figure, person, self, and individual. We talk freely about narrative, but we forget that narrative flows through specific genres. Thus, *characters*, like their forerunners, the Greek heroes, are known by their deeds. Behaviorally oriented psychologists write therapeutic narratives about characters. *Figures*, by contrast, are defined by their place in the drama; they have the traits their roles require, like the classic confidante.

Personhood takes us to a realm beyond both figure and character. Rorty's (1976) concept of *person*—and this is where her ideas become relevant to family therapy—derives from two sources: the person's role and the law. Placed in a structural system, related to others, the person has the power to affect others and bears responsibility for that power. Thus, personhood for Rorty is embedded inextricably in what we have been describing as cultural context. From personhood, it is possible to move to the last of Rorty's distinctions—the *self*. "When a society has changed so that individuals acquire their rights by virtue of their powers, rather than having their powers defined by their rights, the concept of person has been transformed to a concept of self," wrote Rorty (p. 313). Within this overall frame, she argued, Jane Austen described a world of persons "on the verge of becoming selves."

Family therapy frames participants as falling somewhere between the narrative levels of *persons* and *selves*, as if they were characters in an Austen novel. The narrative construction is of people free to act only insofar as their culture and their context allow it, though their assumption of roles is balanced by a pull toward self-definition, expansion, and personal initiative.

Considerably further along on the narrative spectrum are *individuals*, who "begin with conscience and end with consciousness." At the core of the concept of the individual is his or her struggle with society (p. 41). Bruner observed that Rorty described Freud's world as peopled by *figures* struggling within the constraints of a fixed, timeless family narrative, and he has cited challenges to this categorization in the more recent efforts focusing on psychoanalytic "selfhood" by, for example, Schaefer and Kohut. However, it seems to me that it is the members of Rorty's last category of character, that is, *individuals* grappling with societal regimes and expectations and regimens, who function as the protagonists of psychoanalytic dramas.[3]

I have taken liberties with Rorty's forms. If Jane Austen's characters are just emerging into selfhood, then it is rather loosely metaphoric, not to mention anachronistic, to be casting our contemporary, postmodern

[3]Rorty (1976) identified Freud's characters as "figures" who struggle within the constraints of "narratives of family and the plights it creates for the child" (p. 307). Bruner (1986) cited disputation of this categorization, notably the work of Spence and Kohut, who, according to Bruner, shifted the psychoanalytic struggle to Rorty's domain of selfhood. However, as I indicate in the text, I think the contemporary psychoanalytic patient is struggling with the vicissitudes of what Rorty called individuality.

family therapy patients in her early 18th-century milieu. The point is that once we begin to talk about narrative in psychotherapy, we have to think about whose narrative we are telling. Therapeutic praxis is organized around a particular narrative form and its attendant assumptions. The narratives of family therapy and of psychoanalysis tell different stories of self and responsibility to others.

Thus, the setting of couples therapy involves some consensual notions about marriage that are a fundamental aspect of the treatment. Whatever a couple complains about, they are doing it within a fairly closed set of cultural and subcultural meanings. Jackson (1965a) provided four paradigmatic assumptions about marriage in the Western world: (1) that it is voluntary in a culture that regards it as compulsory, 2) that it is supposedly permanent, (3) that it is exclusive, and (4) that it is goal oriented. Thus, marital therapy is negotiated within a permanent structure—somewhere between folk belief and legal stricture.

There are other, more "flesh and blood," descriptions of marital structure available in the family therapy literature. For example, Wynne and Wynne's (1986) model of relational systems proposes that in the course of a marriage the following four major processes or tasks unfold in sequence and then become linked in a circular, rather than linear, manner:

1. Attachment/caregiving
2. Communicating, or exchanging meanings and messages
3. Joint problem solving
4. Mutuality, or "the flexible, selective integration of the preceding processes into an enduring, superordinate pattern of relatedness" (p. 385).

The model emphasizes that these processes determine the day-to-day emotional quality of relating (what is generally described as intimacy by couples). Thus, disputing couples often come to therapy lamenting their lack of closeness or intimacy when what has undermined their marriage may be a lack of skills or a lack of attention to joint problem solving. Wynne and Wynne's sweet conclusion: "If the elusive phoenix bird of intimacy is to return again and again, the relational nest must be in good repair" (p. 393). The point here is that the search for that elusive phoenix bird, which is what most often propels people into couples' therapy, is itself culturally sanctioned, at least in the West.

FAMILY THERAPY IN CONTEXT

The possibility of a therapy designed for the family, courtesy of recent historical developments, creates its own contextual conundrums. These, in turn, intermingle with the conundrums created by that other modern development—feminism. Issues of context thus ramify in both directions, the triumph of a new therapy being both undercut and amplified by the change away from women's traditional roles within families. Let us take the latter issue first. In the past decade there has been a comprehensive feminist attempt to restructure psychoanalytic developmental theory. Concurrently, a perspective on gender relationships has emerged in family therapy that is complementary to the psychoanalytic, a perspective that accounts for participants of both genders and for their interactional acculturated behavior. For example, from the perspective of a couple's division of emotional labor, it is clear that men often contribute technical support to a relationship and women supply emotional support. Psychoanalysts are usually most sympathetic to complaints about emotional constriction and unavailability. However, I think that psychoanalysts often forget the congruence between their own belief system and the feminine perspective; that is, psychoanalysts believe in verbal intimacy and self-revelation, as do most women in our culture. Family therapists, if they stay context dependent, usually look for a balance in the exchange of goods and services, whatever the currencies involved.

However, there have been important critiques of the systems literature itself for being insufficiently context sensitive. Goldner (1988) noted the neglect of gender as a category in most of the fundamental systems literature and argued that an emphasis on issues of hierarchy, but not gender, has been the norm. She insisted that "privileging generational relations by presuming there is anything simple and universal about parents caring for children is anthropologically naive and factually inaccurate" (p. 21). There also is little doubt that African-American and Latino cultures have been too often disregarded as categories in research on families and therapeutic process. Nor have alternative family structures, including lesbian and gay families, been visible, until recently, in the literature. (From a psychoanalyst's perspective, however, the coverage of the aforementioned categories in the family literature is extensive.)

Moreover, the assumptions and history of family therapy in postmodern culture has not been looked at frequently. For Lasch (1977), any kind of psychotherapy invades the haven of the family's integrity and privacy. How much more so a therapeutic that is chiefly focused on doing exactly that—especially when do-good professionals armed with destabilizing interventions often co-opt the very time-honored cultural prescriptions they purportedly respect (and videotape the process to boot!). In a trenchant article tracing the history of the family therapy movement, Brodkin (1980) uncovered what she called the "remodernization" trend in family therapy and the inherent biases of that ideology:

> Family therapy . . . stubbornly retains a traditional allegiance to the "natural" nuclear family group. Furthermore, it preserves the modern assumption of the urgency of a happy private life, away from the inevitable "rat race.". . . It presumes the modern American child-protective stance, and embodies an early modern insistence on the generic naturalness of nuclear family living. It is still individualistic in its own way, presuming that all families, and especially their children, are worth saving. Its "publicity campaign" is conducted with the latest hardware, and it enlists its legitimating metaphors from modern technology as well as pure science [p. 15].

These criticisms notwithstanding, family treatment nonetheless has the great virtue of addressing people in the multifaceted context in which their lives are embedded, a regenerating experience in the postmodern world.

chapter six

Family Patterning

If the music doesn't say it, how can the words say it for *the music?*
John Coltrane

The Browns sit down in a supervisee's office to begin their first therapy interview. They have been married for 14 years. There is a marked sobriety in the room. He is, at the very least, downcast, and perhaps resentful. She is earnest and frustrated. She wants to have a child; he is reluctant. She wants him to get a job ("to put *some* structure in his life, at least"); he feels she is cramping his creativity. Both have had several years of psychodynamic individual therapy. He has been on antidepressant medication in the past, and she, in self-help mode, has explored almost every New Age offering. Both of them talk readily about a lifetime struggle with "neediness."

This couple presents a cornucopia of dynamic issues. The therapist, who has been married a long time herself, wants very much to help. She even lets the session run over so that she can be fair and hear the spouses each present their experience in the relationship. They could do so forever. It is apparent from the once-removed supervisory position that this wife, Julia, has assumed full-time psychological responsibility for the management of her husband, George, and that their presence in a therapist's office is in spite of her best efforts. Julia's responsibility for George's psychic development is one of their family rules, though neither is fully aware of it. Yet until this rule is edited and they become jointly responsible for their relationship, George will not agree to have a baby or get a job and will not really be a psychotherapy client. Thus, the family therapist focuses on the essential configuration of this couple: she is boss and he is subordinate. The therapeutic question is, What are the specific loopings of communication that maintain this hierarchy?

It is precisely this attention to overarching interpersonal patterning that makes working with families seem initially so difficult to psychoanalysts. They sometimes ask family therapists how they can keep track of five transferences. The answer is, you don't; instead, you focus your trained eye on what is transpiring across psyches, not within them.

At the risk of putting the psychoanalyst in the position of Molière's bourgeois gentilhomme (who is thrilled to discover that he has been speaking prose all his life), I want to point out that attention to pattern is, of course, an intrinsic cognitive function for all of us. This attention is deliberately cultivated during therapy training, regardless of theoretical persuasion. Indeed, as Watzlawick et al. (1967) pointed out, "the search for pattern is the basis of all scientific investigation" (p. 36). Patterning is the heart of aesthetic pleasure as well. Rembrandt's power of psychological portrayal resides in his use of pattern—on the arrangement of lines and spaces on a canvas and on his rendering of the movement of light—as much as does any metaphysical capturing of soul; we lose ourselves in his subject matter, but he is carrying us along with his design. In fact, one of the important first lessons in learning to paint is to appreciate the "negative spaces," those lacunae in the composition that are as compelling as any form. The art of entering the world of a couple or family, and of enriching it, is to perceive both the negative and positive spaces in their pattern.

What are the pattern organizers? Each approach to family therapy offers a unique perspective on discerning family patterns. Thus, for example, Bowenians look almost exclusively for triangular formations while followers of Whitaker claim an utterly idiosyncratic sensibility. *All family therapists, however, hear dynamic content as subtext and patterning as primary.*

Relationships are apparent to observers, certainly to therapeutic observers, principally by dint of their communication properties. Communication can be usefully divided into the domains of *syntactics* (forms of transmission), *semantics* (meaning), and *pragmatics* (relationship effects). The psychoanalyst attends to both semantics (dynamics) and pragmatics (transference and countertransference) in a dual-channel hovering attention. Psychodynamic therapists are interested in pattern, but it is the patterning of history to transference, from childhood to current relationship enactment. Thus, a psychoanalyst would be interested in Julia Brown's repetition in her marriage of unresolved and unacknowledged childhood conflicts. The family therapist, by contrast, focuses almost exclusively on here-and-now pragmatics, that is, on the rigid two-step this couple is locked into. What are the feedback loops that maintain it? Are new steps possible? Could George give up his passive submission to Julia's management? Could she accept a more equal, more symmetrical relationship?

In other words, a stronger focus on pragmatics shifts the therapist from an intimate semantic immersion in subjectivity to a wide-angle pragmatic interactional view. This is a very different organizing framework:

Since this communicational approach to the phenomena of human behavior, both normal and abnormal, is based on the observable manifestations of *relationship* in the widest sense, it is, therefore, conceptually closer to mathematics than to traditional psychology, for mathematics is the discipline most immediately concerned with the relations between, not the nature of, entities" [Watzlawick et al., 1967, p. 22].

Accordingly, family therapists attempt to develop a calculus, a new language for the epistemology of relationship systems. The heart of the system, the sender–receiver relation, is feedback, or circular communication: starting point and end point are purely arbitrary designations. Thus, one often deliberately and selectively ignores (although temporarily) any data that distract from the overall pattern of feedback.

In other words, whatever George and Julia discuss—their relationship, their vacation, their breakfast—she will be the manager and he the underling, and that pattern will be the therapist's focus.

Feedback loops are necessarily redundant. It would be impossible to execute any shared human task without some redundancy, predictability being more important than parsimony. However, predictability, which can be so reassuringly stabilizing, can also be constricting. When it is constricting, we most readily notice it in the semantic domain. Thus, Julia Brown's complaints about the psychological cross she bears because of her husband's deficits semantically express evident redundancy. However, pragmatic redundancy—keeping the other in the same old position—is sometimes elusive; in fact, it is often misted over by the fog of semantic redundancy. Thus, Julia and George can spend multiple dysphoric hours discussing their shared dynamic of unresolved dependency. The content can seem fascinating (particularly to a psychoanalyst), but it can mask the fact that the grooves in their relationship pattern are being dug deeper with every word. Only close attention to overall patterning, reflected in the matching of tone, body language, and verbal expression, can preempt the immersion in content. An attentive observer will note that when Julia talks about neediness, George looks distracted, but when George talks about his longings, Julia is riveted in focused worry and concern. Similarly, one notes that Julia talks about her neediness with a demanding sense of urgency, while George does so plaintively and wistfully. For the spouses themselves, their pragmatics are an insignificant manifestation; semantics have preeminence. Not so for the therapist.

What is critical in working with families is recognizing how semantics—however entrancing—serve the pragmatic redundant loop. Few psychoanalysts have been interested in reformulating the calculus of

communication in this way (i.e., with semantics in an entirely secondary role), although many have certainly moved closer to a pragmatic
look at participation. Spence (1982), questioning the truth of remembered events unearthed in the psychoanalytic excavation of a patient's
personal history, invited us to consider the interpretation as a pragmatic communication:

> Whether we think of an interpretation as a special kind of speech act which
> belongs to the category of pragmatic statements or as an artistic product, to
> be evaluated according to aesthetic criteria, we are primarily interested in
> the effect it produces rather than its past credentials [p. 276].

Similarly, E. A. Levenson (1983) pointed out that "in psychoanalysis
the therapist becomes part of what he sets out to cure, and it is the
assessment of his contribution and the form of his amalgamation into
the patient system that gives psychoanalysis its particular power" (pp.
67–68). However, Levenson's (1993) mapping of pragmatics retains a
foothold in a linear epistemology. Like any self-respecting psychoanalyst, he advocates exploration of patient dynamics: who the patient
has been in the past, who the patient is for significant others, and how
he or she participates in the analysis. The patient is the central player;
the analyst, however implicated and unwittingly active, is respondent.[1]

INTERVENTIONS

There are many different ways to conceptualize interventions designed
to change or interrupt the existing pragmatic pattern in a family or
couple. "Punctuation" is one metaphor many family therapists use to
note points of possible intervention in feedback loops. Punctuation in
family therapy works essentially as it does in grammar: it keeps the text
from running on.

Suppose a couple has a marital problem to which the husband
contributes passive withdrawal and the wife contributes nagging criticism. In explaining their frustrations the husband will state that withdrawal is his only defense against his wife's nagging whereas the wife
will label this explanation a gross and willful distortion of what "really"
happens in their marriage and will insist that she is critical of her
husband because of his passivity. Stripped of all extraneous elements,

[1]Levenson (1993) has a radical position regarding analytic participation, claiming, "Ultimately, the patient does not learn from us how to deal with the world.
The patient learns to deal with us in order to deal with the world" (p. 396).

their fights consist of a monotonous exchange of the messages "I with-draw because you nag" and "I nag because you withdraw" (Watzlawick et al., p. 56). As with the Browns, the issue in such a marriage is not the specific content of these sequences of nagging, withdrawal, nagging, and so on ad infinitum. It is not only the nagging and the withdrawal, that is, the pattern itself, but also the way the couple experiences it.

The challenge in punctuation is to identify the principal systemic pattern, which is rarely immediately clear, and then to identify a crucial feedback loop that maintains it. There will be many loops. Which to focus on? Herein lies the artistry of family therapy (in its way it is rather akin to the psychoanalytic ability to notice thematic cohesion in very loose associations). One hopes to identify and punctuate a loop that carries as much systemic loading as possible, that can yield a powerful experience of discontinuous change, but that does not feel so utterly essential to the family's psychological survival that its interruption would lead to total resistance and rejection.

Identifying the principal systemic pattern that might be accessible to intervention is often a complex process. To illustrate, we turn to another clinical example.

Ruben, 32, and Agueda, 30, are Puerto Rican. Their son, who is three and a half, has been brought to a few sessions. They are attentive and competent parents, and the little boy is adorable. Their presenting complaint was Ruben's depression about his lack of initiative. They have been in therapy for about six months, and a new therapist is just taking over the treatment. As a supervisor I am impressed by the multiple dynamic narratives that one can construct about this small family:

1. Ruben comes from an intact family of seven children and describes both his parents as loving. Agueda's biological mother abandoned her to her father and stepmother, who did not want her. She was reared by a cold grandmother. She was attracted to Ruben's family's warmth.

2. Agueda is a college graduate with a major in communications and an eye to a Ph.D. Ruben is a would-be artist who works during the day as an office clerk. Agueda is critical of Ruben's inability to "catch on" to ideas and to articulate them.

3. Ruben was badly burned in a household accident at age 13. The skin on his legs is discolored and scarred, and he is obsessed with it, almost like the clubfooted protagonist of Somerset Maugham's *Of Human Bondage*. He will not go to the beach and talks about his disfig-urement a great deal.

4. Ruben cannot decide if he loves Agueda. What is love? he asks himself. He is fiercely attracted to a woman at the office and has discussed this "passion" at length with Agueda.

5. Agueda complains that Ruben does not help her with their son. He says he needs space.

We could approach this couple by emphasizing dependency needs springing from their experiences in their families of origin. We could focus on psychic trauma. We could think about cultural and gender issues or focus on Ruben's discussing his passion for the woman at the office from a perspective of differentiation. But I am struck by the therapist's observation that no matter what they talk about, Agueda criticizes Ruben and he defends himself, becoming so preoccupied with himself in the process that he almost erases her existence. Once criticized, he talks only to the therapist and demands the therapist's total attention. Agueda's only contact point is her criticism of him, but avoiding her criticism becomes Ruben's reason for needing space from her. In other words, this patterning includes all the separate dynamics, it can be explained by all of them, and it transcends them. In considering how to interrupt this pattern, several possible therapeutic points of entry can be highlighted. The therapist might give the couple a task that requires symmetrical, rather than complementary, participation. For example, Ruben might be asked to inquire about something that Agueda says, making her the subject of his positive attention in an interchange in which he takes the initiative.

In general, family therapists try to capture the essential and natural punctuation of a family's organization. They work with families to formulate explicit notions about that punctuation. Two basic approaches to highlighting punctuation will be discussed here (others will be discussed in Chapter Nine): eliciting a central metaphor and family sculpture. Family therapists think about organization in a distinct fashion; a concept that orients the therapist in considering punctuation is that of boundaries—boundaries that surround each member, the key subsystems in the family, and the family as a whole.

Eliciting a Central Metaphor

The experience of Julia and George Brown with whom we opened this chapter might be captured in an image of a huntress, Diana, who has cornered her prey. Altering that punctuation might open possibilities for them. The therapist might begin simply by attempting to highlight this punctuation. She could invite the couple to make sure they understand each other. In asking each to question the other for clarification and to attempt to understand the implications of the other's position (i.e., she is entrapping, he is hunted), the therapist introduces parity and a crisper syntax. Julia and George are less likely to act out the same old story of pursuit and retreat.

With a couple similarly organized, I used a metaphor spontaneously introduced by the fiancé, who talked of feeling that he had a yoke around his neck. I took the image seriously and addressed it as a relationship configuration, not as a distorted perception or fantasy. And in what is characteristic of family work, I drenched the session with this metaphor. "Is the yoke loose or tight, long or short?" I asked. "What are the pleasures of being so constrained?" "Is it safe?" Thus building on D. N. Stern's (1985) finding that fantasy follows reality, I explored the possibilities for transformation by boldfacing the punctuation of this couple's relationship.

Children understand punctuation readily, particularly when it is cast metaphorically. In work with a troubled family with two sons, one withdrawing and the other overly active and requiring his divorced, adversarial parents to become involved with each other, I described one son as a "red light" and the other as a "green light," inviting parental reinvolvement. The boys got the point and from then on played with it, implicitly reminding their parents how much their conflict had been dividing their sons.

It is important to repeat that we are not talking about punctuating verbal statements but, rather, whole relationship systems. And relationship systems are talked about and "talked" in two different modes: The analogic and the digital. In a digital mode of communication there is an arbitrary assignment of sign to thing; all human language systems operate digitally (or, in other words, arbitrarily and abstractly). In the analogic mode, as with a thermometer, the sign and its directionality are homologous with what is being measured. Analogic modes of representation make sense (e.g., a clenched fist signifies anger). Analysts deal with the juxtaposition of the analogic and digital every time they listen to a dream description. The dream was experienced in the analogic mode but the patient codes it in digital language to report it, thereby likely losing accuracy and immediacy in the service of interpersonal communication.

Oliver Sacks (1985) described listening to a Reagan presidential speech in a neurology unit: "*What* was going on? . . . There he was, the old charmer, the actor with his practiced rhetoric, his histrionics, his emotional appeal—and all the patients were convulsed with laughter." Sacks went on to explain that on this aphasia ward (where patients have become uncomprehending of words but have become, in a compensatory manner, exquisitely sensitive to tone and gesture, that is, to total expression) "the grimaces, the histrionisms, the gestures—and, above all, the tones and cadences of the President's voice—rang false for these wordless but immensely sensitive patients." Sacks contrasted the aphasics' response to that of a woman with tonal agnosia (who had lost the ability to perceive the timbre and feeling of tone) who also had difficulty seeing clearly. Focusing on the precise use of the President's word usage (i.e., stripped of any analogic coloration), she, in contrast, frowned and stated, "He is not cogent." Reagan's speech was well accepted by the public, Sacks noted, it being a marriage of "deceptive word use combined with deceptive voice," which left only the brain-damaged undeceived (p. 29).

When the digital and the analogic are well married, as in the presidential speech, communication is received comfortably and inattentively. The difficulty—and it is a frequent and dense problem in intimate relationships—is that the matching is often puzzling and mystifying. Family therapists have been fascinated with the relationship of analogic and digital communication because they have to be. Relationships are coded on both levels.

Family members typically take their digital communication most seriously; it is the stuff of which we construct our personified selves. A wife says to her husband, "I need more space." He panics, fearing abandonment. He is listening in the digital mode, underattending the central analog configuration of their relationship, which is that he regularly asks for a precise accounting of her whereabouts and interrogates her about her professional liaisons. Does he hear abandonment in her digital communication because he senses, on a more global analogical level, how furious she is? Is she on her way out of the relationship because he is so invasive, but would she stay if he pulled back? What is most salient for this couple's family therapist is the gestalt of anxious smothering, and it is this relationship patterning that must be addressed.

Repunctuation often requires bypassing insight, however earnestly pursued and accurately produced, and this can be difficult for the psychoanalyst new to family work. But note that Julia Brown knows that she is controlling and that she freely reports that she became so in relation to an invasive mother with whom she identifies. George Brown knows that he has low self-esteem and can poignantly trace its origins. Yet the articulation of these dynamics does little to modify the current patterning of their relationship. In fact, it is a characteristic of their relationship pattern that Julia demands this kind of self-revelation from George, thereby rendering any of his insights pragmatically impotent.

How can a psychoanalyst live with bypassing insight? It is true that in today's climate of opinion, the therapeutic relationship is now viewed as sheltering under its broad wings the previously feared "corrective emotional experience," a phenomenon often associated with minimizing the therapeutic action of insight. However, the suggestion here is more radical; family therapists propose that a shift in patterning is the *sine qua non* of change in relationship systems.

The basis for this supposition is twofold. First, some of the most rigidly binding feedback loops organizing family members have been serendipitously, rather than profoundly or irrevocably, organized. For example, imagine a family in which the essential systemic dysfunction lies in an imbalanced closeness between daughter and mother that excludes father. This pattern can take a variety of forms. The fact is that daughter and mother might express their imbalanced closeness either by criticizing father, by infantalizing him, or by "revering" him (as an icon, not as a husband and father). Why any particular expression has become established and second nature reflects a complex welding of three different personalities and character structures. In a sense, symptoms in an individual patient, considered as a compromise between impulse and defense, are subject to the same serendipity. When more than one psychic structure is involved, however, the mathematical permutations expand considerably and settle somewhat more arbitrarily. However, once a particular loop is in place, it is experienced as essential and true by the family members; all their personifications of self and other become tied to it. Dysfunction is then denied. Let us assume that in the aforementioned family the dominant organization or loop that protects the triangular imbalance is that dad is considered all-knowing, a guru to be consulted only on important matters, like the national deficit, while inessential things, like the family vacation, are left to mother and daughter. If one inquires why mother and daughter treat dad as a distant guru, they will elaborate, perhaps quite insightfully, about their own deficiencies and his wisdom, but they will not loosen their overattachment. If you probe their closeness further, unless they are particularly insightful and flexible, they will likely retreat to an even more determined description of deficiency and neediness. The therapist's task is to fashion an interruption in the cycling of this predominant loop. If the next episode of reverential advice seeking from dad is cast in a totally different light, the systemic dysfunction will be exposed. The operations that keep it running and covert will be short-circuited.

This kind of punctuated interruption is generally referred to as discontinuous change in family therapy; it is a thrust at interrupting the overly redundant behavior that protects systemic dysfunction. It is discontinuous because it is not built gradually, by accretion, as psychoanalytic change is; instead, it is punctuated, or interrupted.

Peter and Doris Cooper are a couple in their mid-50s. They have been married for 16 months. Doris has a son by her first marriage: Donald, age 20. He and Peter have accepted each other to an extent that delights all three of them, but Doris senses a lack of commitment to her from Peter. Recently, they have returned from vacation, and in the following dialogue excerpted from a therapy session Doris is collapsing two episodes into one denunciation of Peter's "general attitude." In the first episode, which occurred while they were visiting Doris's parents, her father walked into their room early in the morning; Peter was embarrassed and furious, and he "was in a bad mood all day." Subsequently, on a shopping trip with Donald, Peter wanted to look at a sweater for himself but Doris didn't think they had time.

> *Peter:* I didn't see why we couldn't take fifteen minutes . . .
> *Doris:* So find a way to say it nicely! It's just like what happened with my father. He only wanted to talk to me. So if it bothers you, say so! Whenever you don't like something, you lose your temper. Then I get uptight, and we can't talk to each other!
> *Peter (to therapist):* I feel whenever we relate to other people, my wishes are the last to be consulted. Well, no, probably it's Doris's wishes, but she doesn't mind. But if I object . . .
> *Doris:* I wouldn't mind if you objected. But find a nice way to do it! You throw your hands in the air, and storm off!

Listening to this, the therapist realized that Peter does not object to Doris's criticisms and entreaties. To him this is attention, a warm engagement much to be preferred to what had been a very lonely bachelorhood. And Doris certainly does not object to Peter's providing some space between her and her parents (she thanked him for it in previous therapy sessions). Yet the loop remains intact. Doris cannot competently manage her own relationships, and Peter cannot make her hear his plea to attend to him and his needs.

> *Peter:* Whenever I object, you just say, "What do you want me to do?" All I'm doing is speaking up for myself, and suddenly I'm the bad guy. Yes, I was upset when your father walked into the room. And maybe I was wrong to lose my cool. But I don't see why you're so pissed at me.
> *Doris:* I don't object when you don't like things. I object to your losing your temper. Find a nicer way . . .
> *Peter:* You push the right buttons and then sit back. You're Ms. Innocent, and I'm Mr. Bad Guy.

Doris: No! Anything that says no to you pushes a button!

Therapist: I think you do push Peter's buttons, Doris. You are a sensitive woman, and you're experienced with marriage, parenting, in-laws. This is all new to Peter. He was probably shocked when your father walked into the bedroom.

Doris: Were you really shocked?

Peter: I couldn't believe it!

Therapist: Why don't you help him understand his pushy in-laws?

Peter: Well, I don't know that it's her job . . .

Therapist: You know, that is really a very nice thing. I criticized Doris, and you defended her. He's acting like a husband, Doris. And he's getting good at it. But you could help him more.

Doris: Well, what I don't understand is why he can't find a *nice* way to . . .

The therapist has succeeded in involving Peter and Doris in a new interest in mutual helpfulness, but their grasp of how to sustain this way of relating seems tentative. How can the therapist highlight the pattern of dual deprivation this couple is experiencing? An emphasis on temporal patterning, beyond content, supports the new interpersonal perceptions:

Therapist: No! Stop. Think. Count to twenty. Let it percolate. You're not helping Peter. He makes what he thinks are the right moves, to be a good husband. But he has to enter slowly, feeling it out. And you are not helping him. You're very fast—staccato, like jazz. Whenever anybody says anything, you are already cooking the answer. You're such an expert, you respond so quickly, that you're not helping him. (*Peter looks at Doris intently, as if willing her to respond to this characterization of their relationship pattern. Doris looks at him, then away.*)

Doris: I've tried to . . . I guess I never thought about it that way.

Peter (prompting her): It's like when I helped you with your mother.

Doris: I couldn't handle it. (*smiles*) And you told her off, and I started to cry. No one ever helped me before, with her.

In this couple the wife set the rules and responded so fast that the husband's efforts went unrecognized. By capturing Doris's impatience in the metaphor of staccato communication, the therapist was able to slow her down and make her recognize both her own strength and her husband's effort, thus providing the couple with the crucial experience of awareness. The metaphor of Doris's "staccato" communication seemed to get her attention and to break her automatic, fussy control.

The punctuation was changed in a way that made Doris view Peter more positively, and his own self-perception improved. The next step in attempting to involve this couple in a more or less comfortable sequence of change would perhaps be to address what Peter wanted from Doris.

Family Sculpting

An extremely evocative means of exploration of patterning, with a net wide enough for a full analog set, is the family therapy technique of sculpting. Sculpting was developed by David Kantor and Fred and Bonnie Duhl, at the Boston Family Institute in the early 1970s. When family members are asked to "sculpt" their relationship, they provide a nonverbal spatial representation of it in ideal or real form or represent a concrete aspect of the relationship, such as wished-for distance or closeness. Usually, partners create a comparable sculpting. Because of time limitations, one or two members of a larger family create a sculpting that functions then as a "common external metaphor against which . . . [family members] compare [their] own private internal understandings and images of the family they had been talking about" (Duhl, 1983, p. 216). Some therapists encourage sculptings-in-motion, that is, a silent flow of movement between family members dramatizing a problem interaction. Sculpting can be particularly useful with couples who take their digital (i.e., verbally coded) statements to each other too seriously. I invited each of the Browns to sculpt a physical configuration that would represent the specter that haunted them both, namely, George's depression. How could they represent the depression? George put Julia far across the room with her head bent, defeated and detached. What a change from a stalking pursuer! Julia, in her turn, asked George to lie on the floor; then she stood over him, creating a living sculpture that moved this highly intellectualizing, blocked couple to tears. Did George put Julia across the room because he, on some level, recognized her emotional distancing in spite of her hyperinvolvement? Supposedly involved, she was really terrified of his sadness and worried about how she might be contributing to it. Similarly, her sculpture was revealing: it was aggressive and dominating and laid bare the anger (defensive of her fear) behind her oversolicitous concern.

"Explanatory language tends to isolate and fragment, to describe one event followed by another in a linear fashion," wrote Papp (1982). "Figurative language tends to synthesize and combine. It is capable of uniting different levels of thought, feeling and behavior into a holistic picture" (p. 454).

Juan and Ana Restropo applied for marital therapy because they were unable to communicate anymore. They had two boys, aged 13 and 7, who were still living in Colombia with Ana's parents. Juan had come to New York three years before to pursue his doctorate. For the first year Ana remained in Colombia with the children. During that year Juan had an affair. He also began to realize how unhappy he was in his marriage and how much he needed to focus his energy on himself. He became involved with Adult Children of Alcoholics because his father was an alcoholic; at one point he was attending up to 17 meetings a week. There he learned that his recovery must take priority over everything else and that he had to be in an environment where he could feel "safe" and not "invalidated." When Ana came to New York to be with him, saying she had missed him terribly, Juan lost no time in letting her know about his affair and in making it clear that he felt repelled by her demanding, suffocating behavior toward him.

This is another couple who tended to talk at each other without listening. Juan delivered long, intellectualized monologues. Ana cried. In an effort to punctuate this pattern, the therapist asked them to imagine a sculpture of their ideas of closeness in a relationship. Juan chose two birds in a cage. Ana chose two mirrors bordered by glittering lights, each rotating on its own axis; the rotations sometimes resulted in complete darkness.

The couple and their therapist were able to use these sculptures as a way to reframe the entrenched notion that Ana was an inadequate wife who was about to be left by her husband. The sculpting imagery enriched the inquiry and the interventions of subsequent sessions. The therapist playfully suggested that although caged birds are imprisoned, they are also well fed and protected by caretakers. She also noted that Ana's rotating illuminators often left Juan in total darkness, an observation that cast doubt on the idea that Juan was the powerful partner who was threatening to leave the marriage. Instead, his provocative behavior was seen as rebellious and perhaps anxiety-driven.

The therapist asked Juan to think of something he really wanted and to ask Ana to do it for him, so he could experience her full attention. But she encouraged Ana to occasionally leave the apartment without telling Juan where she was going. Juan later reported feeling "traumatized" when she did so and was visibly depressed as he spoke of this experience. This was interpreted as part of the same reframing, with Juan needing warmth from Ana and needing to take an active role in getting that warmth. Now it was possible to begin a new phase in therapy, one that would focus on realigning the axis of dependence and independence in this relationship.

Boundaries

Another essential patterning template in family therapy involves the concept of boundaries. Proposed originally by Minuchin and Fishman (1981), boundaries are figurative dividers between or among systems or subsystems. Within the family, boundaries are maintained by an implicit rule system defining how family members participate in a given subsystem and what the parameters are for entering and leaving the interactional sphere of other subsystems. It is important that boundary membranes be permeable (i.e., flexible and adaptive), whether these membranes encase individuals within subsystems, subsystems within the family, or the family itself in its larger social context.

Consider the case of Veronica and Cecilia, the mother and grandmother who shared the responsibility of raising Veronica's child, Jared (this case was introduced in Chapter Five). The grandmother's participation in child rearing was a adaptation to the challenges of single mothering and created the parental subsystem of grandmother-and-mother. Recall that Cecelia's overinvolvement was undermining Veronica and causing her to try to distance the grandmother in a way that made the grandmother feel estranged from both her daughter and the grandchild who had been like her own child. The therapist's intervention (inviting the grandmother to compliment her daughter and to relax and enjoy the fact that she had raised a daughter who was a competent mother) was a boundary-making intervention. By indicating that the mother had to take the major responsibility for parenting at this stage and was fully capable of doing so, the therapist allowed the mother a realization of her own competence and redefined the parental subsystem boundary in a way that rewarded the grandmother instead of excluding her.

The family systems perspective has always posited an inherent mutual organizing and penetrating influence between members of family groups. The boundaries it postulates are necessarily permeable ones. Minuchin has delineated a range of boundary strengths, from extreme enmeshment to extreme disengagement, with a very wide normal band in between. In sessions he often works with the family to reshape and reinforce boundaries. For example, he might make too enmeshed a relationship between parents and children spatially explicit by asking children who are overinvolved in their parents' lives to turn their chair around during a family therapy session with their back to their parents, explaining to them, "You don't have to be part of your parents' fight." A mother inappropriately distant from a child might be asked to move her chair closer. "Sit next to Beverly," Minuchin might say. "She is only a little girl, and she needs you to take care of her."

What makes boundary- and alliance-formation so interesting is that the structural problem is often masked, as with the pragmatics of feedback, by the semantic communication. Psychoanalysts who watch a family with a bitterly abusive father and son at each other's throats are often dismayed by the lack of modulation, by the rage and the accumulating trauma. Of course, they are correct in insisting that both collectively and individually these affects must be addressed. But early on in thinking about families, they often miss the closeness, the alliance, between the members of this dyad, from whose intensity other family members feel woefully excluded.

The phenomenon of boundary maintenance observed in families is particularly thought provoking from a psychoanalytic perspective. For a long time in the history of psychoanalytic theorizing the concept of a personal boundary was equated with self-protection and autonomy and, as such, with psychological well-being. Thus, the concept of a personal boundary found a place in psychoanalytically informed infant research, which emphasized the child's stimulus barrier. In clinical theory, boundary invasions were emphasized by Kernberg (1975) and others in the delineation of borderline pathology, which was generally discussed as a tendency to confuse self and object representations, particularly as projected onto the therapist. More recently, a place for boundaries as both permeable and robust has been found in psychoanalytic theory because of the feminist challenge to the assumed equation between autonomy—or hyper-boundary-maintenance—and psychological health. In family work, one sees rigid and flexible boundaries, permeable ones and impermeable ones, as part of a pattern that is shared and redundantly organized in ways that go well beyond the individual.

PATTERNS IN PSYCHOANALYSIS

There is pattern matching in psychoanalytic work, but it is different. The match moves across transference and the extratransferential material of history and current circumstance. The theoretical template used for the pattern matching (e.g., oedipal issues, the power of internal objects, dissociated self-experience) depends on the dynamics favored by the particular psychoanalytic orientation. The dynamics are generally organized diachronically in time, from infancy to adulthood, and they are generally investigated in an analogous linear manner, from appearance down to underlying structure. This tracing can be extremely challenging, and the particular talent of synthesizing a mixture of symbolic, biographical, and free associative communications has probably not been adequately defined. Spence (1982) has made it altogether clear that the activity of patterning on the part of the psychoanalyst is far more proactive than we ever imagined. He notes that "instead of finding a true instance of structural correspondence, we are often generating a similarity by a clever application of language to a pair of random events; given the flexibility of language, we can almost always succeed" (p. 157).

I think that an immersion in systemic patterning, as described in this chapter, can have a salutary effect on efforts to grasp psychoanalytic process. The report and command aspects of family communication (what Olga Silverstein [Keeney and Silverstein, 1986] dubs the "semantic and political" aspects of communication) are often not struggled with directly by psychoanalysts.

An analyst reports battle fatigue from a patient who complains that the analysis is useless but never misses a session. The analyst finds himself or herself, with some chagrin, wondering why the patient won't just go away. One could describe the situation in dynamic terms—perhaps the patient views the analyst as an exciting but dangerous object—but what is often missed is that the more the analyst attempts to be reassuring, the more exciting he or she becomes, which results in yet greater efforts to assuage the patient's fears. It is as if the command aspects of the relationship have utterly swamped any possible reporting of newness. In many such frustrating transference and countertransference struggles the only truly helpful, as well as honest, move to make is one of expressing helplessness or anger, responses that can be viewed as nonanalytic in that they are "acted-in" rather than interpretive.

I think these unorthodox moments of enactment are potentially mutative because they are inherently redundancy interrupting. The talking cure runs out of steam when words can carry no news of a difference, in Bateson's terms, but simply carry the same command over and over. The analyst must enact a new relationship configuration, though, one hopes, not impulsively and not unsympathetically.

Note that this is not the patient's enactment; the spontaneity emerges from the analyst's center of action. Pushed to the edge of entropy, of meaninglessness and redundancy, the analyst must seek order. We hearken back to the inherent order seeking of complex systems postulated in chaos theory. A family therapist in an equivalent situation, that is, faced with a group of people locked in a collectively organized emotional position of coming to family sessions only to decry the ineffectiveness of therapy and of the therapist, might feel the need for a paradoxical prescription to loosen the rigidity of the system. He or she might, for example, congratulate this group on their ability to band together and protect themselves from alien ideas that might cause confusion.

In the sweep of the analytic literature of the last two decades we find one clinical theorist, Andreas Angyal, who bases his conception of personality structure and change on systemic patterns with as much conviction as family therapists do. Angyal was influenced by Kurt Goldstein and thus by the thinking of Gestalt theorists in the 1940s. What is unique about Angyal's theory is his conception of health and neurosis as alternatively patterned organizations of the same personality characteristics. Angyal (1965), who defines personality as an "ambiguous Gestalt," stated:

> Health and neurosis are to be thought of as two organized processes, two dynamic Gestalts organizing the same material, so that each item has a position within two different patterns. There can be shifts between the two, lasting or short lived, in either direction, but at any given moment the person is either healthy or neurotic, depending on which system is dominant [p. 102].

What is crucial about this formulation is the abandonment of a view of neurosis as, in Angyal's terms, "a rotten part of a healthy apple" (p. 103). For Angyal, every aspect of personality finds a systemic niche in either the healthy or neurotic gestalt. Working within an individual psychodynamic orientation, Angyal stresses the mutative effects of reliving early traumatic experiences and of powerfully experiencing the transference relationship. Although his praxis is traditionally psychoanalytic, his thinking is inventive and somewhat radical. To Angyal, massive resistance on the part of the patient is indicative not of unmitigated pathology but of latent personal strength, with resistance being the neurotic manifestation of it. Similarly, Angyal is opposed to guarded and muted therapeutic engagement. He believes that the best therapists offer a sense of drama, thus preventing the patient from dissociating from the urgency of his or her needs. The essence of his holistic view—that psychological growth derives from a reorganization of the separate elements of character, not from a transmutation of those elements—offers a very close analog to family systems theory.

chapter seven

Development from a Family Perspective

Each man's memory is his private literature.
Aldous Huxley

The family systems model of development, that is, the family life cycle, describes an aggregate of individuals each of whom is following his or her own separate developmental course. Because it thus involves a part-to-whole relationship, family developmental theory is particularly heuristic for moving back and forth between individual and family concepts. In fact, we propose that family systems models of development, which organize the complex data of a multiperson system, can also expand the developmental perspective of a therapist charting the life story of an individual patient.

Psychoanalytic theory is conceptually anchored by its developmental perspective. Freud's dominant emphasis on historical reconstruction reflected the excitement of 19th-century German intellectual life, which had been sparked by Darwin's radical evolutionary theory and major discoveries in archaeology and paleontology (Horner, 1991). This developmental perspective has experienced its own multifaceted development; it has been essentially reshaped by every orientation within psychoanalysis and has recently risen to the challenge of deconstruction and narrative theory. Development from a family systems perspective, however, is an altogether different matter. Developmental constructs within family therapy are suited to a focus on the interactive and on the here-and-now.

A heuristic schema from which to compare sets of developmental data was offered by Wrightsman (1988), who divided developmental theories into three categories: (1) early formation theories, which stress the first few years of life; (2) stage theories, which focus on tasks germane to each stage of development; and (3) dialectical approaches, which chart an evolving but endless struggle between basic polarities in personality structure. Dialectical approaches chart a timeless oscillation and interpenetration between opposing areas of experience. An example of the dialectical approach—that development involves a struggle between the press of autonomy and the need for dependence and community—lies at the heart of considerable controversy within psychoanalytic theory today. Inherent in the early formation model of development is an emphasis on conflict resolution via structuralization. Similarly, stage theories postulate reasonably successful resolutions of earlier conflicts as the doorways to continued epigenesis. What is distinctive about the dialectical perspective is an emphasis on the instability of conflict resolution.

How do psychoanalytic and family systems perspectives compare with one another according to Wrightsman's schema? Psychoanalytic models characteristically emphasize developments early in life. To be sure, most orientations within psychoanalytic theory wed a focus on early formation to a stage theory of development, though there is variation in how far into the life span the stages reach. Family models of development are more clearly stage oriented, but they, looked at closely, also have a strong dialectical component. The dialectical, or cross-sectional, component grows out of a systems emphasis on family structure (i.e., subsystems and hierarchies) and communication as inherently circular in nature. The differences in how the developmental framework is organized within the psychoanalytic and systems paradigms determines how lives are narrated and "storied" within these two perspectives. Once we consider development from a systems perspective, we are naturally stimulated to look anew at the genre of psychoanalytic narrative, reflecting in particular on its timing and pragmatics. Ultimately, one conceptual crossroad where the two different foci on development meet and intersect is along the newly blazed path heading toward the postmodern distributed sense of self.

Let us briefly review the major psychoanalytic developmental perspectives. The classical position rests on the genetic foundation of the psychobiological drives, which shape a rather robust character structure by the completion of the oedipal stage. Object relations theory focuses on the child within the adult, awaiting discovery and healing. In the self-psychological orientation, the self is, in Goldberg's (1986) term, "pre-wired"; needs for mirroring and idealization are either satisfied early or remain rents in the fabric of the self. These are all in their different ways early formation theories. Interpersonal psychoanalytic theory, by contrast, journeys as far as young adulthood, and since it allows for transformation at the cusp of every new stage, it is a stage theory to a large extent. There is, in the interpersonal sector, considerable controversy between those analysts who emphasize a necessary return to the site of initial dyadic bonding in order to effect the transmutation of "bad me" personifications (Bromberg, 1979; Schecter, 1983) and those (E. A. Levenson, 1989) who scan later childhood experience for confusion and mystification.

Recently, there has been some new work in the area of psychodynamic developmental theory that addresses the rhythm of development in terms of dialectical forces. Franz and White (1985) criticized Erikson's stage theory as too linear, too committed to a "single developmental pathway" (p. 225). They further argued that the linearity is phallocentric, weighted more heavily on autonomy than intimacy. They thus proposed a weaving of the negotiation of intimacy versus autonomy within the prominent developmental task at each stage. That is, to the stage of early childhood, which Erikson (1959) pivoted on "autonomy versus shame and doubt," they added "secure attachment versus narcissism," and for the age of toddlerhood, to Erikson's "initiative versus guilt" they added "imaginative playfulness and identifications versus inhibitions" (p. 244).

Psychoanalytic developmental theory, as embodied in the classical, self-psychological, and object relational approaches, can be assigned to Wrightsman's category of early formation theory. In postulating a preemptive impact to early development these psychoanalytic theories ultimately trace their lineage to late-19th-century theories of sexual development, most especially concerning fetishism and perversion, which stressed early fixation of the drives (Sulloway, 1983). More recently, such formulations have drawn additional support from theories arising from ethology that stress critical or sensitive periods in development and take as their theoretical touchstone the phenomenon of imprinting. To be sure, analysts do not often use the ethological terms directly, but more recent revampings of their models implicitly show the ethological influence. Today, however, we are in the throes of enormous controversy regarding the preemptive effect of early experience. Cohler (1980) has charted the lineaments of this controversy. First, he questions the relevance of childhood experiences to more complex, and certainly quite different, adult personality functioning. For example, he scorns attempts to apply Piagetian notions of early concept formation to "adult analysands who function well at the level of formal operations" (p. 155). Second, he notes as problematic the psychoanalytic emphasis on putative critical periods in childhood, citing extensive research regarding the reversibility of childhood deprivations. The third issue Cohler raises concerns one of the thorniest issues in psychological theory today, namely, the question of memory storage and retrieval. How accurate is the retrieval of early memories? Does accuracy mean photographic imaging? Does the memory of traumatic events differ from the memory of benign happenings? Is memory stored in batches or scripts? It is Cohler's position that Freud, more than his followers, clearly recognized that "the life biography is successively rewritten at transition points in the life cycle in order to achieve the consistency which is necessary for continued adaptation" (p. 157). Discussing Freud's (1937) "Constructions in Analysis," Cohler notes that "the test of the validity of reconstructions was not actual recall of events, for clearly such recall was not possible. Rather, the test was the development of a 'sense-of-conviction' on the part of the analysand of the reconstruction" (p. 184).

The problems inherent in the early formation theories are not salient in the family systems model. The family approach to development is essentially a stage model that extends into later adulthood, and it relies considerably less on memorial data. However, although psychoanalytic developmental theory emphasizes early formation concepts, in practice it can and does offer a reservoir of dynamic hypotheses for family therapists. In particular, when children are present in the treatment, these dynamics can be explored *in vivo* and, more importantly, shifted. Jay Haley (1976) has provided a transcript of a case he supervised, one he calls "A Modern 'Little Hans.'" The intervention in the case is traditionally viewed as an exemplar of strategic technique, but it is equally illustrative of the intersection of family structure and psychoanalytic developmental theory. Freud (1913) summarized the original case of Little Hans as follows:

> The boy had a phobia of horses, and as a result he refused to go out in the street. He expressed a fear that the horse would come into the room and bite him; and it turned out that this must be the punishment for a wish that the horse might fall down (that is, die). After the boy's fear of his father had been removed by reassurances, it became evident that he was struggling against wishes which had as their subject the idea of his father being absent (going away on a journey, dying). He regarded his father (as he made all too clear) as a competitor for the favors of his mother, towards whom the obscure foreshadowing of his budding sexual wishes were aimed. Thus he was situated in the typical attitude of a male child towards his parents to which we have given the name of the 'Oedipus complex" and which we regard in general as the nuclear complex of the neuroses [pp. 128–129].

In Haley's case the little boy is afraid of dogs. Rather than focus on the boy's dynamics, Haley moved directly to a consideration of the current family structure:

Arbitrarily choosing mother, father, and child as a unit, leaving out other family members, one can say that when a child has a problem that handicaps him, usually one parent is intensely involved with the child. This parent often speaks for the child, hovers over him, and is both overprotective and exasperated with him. The other parent is more peripheral, tending to be disengaged from both the child and spouse [p. 227].

In this particular case, perhaps somewhat too stereotypically, it is the mother who is overinvolved and the father who is peripheral. Haley's quintessential systemic view of the child's fear of dogs is that it serves a function in the family system, in this case both to distract the parents from their marked uninvolvement with each other (largely due to unresolved bitterness about a marital infidelity) and to absorb the mother's need for contact, which the father suppresses altogether by working two jobs from dawn to dusk. The interventions are carefully planned both to respect the family's concern about the symptom and to remove the symptom from the system, which by necessity must itself be restructured to facilitate the removal. A variety of different kinds of restructuring interventions are introduced. For example, in the second session, when the mother leaves to take the daughter to the bathroom, the therapist, at Haley's direction, carefully interviews the father about his own precautions with regard to strange dogs (the father is a mailman). For the first time, father and son become intensely and atypically engaged with each other around the issue of personal vulnerability and aggression. In the following transcript excerpt the therapist is pursuing father–son closeness as a way of extricating the mother from an overinvolvement with her child, this being a necessary first step toward reconnecting her to her husband:

Father: If you take your hat and you put it in front of a dog, and the dog grabs ahold of the hat, he's gonna grab the hat, he's not gonna pass the hat and grab your arm. He's gonna grab the cap. Right?
Boy: Uh-huh.
Father: You kick him under the chin, while he's grabbing hold of the hat.
Boy: You kick him under the chin?
Father: Uh yeah.
Boy: That be . . .
Father: It fits real nice, you see. (*shows foot movement*)
Boy: Yeah.
(*Mother entering the room with daughter*)
Mother: We got lost.
Boy: So isn't that cruel?

Father: If the dog is trying to bite you, nothing is cruel.
Boy: Uh-huh.
Father: Nothing is ever cruel if the dog is trying to bite you; defending yourself is not cruel.
Therapist: You see, I think maybe you haven't thought that you have an expert on dogs right at home.
Boy: I know.
Therapist: Your father deals with dogs every day [pp. 230–231].

In the end the boy totally overcomes his fear of dogs, and his parents become closer. Note, however, that there is no therapeutic interest in the content of the child's fears or in his dynamics.

Certainly, one can look at the conversation between father and son and reflect that this is the stuff—wanton aggression and appropriate self-defense—with which oedipal crises are resolved. And one could note further that this father and son are resolving the son's underlying conflict in here-and-now reality. With both psychoanalytic developmental and systemic lenses in hand one can look at a young boy's phobic displacement of aggression onto animals in two ways: as an expression of his libidinal conflicts and as a structurally determined triangulation. Having both lenses allows for more flexibility in developmental assessment.

In principle, any inquiry into a family's "culture," as Bruner designates it, can be informed by psychoanalytic constructs. Indeed, psychoanalytic developmental theories potentially offer a rich yield of useful hypotheses in couples work and in the treatment of families with older children. The problem is that these formulations—for example, psychosexual fixations (classical theory), mirroring functions (self psychology), tantalizing objects (object relations theory), chumship experiences (interpersonal theory)—can obscure the clinician's focus. Individual-based developmental theories may leave the clinician working with families feeling unfocused, much like having the experience of sitting ringside at the circus, mesmerized but somewhat disoriented by the three-ring activity. A clearer viewpoint can be secured by subsuming psychoanalytic formulations within family systems developmental conceptions, but this requires a familiarity with the latter and a clear sense of how they can usefully encompass the former.

THE FAMILY LIFE CYCLE

What sort of developmental model is provided in the family literature? The family developmental model is almost by necessity stage constructed. The family brings people of all ages simultaneously to the therapist's office; what is critical is a template or schema that systemically catalogues their individual life stage experience in terms of a stage theory that will encompass them in the aggregate.

There is an overarching structure to family life, winding around individual development as we know it. Carter and McGoldrick (1989), who are noted for their contribution to the theory of family development, have described the life cycle perspective as follows: "The central underlying process to be negotiated is the expansion, contraction, and realignment of the relationship system to support the entry, exit, and development of family members in a functional way" (p. 13). Cecilia Falicov (1978), also a noted family developmentalist, specifically identified three criteria by which the life cycle of the family can be divided: changes in family size, changes in age composition, and changes in the work status of the breadwinners. For Carter and McGoldrick as well as for Falicov, family stage theory must be qualified by a consideration of individual data; by the recognition that any given family exists within a multigenerational field; and, in particular, by the therapist's awareness that gender redefinitions have radically transformed family life within recent decades. There are many choices not covered in the family life cycle schema, including, just for a sampling, singles who never leave home, those who never marry, and the voluntarily childless couple.

In the family life cycle model, the family moves through six stages: (1) single adulthood, (2) the joining of families of origin through the marriage of the young couple, (3) families with young children, (4) families with adolescents, (5) families launching children, and (6) families in later life. Carter and McGoldrick have charted the tasks that must be completed within each stage, as reflected in the schema of Table 7-1.

There is a commonsensical quality to this "must do" list, but it offers a useful framework for viewing the presenting problem of the family. Interestingly, Combrinck-Graham (1985) has welded this stage model to a dialectical schema. She describes the alternating centripetal and centrifugal forces that hold the family in dynamic tension as it moves through these stages, like a plant that expands and contracts in growing and fallow seasons. Thus, looking simultaneously at expectable shifts at three (different) generational levels, Combrinck-Graham notes that a typical centrifugal system configuration occurs when a child enters adolescence, when her parents will most likely be entering a midlife transition and her grandparents will be preparing for retirement. This is in sharp contrast to the centripetal cluster of childbirth, which typically brings parents and grandparents into closer bonding with each other.

Table 7-1. The Stages of the Family Life Cycle*

Family Life Cycle Stage	Emotional Process of Transition: Key Principles	Second-Order Changes in Family Status Required to Proceed Developmentally
1. Leaving home: Single young adults	Accepting emotional and financial responsibility for self	a. Differentiation of self in relation to family of origin b. Development of intimate peer relationships c. Establishment of self re work and financial independence
2. The joining of families through marriage: The new couple	Commitment to new system	a. Formation of marital system b. Realignment of relationships with extended families and friends to include spouse
3. Families with young children	Accepting new members into the system	a. Adjusting marital system to make space for child(ren) b. Joining in childrearing, financial, and household tasks c. Realignment of relationships with extended family to include parenting and grandparenting roles
4. Families with adolescents	Increasing flexibility of family boundaries to include children's independence and grandparents' frailties	a. Shifting of parent child relationships to permit adolescent to move in and out of system b. Refocus on midlife marital and career issues c. Beginning shift toward joint caring for older generation
5. Launching children and moving on	Accepting a multitude of exits from and entries into the family system	a. Renegotiation of marital system as a dyad b. Development of adult to adult relationships between grown children and their parents c. Realignment of relationships to include in-laws and grandchildren d. Dealing with disabilities and death of parents (grandparents)
6. Families in later life	Accepting the shifting of generational roles	a. Maintaining own and/or couple functioning and interests in face of physiological decline; exploration of new familial and social role options b. Support for a more central role of middle generation c. Making room in the system for the wisdom and experience of the elderly, supporting the older generation without overfunctioning for them d. Dealing with loss of spouse, siblings, and other peers and preparation for own death. Life review and integration

*From Carter and McGoldrick, *The Changing Family Life Cycle.* Copyright 1989 by Allyn & Bacon. Reprinted by permission.

In the next chapter I focus on diagnosis, and there the implication of developmental stage dislocations for psychopathology will be discussed in greater detail. Here it is useful to note that inevitably there will be a relationship between family development and presenting symptomatology. There are several useful concepts for linking symptom formation and developmental stage theory. Falicov (1978) summarized these as follows:

> One way to think about this connection is to view the symptom as a manifestation of the stress that the family is experiencing around the transition events. Another way is to observe that the family is rigidly organized and cannot change its organization to fit the new developmental requirements. A third possibility is that a symptom has a meaning or a function or acts as a "solution" that serves to maintain stability in the face of impending change [p. 40].

A Case Example: The Baker Family

The Baker family was referred to me because their 11-year-old son, Clyde, was displaying worrisome behavior not only at school, which they were accustomed to, but also outside the school, with newly initiated petty thievery from neighborhood stores and the household kitty. He had been evaluated initially when he was in third grade because of concentration and attention deficits in school and general recalcitrance at home; an extended evaluation and intermittent consultation had led to a course of Ritalin, which was currently being reevaluated. The younger child, Anne, a second grader, was noted for being verbally aggressive, almost assaultive, at school (although she was agreeable at home). The Bakers were an affluent family, enjoying a fairly charmed life involving good looks, admiring friends, and enviable diversions.

Treatment for the Bakers occupied a total of 12 sessions. Their son initially staged a therapy strike by refusing to participate in the sessions, clowning, and distracting the others. The parents seemed totally at a loss, with dad faintly contemptuous and mom both ashamed and empathetically distressed. Mom vacillated between imploring Clyde to talk about his feelings in the sessions and imploring me to help him do so. Dad issued brief, rather perfunctory bulletins to Clyde regarding correct behavior. As the sessions progressed, Anne started acting up a bit, growing ever more defiant. She seemed to be enjoying a rather new "bad girl" affiliation with Clyde.

The Bakers are clearly in Carter and McGoldrick's third stage of the family life cycle, and they are stuck. For families with young children the key tasks are the following: (1) adjusting the marital system to make space for the children; (2) joining in childbearing, financial, and household tasks; and (3) realigning relationships with extended family members to accommodate changing parenting and grandparenting roles.

Let us consider the task of adjusting the marital system first. Embedded in the definition of this task lies a rather mythic achievement: the balancing of spousal and parental functions. In the psychoanalytic literature this balancing is considered expectable and somewhat uneventful. Even in the nonpsychoanalytic developmental literature only the transition to parenthood is identified as difficult, not parenthood itself. Our canonical psychoanalytic parable, the Oedipus legend, chronicles the destructiveness wrought by a child usurping parental place and prerogative. The actions of the father remain subtextual in this parable, and indeed they are subversive to our tradition of emphasizing the vicissitudes of childhood sexual longings. Yet the fact is that Laius, the father, terrified by the oracular prophecy that his son will replace him, *abandons Oedipus, his infant, to a death on the barren hills of Thebes!* Our canonical reading of the legend, focused on the fantasied and forbidden longing for erotic possession of a parent, might well be shifted to a reading that stresses the father's conflict between erotic coupling (Laius fears that Oedipus will take his wife, Jocasta) and the injunction to protect his offspring (which Laius disobeys). In the family literature this struggle between parental role and marital relationship is recognized. The focus clinically is on adjusting the spousal relationships so that it may be a complement to and facilitator of the parental relationship. Thus, inattentiveness to the needs of children can result from either a high level of parental conflict or a high degree of spousal overinvolvement. The imbalance can be subtle, but it is easily registered by a sensitive child. In the Baker family, it was the latter constellation, spousal overinvolvement, that was the problem. The parents had bifurcated their pleasures in life. Their working rule was to derive pleasure in their marriage and offer dutiful (and fairly joyless) commitment to their children. In the first session Clyde drew a picture of his family that depicted his parents facing and smiling at each other while he and his sister were staring blankly ahead in another section of the paper; there was a separate space for the children, but it was cordoned off, emotionally bleak.

The tasks proposed for each stage of the family life cycle function as a set of normative expectations; they serve as a template for viewing individual psychodynamics. Yet there are also out-of-phase events regarding childbearing that specifically require individually textured formulations. Having a child in midlife raises issues that are different from those associated with procreation at a younger age. Parents older than the Bakers (a couple in their late 40s), who are dealing with the debilitation and death of their own parents, might well turn to their children for playful relief. Then again, the inevitable sense of psychic loss that is part of the midlife readjustment of one's dependency on one's parents could lead to a desperate need for restitution from off-spring. Indeed, in a worst-case scenario, the parents might bitterly resent the additional responsibility of child rearing. The point here is that some intriguing possibilities emerge from a scanning of family configurations, possibilities that invite supplementation by psycho-dynamic formulations.

From the opposite perspective, the wide view of family stage development theory can offer hypothesis-generating possibilities to the psychoanalyst. Because of the early-imprinting bias of psychoanalytic theory, we too often ignore the changing complexion of family experience and at times forget that sometimes psychic change can be evoked by external rather than by internal shifts. Thus, mom and dad can stay as neurotic as ever but if they become more successful in their work, their adolescent children may feel better able to step out onto a developmental launching pad. Having parents who are embittered is different from having parents who are too involved but pleased with their lot in life. In a sense, the interiority of psychoanalytic theory, which is its great strength, has shielded us from a healthy respect for life context.

No issue so captures the relevance of developmental context as the issue of differentiation, particularly at adolescence. Every family therapist has had the experience of recommending family therapy for a troubled adolescent only to receive an alarmed phone call—"He needs space!" (i.e., individual therapy)—from a guidance counselor, an individual therapist, or even a parent on behalf of the troubled adolescent. This equation of psychological differentiation and psychotherapy mode can reach to the upper limit of what is a remarkable concretism, truly magical in nature, as if removing parents from the treatment room could unclench the fierce hold they have on their offspring. The adolescent is not just furious enough to want to leave them; he or she is also terrified of doing so. Though it may seem highly counterintuitive at first glance, the delicate disentangling of troubled adolescents from their family of origin is, in my experience, best and most lastingly explored with all participants present.

Let us now return to Carlo, the teen introduced in Chapter Five whose father expressed the wisdom and long-range commitments of middle age compared to the "quick solution" orientation of youth. It is now later in the course of therapy. Carlo has become less uncontrollably angry and aggressive (he was originally referred because he started a minor fire in his school). He has entered a new developmental phase of modulating attachment and separation from his parents, and the therapist gently supports this effort. Though in this session the therapist is seeing Carlo by himself, she has her eye on and her ear tuned to his structural position in the family:

Therapist: How are things at home?
Carlo: Pretty normal, actually. Mom's an invalid, and Dad's always angry. No, not angry. Indifferent. Mom nags, but I've become zombie-like. "Clear the table!" I just do it. It's easier. Well, sometimes I explode, but mostly I don't fight with my mom because she's too stupid to understand. I just avoid her. She thinks I'm some kind of animal. She thinks I have no human qualities, but I don't care.
Therapist: Why have you changed?
Carlo: It's easier. She's like a little kid. I do what she says; it's easier. Dad is stubborn. He has rules: "You will study now." But he leaves me alone most of the time. His idea of life at my age is wake up, go to school, come home, study five hours, eat and go to bed. My dad's a nerd. I don't give a shit what he did when he was seventeen. This is me! "Why are you failing? You're not an idiot!" Shut up! I just don't care.
Therapist: Maybe he talks that way to you because he thinks that's a way you can understand him.
(*a little later in the session*)
Therapist: You don't sound to me like a kid who doesn't like his parents.
Carlo: I think my dad is disappointed in me. My mother loves me, but that's because she's a sucker.
Therapist: You think he's disappointed in you, but what about loving you?
Carlo: I don't know.
Therapist: It's interesting for me to realize that it's not as clear to you as it is to me that they care about you.
Carlo: Maybe that's the problem. Maybe they should shut up and butt out. I can see myself years from now, when I'm twenty-five. They'll still be —
Therapist: But you're not twenty-five. You are seventeen.
Carlo: I'm not five either!
Therapist: No, you're not five. But there's a difference between negotiating at five and seventeen. And they are having trouble with that.
Carlo: They'll still be running my life when I'm twenty-five.
Therapist: Probably.

Carlo: I can see myself. I come in late on a Friday, and they're like, "How can you come in so late, and—"
Therapist: No. The conversation will be very different. You'll laugh. "I'm not seventeen anymore. You're forgetting that I'm twenty-five now." Things will look different.

Note that the therapist does not plumb the depths of Carlo's rage, his contempt, or his projected self-contempt. If she did so, the teen would likely escalate his attacks on his mother and then on his father for protecting her; his anxiety about injuring his attachment to them would then be exacerbated, and this anxiety would eventuate in his levying even more debilitating attacks on them. Expressive anger is his everyday wear, but emotional ambivalence and modulation are new apparel for Carlo.

Analysts sometimes find the stage theory requisites of the family life cycle schema too prescriptive and view its lockstep normative progressions as a dismissal of the complexity of interior experience. However, it is quite remarkable how psychoanalytic developmental theory, as a narrative of unfolding events based on object relations and/or drives, becomes a normative curriculum itself. Indeed, psychoanalysis is committed to its own set of normative end points for specific developmental stages, a commitment it shares with developmental psychology in general. William Kessen, a noted developmental theorist, stated:

> To a remarkable degree—and this has become so clear to us that it approaches a platitude—the last 100 years have been motivated by the spirit of Charles Darwin, or by his idea, or even by his data, and nowhere more critically, more formatively, than in developmental psychology. In the crude forms that can be found in Spencer and Hall, or in the somewhat more subtle forms of Piaget and Werner, or in the richly ambivalent forms of psychoanalysis, developmental psychology has been committed to the proposition that human development is regular and progressive. The notion of progressive development necessarily implies a goal, and as Kaplan (1967) pointed out a long while back, all developmental theories are held together by the specification, implicit or explicit, of an endpoint, the goal toward which progressive development is going [Bronfenbrenner et al., 1986, pp. 1218–1219].

As Kessen has suggested, psychoanalytic developmental theories of all complexions postulate various end points of psychic health, whether these be designated as cohesiveness of the self, as the fulfillment of the capacity for intimacy, or as the achievement of a reasonably conflict-free capacity for love and work. Nor are psychoanalytic stage theories less

preoccupied with these implicit norms. Thus, psychoanalytic developmental theory is often tacitly, though not explicitly, prescriptive. Would
we not cast a worried eye on a latency period fraught with active erotic
fantasizing? Have we not come to expect—and, it turns out, perhaps
altogether incorrectly according to current developmental research—
that adolescents should be stormy and irrational? It seems that it is
rather impossible to talk or think about a sequential process without a
schema of expectancies, ergo norms.

Before we leave stage theory, let us return to the Baker family. What
was helpful to this family was a reorientation to one of the stage
prescriptives of the family with young children, namely, loosening the
marital dyad to make room for the children. Here, of course, the parents
thought they had adequately done so by a dutiful but joyless set of
"quality time" arrangements. However, the children knew that they
were an onerous obligation and that the parents resented them for
being one. Moreover, there was internal dissension between the couple
around over- and underperforming in all their interpersonal roles,
with mom exhausted from overextension and dad withdrawing in
resentment, dissension that had, unfortunately, extended to parenting.
Exploring this dissension facilitated its containment in the marital
subsystem—and helped decontaminate the emerging sphere of true
parental involvement with the children. That in turn allowed Mr. Baker
to begin setting firmer rules. Clyde, the erstwhile petty thief, was not
the protagonist of this therapeutic journey, but he may have been the
clearest beneficiary of its rewards.

FAMILY STRUCTURE

Families, and family members, do not just pass through stages; for
a time, they live there. The family therapist must inquire about and
reflect on the experience of clients who inhabit a particular stage of the
family life cycle. Along what dimensions does the therapist locate the
family's reported experience? The family therapist does not enter any
stage of the family life cycle empty-handed or empty-headed but,
rather, comes with a set of paradigmatic constructs. Ringing in the
family therapist's developmental ear is, above all, the theme of structure
and all its variations.

Family therapists, particularly structural family therapists, emphasize that children need both love and structure and that, in fact, parents
can often most clearly express their love by creating a structure in a
child's life that yields both freedom and safety for the child's ongoing

experience. Within family systems theory there is a pervasive emphasis on hierarchy, of parents taking the helm of family functioning. This emphasis is the hallmark of the structural model, and it is also implicit in the power relationships emphasized by the strategic school. Parents are regarded as fundamentally in charge, as executives, while grandparents are viewed as loving consultants.

Here we can revisit Cecilia, grandmother of Jared, who lost her role as primary caregiver when her daughter, Veronica, wanted to reclaim the raising of her son. The therapist's task was to help grandmother redefine a role in her three-generational family system. This invited redefinition had to be extended with respect for the contextual realities of African-American family structure, where intensive grandparental involvement is typical. Research indicates that a key benefit of extended family support is to unburden parents, who can then pursue areas of their own self-development (Wilson, 1989). Empowered by the realization that Cecilia's defensive criticism in response to her demotion was both subculturally and systemically off-kilter, the therapist was able to probe about for a new configuration:

Therapist: Clearly, you're both so attached to Jared. I'm thinking of last week and how you, Cecilia, worry about Jared's report card, his nervousness, et cetera. I'm thinking that this is now how you show some of your attachment to Jared, because you raised him practically as your own son for three and a half years.

Cecilia: I am attached to him. I still feel he's almost my own child. I worry because I know Veronica has high hopes for him, and I don't want her to be disappointed. Some things will be corrected, some not. I feel she will be quite upset.

Therapist: You know—I'll put it dramatically—but it's almost as if Jared was torn from your breast at age three and a half.

Cecilia: I miss him. I didn't have a home life myself. I always wanted to raise kids in a stable home.

Veronica: I think she feels that way. But I don't think she expected me to be as good a parent as I am. I think she expected me to lean on her more because we always had a close relationship. I think she doesn't feel I give her credit—I'm grateful. But that's five years ago; give me credit now!

Both women were passionate caregivers, but the lack of generational resolution concerning primary mothering was injurious to Jared. Grandmother had staked her claim to her grandson on the basis of his increased psychopathology under her daughter's care. The therapist intervened by asking the daughter to be more responsible for her mother's enjoyment of grandmotherhood, that is, by sending Jared to her with interesting projects for them to do together, with tickets to events, and so on. This became an additional source of competence to the daughter and more clearly supported the newly differentiated roles in this family.

Of course, psychoanalysts know that parents guard the hearth and pay the bills, but there is a subtle leveling of generational difference in much psychoanalytic developmental theory. Parents are rarely recognized for their developmental achievements or for their relative success in executing their sometimes burdensome responsibilities, whether protective, administrative, or supportive (financial and emotional). Rather, they are too often faulted for what they have failed to provide, with these failures then often targeted in a linear way as leading to the difficulties of their offspring. By contrast, the structural mapping of family therapy creates a heightened awareness of responsibilities and roles, and that map in turn becomes an aid to thinking about strengths rather than deficits.

Beyond the heuristic virtue of recognizing strengths, there is the potential psychological benefit to be had in clarifying structure, that is, in recognizing in a family forum just who is the authority. Parents today underestimate the degree to which they can relieve their children's anxiety simply by exerting consistent and meaningful control over childhood impulses. In fact, it is partly a pervasive psychoanalytic influence in contemporary culture that has diminished awareness of the benefits of parental authoritativeness; in our efforts to heighten the expression of desire we have reduced our shelter over childhood anxiety.[1] Psychoanalytically oriented play therapists usually then spend the bulk of their concomitant parent advisory time trying to help parents see the world through their children's eyes, hoping to reduce childhood distress through parental empathy. Family therapists, on the other hand, most often encourage parents to take charge, sympathetically but definitively. The hope of family therapists is that children will spend less of their creative energy finding pressure zones in their parents' wobbly structure and will, instead, move on to exploring what the world has to offer.

My most salutary intervention in the work with the Baker family involved challenging the haughty and disengaged father's derelict

---

[1]Lasch (1979) has attributed an increased narcissism to parental abnegation, which he avers has shifted expectable conscience formation into harsh and archaic superego surveillance.

stewardship of his son. I highlighted, even parodied, his difficulty in getting his son to do anything. I urged him to reverse the skewed hierarchy in the session then and there. He was stiff and wooden at first but adopted a kind of flexible authority before long. Of course, once his son was under control, he had to face another issue: increased involvement with his wife. They each had a multiplicity of distractions keeping them from forming a close relationship (their son's "bad" behavior being particularly functional in that regard).

Writing from a family perspective, Kenneth Kaye (1987) has suggested that overly permissive parents (like the Bakers) have an easier time shifting their parental style than do overly controlling parents. Why should this be so? Is it a question of the parents' defensive structure? Of their identification with their own parents? How could we intervene more effectively? This is a crucial issue for both child and family therapists, and it is clearly the kind of issue that invites psychoanalytic conjecture as an enrichment of systems theory.

Lest we follow the traditional psychoanalytic bias of representing the axis of development entirely as a function of parent–child interaction, we would do well to include sibling structures in our discussion. With the exception of a paper by Lesser (1978), the critical effect of sibling relationships has been relatively neglected in the psychoanalytic literature. Lesser noted that because of Freud's original conception of sibling relationships as fundamentally competitive, positive sibling interactions have been undervalued. In fact, if we stop to think about it, since siblings are not only idealized but mirror and perform the full host of crucial psychic functions for each other that their parents do for them, they can mollify or intensify parental dispositions.

Beyond a clarification of siblings' impact on one another, a focus on the sibling system can also provide a means of reexamining parental expectation. A family came for treatment because the 12-year-old daughter was "going bad." She had always been the beacon of hope to her mother, compared to her brother. Her mother was desperately clinging to a middle-class dream of achievement, being the lone survivor from a large family of siblings who had failed (through addiction, trouble with the law, etc.) to achieve respectability. It seemed clear that the daughter had important issues to resolve regarding her mother's overly intense preoccupation with her. However, it was not an exploration of the mother–daughter identification but, rather, of the daughter's deep sense of guilt at abandoning her own brother to the street and then implicitly participating in his denigration, an inadvertent consequence of her precocious success, that provided the fulcrum of liberation for her. In fact, viewing her daughter's loyalty to her 15-year-old brother enabled the mother to experience her children as related to each other. This obvious but up-to-now dissociated reality seemed to help the mother feel more separate from them, generationally and psychologically. What is more, with the acceptance of that separation, she started to reclaim some of her own ambition and assertiveness for herself and no longer needed her daughter to carry it for her.

CIRCULARITY

The structure of much of psychodynamically oriented child therapy is inherently linear in conceptualization. Children are seen in play therapy in order to evoke and, one hopes, resolve their conflicts. These conflicts are then discreetly discussed with parents in intermittent parent counseling sessions. Parents are enjoined to change their relationship style to suit their children's difficulties, sometimes as if their own conflicts could be contained or erased. It is true that within the traditional child therapy model, parent and child dynamics are viewed as interrelated, but from a family systems perspective, these dynamics are not simply associated with each other but, rather, form one continuous and organic circle. A rare exception to the general linearity of psychoanalytic development theory, and thus a good illustration of a circular formulation in general, is Sullivan's (1953) description of the malevolent transformation:

> The child learns, you see, that it is highly disadvantageous to show any need for tender cooperation from the authoritative figures around him, in which case he shows something else; and that something else is the basic malevolent attitude. . . .
>
> A start in the direction of malevolent development creates a vicious circle. It is obviously a failure of the parents to discharge their social responsibility to produce a well-behaved, well-socialized person. Therefore, the thing tends to grow more or less geometrically. Quite often the way in which the parents minimize or excuse their failure to socialize the child contributes further to his development of a malevolent attitude towards life—and this is likely to be on the part of the mother, since it is difficult to picture a malevolent transformation's occurring at all if the mother did not play a major part in it [p. 215].

Sullivan here establishes a circle, but its circumference can be stretched further. Chrzanowski (1978) noted that in Sullivan's concept "the malevolence is *not* viewed as an inherent mean streak in a person but [as] an exaggerated *security operation* designed to protect the person from mutilation, painful ridicule and other forms of rejection" (p. 406). However, what is not emphasized by Sullivan and rarely by analysts is the humiliation a parent experiences by having an embarrassingly difficult child. Once the embarrassment has set in, the parent feels the need to deflect it; sadly, this deflection sometimes takes the form of persistently and compulsively identifying deficits in the child, to avoid sinking deeper into parental shame. Even more poignantly, the "malevolent" child, accustomed to anxiously critical parents, will feel the need to create and sustain his or her "badness." The parents' reliability is dependent on the child's proving and making badness for them. From this systemic perspective, the parent–child relationship is tightly coiled, offering few degrees of freedom for new experience.

One of the most dramatic moments in family therapy can occur when parents are congratulated—some realistic basis must be found by the therapist—on their success in raising what they had hitherto believed was an utterly impossible child. It is as if the therapist has released a coil locked in a strained position, which then rapidly rewinds; once the parents' sense of their own humiliation and embarrassment is relieved, information then travels in the reverse direction. In the context of a more positive appraisal of their own performance, parents sometimes dramatically become more appreciative and complimentary toward their child. A case example: A couple in treatment were facing their second year of negative school reports regarding their only son's faulty peer relationships. Convinced that he was socially inept, they rarely encouraged him to play with friends but hovered about him diagnostically and reprovingly, thereby binding him to their negative expectations and appraisals. The child did have a zany sense of humor, but this gift had thus far landed him only the unenviable position of failed class clown. However, in the therapy session, where it was clearly in evidence, the therapist (knowing that the parents valued this quality in themselves) spontaneously admired their son's imaginative sense of humor. Without too much strain, probably because it offered narcissistic gratification as well as assuagement of parental guilt, the parents began to view their child increasingly more positively. They clearly were still prone to view him as their mascot, but their newfound pride, rather than shame, gave their son the courage to move away from them toward other relationships. When the guidance counselor stopped calling them, they grew even fonder of him. A new loop of appraisals began to be forged.

Attending to the circularity of process generally makes a therapist especially cognizant of the deleteriousness of blaming. For example, as long as Mr. and Mrs. Baker considered Clyde unmanageable, they

vacillated between faulting him for his unruliness and being held
hostage by his dysfunction. The guilt he accrued from either alternative
paralyzed his development. There was no way to relieve Clyde of this
guilt. He acted out of control because his parents permitted it and then
blamed him for it.

How is the circular view useful to analysts working within an analytic
framework? In fact, analysts can use their constructive lenses inter-
changeably, as creative photographers do. At times, intense empathy
for a patient's recollected disappointment is most important. Memories
of a mother who ridiculed one's attempts to be self-expressive or true to
one's self represent traumas warranting empathic recognition. However, at other times the analyst can more readily empathize with the
mother's reaction, particularly in the wake of strong countertransferential feelings. Analysts too often stifle their empathic response to the
reciprocal partner standing in the shadow of a patient's complaints.
Thus, for example, a supervisee reported being irritated at a patient's
dismissive behavior, for example, extremely late appointment arrivals,
personal profligacy coupled with bill payment defaults, and minimal
therapeutic involvement. The supervisee was involved in an intricate
exploration of the failures of the patient's inattentive and distracted
mother. The supervisee had four grown children of her own and was
familiar with the travails of motherhood. When I inquired about
whether she felt the patient's mother might have grown avoidant and
disrespectful of so dismissive a daughter, her grasp of the daughter's
dynamics took a quantum leap. She had assumed that her analytic task
was to singularly and empathically view the experiential world through
the eyes of her patient. To be sure, this is a demand characteristic of
psychoanalysis, but it is one that can well be suspended at times in an
effort to understand the relational world of the patient. Quite clearly,
analysts *do* look for signals in themselves, including countertransferential identifications with significant objects, in order to grasp patient
dynamics. However, I think we rarely look first to what the experience
of a parent might be, and here a family perspective can extend the range
of analytic recognition.

The systems perspective offers an even wider-angle lens. For example, mothers who rely on ridicule are sometimes the butt of family-wide
contempt just out of earshot. Similarly, fathers who cannot express
tenderness to their children are sometimes deeply discouraged by their
wife's inability to accept tenderness from them; their sense of emotional incompetency first takes root in marriage and only later general-
izes to parenting. We can widen our focus still further to include the
cultural context. Here I would mention only Erikson's position that

competence and confidence in parenting derives from a coherent cultural framework regarding child care. With such a framework, parents feel that their responsibilities are consensually defined and meaningful; without it, they flounder.

From a systems perspective, much of what we consider individually lodged symptomatology is both created and maintained in family cultures. Sullivan (1940) rooted several of his developmental syndromes in family cultures. For example, the obsessional dynamism was believed to typically originate in a family known for its verbal disguises and acrobatic rationalizations:

> No matter what aggression anyone perpetrates on another—no matter what outrages the parents perpetrate on each other, or the elder siblings perpetrate on each other, on the parents, or on little Willie—there is always some worthy principle lying about to which appeal is made. And the fact that an appeal to an entirely contradictory principle was made 15 minutes earlier does not seem to disturb anybody. The members of a group like that might be called by unfeeling neighbors "damned hypocrites." Here is a situation where it has been found that it is better to have this limited verbal magic than the only other thing one could have—an awful lot of fairly open hostility and dislike and hatred [pp. 230–231].

Undeniably, family shaping of character and of symptomatology begins at ground zero. The press of unresolved conflict and disassociation in family members finds no sadder but also no readier target than the tabula rasa of a new family addition. In this context, James Framo (1972) lucidly described the process of irrational role assignment in which parents project onto their children characteristics of their own parents in order to avoid loss and individuation. The child caught in this system of irrational attributions can react according to a range of possibilities: absorption, negation, or fighting, each of which becomes irrevocably organizing. The point is that once the patterning is enacted, it can become indelible in rigid families. According to Framo, "the 'family way' of seeing and doing things becomes automatic and unquestioned, like the air one breathes. The assignment is further reinforced by family myths and rules and is ritualized into family structure" (p. 208).

One of the real reasons that patients' persisting amnesia about their early years seems so ambiguous in psychoanalysis—beyond the important controversies about memorial processes—is that we often do not want to or actually cannot cognitively reconstruct the gestalt of the irrational role assignment. A patient's behavior, based on the role assignment, may have a kind of surreal plausibility at the same time that the patient is enraged at the need to enact it. The underlying irrational role assignment can remain undetected for a long time. Thus, an analytic patient who spent most of his childhood and youth in self-defeating behavior had a deep conviction that he had simply given up hope for himself at a young age. He could not fathom why. Was it cognitive processing difficulties that he had not been adequately evaluated for? (He *was* evaluated during his course of treatment with me, and the deficits proved to be mild to moderate, insufficiently accounting for his failures.) Was his an unconscious identification with a demeaned father who was ridiculed in the family for his business failures? This hypothesis was persuasive but not transforming. At the very end of treatment, when we were hashing out for the last time my "nagging" and his "resentment," he commented (to his own amazement) that he actually felt he didn't *"have* to put out any effort." When I called this an "aristocratic" attitude, he agreed (with baffled enthusiasm). It occurred to me that this was an example of irrational role assignment. I conjectured that his demeaning mother and denigrated father probably shared an overlapping view of their firstborn as regent or heir apparent or perhaps as an idealized version of one of *their* parents (it really did not matter). The personification likely succeeded in containing the parents' angst and anxiety, but it left my patient living—but not "owning"—a strange identity.

This kind of material is often the fruit of a well-seeded analysis. However, the flowering can be very late. Within the process of family work, with all the key personae present at once, self-realization regarding attributions of others can occur earlier.

THE PLACE OF PERSONAL HISTORY
IN THE FAMILY SYSTEMS PARADIGM

Autobiography is the essential developmental narrative within the psychoanalytic paradigm. In the family systems paradigm, autobiography is subsumed under a collective narrative of family development. This allows personal narrative, when it emerges, to take on more clearly visible pragmatic significance in the eyes of the family therapist.

From an analytic perspective—and in Western culture in general—we assume that a personal individual narrative is an essential aspect of identity. Within the psychoanalytic paradigm, it is interesting to note when patients feel the need to return to talking about their history; our working assumption has been that this occurs at the time of nascent self-realization or insight. However, it is most certainly true as well that a sense of personal historical continuity provides a sense of coherence to the self, a kind of homeostatic equilibrator to the unexpected (whether delightful or threatening). Thus, to the degree that auto-biography is equilibrating, it also functions as resistance. A patient of mine, whom I have identified as moving to a historical perspective when she feels threatened by new self-realization, quipped recently as she was about to make this characteristic detour, "Listen, I'm going to talk about my parents. What the hell, this is therapy."

The same double-edged function of serving both personal coherence and resistance is true of individual narrative within the family inter-view. There are moments of pronounced autobiographical irony in family therapy. Personal history can serve the oddest of systemic pur-poses when told in the presence of other family members. Perhaps the most farcical function is that of autobiographical competition. In cou-ples work especially, this sometimes takes the form of insisting that one's own family of origin is much healthier than the partner's—or for those in a dedicated one-down position, much sicker! The field of inquiry makes a difference in a way that brings us back to Bruner's conception of the self as "distributive." Bruner (1990) eschews a concept of an observable self

[as] if Self were a substance or an essence that preexisted our effort to describe it, as if all one had to do was to inspect it in order to discover its nature. Psychoanalysis, of course, was a principal essentialist sinner: Its topography of ego, superego, and id was the *real* things, and the method of psychoanalysis was the electron microscope that laid it bare [p. 99].

Bruner asks a crucial question: "Does 'Self' comprise (as William James had implied) an 'extended' self incorporating one's family, friends, possessions, and so on?" (p. 100). For Bruner (1990), the context of self-identification is, in fact, inseparable from the content or imagin-ing of self. He notes that Gergen (1982) has persuasively argued that who we are emerges from who we are *with* at any given time and that this plasticity is a product of two human capacities: (1) the capacity to be "reflexive," that is, change the past in terms of the present, or vice versa, and (2) the capacity to "envision alternatives," or multiple ver-sions of our experience. Bruner (1990) concludes, "In the distributive sense, then, the Self can be seen as a product of the situations in which it operates" (p. 109).

In the distributive field of family interaction a family member recount-ing an overly familiar individual narrative is offered new possibilities for expansion, for reflexive and alternative constructions. Sometimes, inter-estingly, a redundant and restrictive narrative statement will represent the last hurrah of a long analysis that preceded the family referral. I think that one hedge against the interminableness of analytic exploration is to develop a kind of tunnel vision of one's history, to fixate on one narrative version as true and compelling. Family work, on occasion, can provide a flexible forum for reevaluating these narratives. For example, work with one couple involved exploring why the wife felt dread about her husband's expressing anger toward her. She explained her reaction in terms of her analytically derived conviction that she had suffered persistent childhood terror at her father's explosions of rage. She thereby assumed the legitimacy of equating male anger across rather disparate personalities (her father's and her husband's). Highlighting their differences enabled her to spin off reflections on how she in fact was forced to participate in calming her father down because of her mother's abnegation of this responsibility, with mother's abdication being no less a factor in her coming to believe male anger was impossible to deal with. What emerged was a new gestalt about her historical trauma regarding anger.

Family work can be a rich source of grist for the mill of individual treatment. Spouses hear their significant other's same old story in new ways in the family therapist's office. What is heard for the first time almost always reflects the major theme of ongoing therapeutic work in their own analyses. For example, a husband who thought he knew every detail of the story of the family of his wife of 15 years noted for the first time in individual treatment that there were, in fact, very few successful men in his wife's family. He noticed this Batesonian difference precisely because he had been currently exploring in couples therapy a fledgling sense of his own professional competency in his marriage.

It is particularly striking that when collecting autobiographical information, a family therapist can uncover information that has been unavailable to an individual therapist working concomitantly with one of the family members. I once worked with a young couple struggling with the male partner's difficulty with commitment. One of his key complaints was that the young woman had very little self of her own and that her existence orbited around him. Of course, he was an extremely self-absorbed fellow who yearned for a woman who was both dazzling and exquisitely sensitive to his needs. Both partners were seeing individual therapists, but I met with each of them alone (as I sometimes do, in addition to seeing them as a couple) to explore facets of their relationship that I thought might be unavailable in couples therapy. I found that in individual sessions the young man focused on his yearnings for an ideal mate and left his more obscure dynamics considerably beyond my reach. However, meeting with his somewhat overly desperate companion had a richer yield. In my first session alone with her she reported that her father's basic vision of a woman's destiny was clear and singular: her life's work was to actualize her husband's strengths and talents. She had always known this; it was consciously coded information. I inquired about her mother's success at this task. In fact, her mother had failed, and her father felt bitter that he had had to achieve his very marginal and disappointing level of success unsupported. Father's disappointment was hitherto less consciously available to my client. I wondered aloud about the satisfaction my client might derive from succeeding where her mother had failed and whether her virtuoso attempt to subvert her own interests in order to fan the ego of her current (and reluctant) partner was part of this drama. She was shocked to think that she might be stepping in where her mother had failed, that her current desperation might in fact reflect a version of competitive striving. This possibility interested both of us, and part of its intrigue was the fact that it had not arisen in the context of her individual therapy with a very talented analyst. It was as if her dissociation from this dynamic could only be dissolved in the presence of a witness to its enactment.

This brings us to another aspect of history in family therapy. Personal history is often considered, particularly by structural family therapists, to be a cognitive reinforcement for an ongoing intervention. It serves an instrumental function of strengthening the press and meaning of change for the family. This somewhat instrumental approach to therapeutically derived narrative has been suggested within psychoanalysis by Schafer (1981), who summarized his new narrative perspective as follows: "Let's see how we can retell it in a way that allows you to understand the origins, meanings, and significance of your present difficulties and to do so in a way that makes change conceivable and attainable" (p. 30). In couples work, for example, when a woman is immersed in her narrative of childhood neglect and misunderstanding, I am most struck by the fact that it forces her to walk on her own narrative path and to desist from blaming her partner for his neglect and abuse of her. When the partner then responds with more directly expressed sympathy than I have heretofore witnessed from him, is it because he is moved by her story (the semantics of her presentation) or by the fact that its telling precludes her finding fault with him (the pragmatics of her presentation)? Can these be separated? Perhaps not, but the therapist can choose to invite autobiography for pragmatic purposes alone. The point is this: Analysts have to guess how the narrative being fashioned in their office is being used outside of it, while family therapists get to see firsthand.

We are left with several questions that can happily take a lifetime of clinical work to ponder. When do individuals seem most pressed to organize their experience in historical and developmental frameworks? How do individual narratives intersect family-constructed narratives?

These questions emerge for us in the flux of clinical process. However, definitions of selfhood are tugging at scholars working in the social sciences and humanities today. In fact, these two perspectives— psychoanalysis and family systems theory—meet in the arena of postmodern constructivist views of personality and personality change. We turn to a postmodernist for a sighting at this horizon: "the final stage in [the] transition to the postmodern is reached when the self vanishes fully into a stage of relatedness. One ceases to believe in a self independent of the relations in which he or she is embedded" (Gergen, 1991, p. 17). The psychoanalytic clinician is enjoined by postmodernism to expand the personal perspective of the patient so that new opportunities for self-organization and relationship are both imagined and experienced. It turns out that to do so, there is really no place like home.

chapter eight

Diagnosis in Family Therapy

I was crazy when being crazy meant something.
Charles Manson

Psychoanalytic treatment has always been linked to psychodiagnosis, though some analysts find diagnostic notions abhorrent. Freud first proposed his theory as a radically new perspective on a set of theretofore mystifying psychiatric syndromes, which he grouped together as the "psychoneuroses." Though the treatment was originally deemed inappropriate for individuals suffering from severe ego pathology, psychoanalytic diagnostic schemes have subsequently expanded to include categories previously deemed unanalyzable. Major new therapeutic approaches have developed under the aegis of this expanded psychoanalytic view. Kohut's self-psychological approach, though originally focused exclusively on narcissistic personality disorders, is now a fully inclusive psychoanalytic orientation. Similarly, Fairbairn's and Guntrip's original focus on schizoid disorders serves today as a fully developed object relations approach for all psychoanalytic encounters. For many analysts today, diagnostic considerations are most relevant in defining the structure, or parameters, of the treatment relationship.

Diagnosis in family therapy has had a very different history. Largely viewed as a suspect enterprise, one representing linear, noncontextualized thinking, diagnosis was initially eschewed altogether, or else broadened to cover the whole family. As a result, family theorists have had to construct new templates for referencing data describing an individual family member's deficits. The tricky issue has been to delineate the difference between actual deficits and those identified as operating in the service of maintaining systemic dysfunction. This chapter presents the various challenges to traditional psychiatric diagnosis that have been developed within the systems model, whose basic tenets are that system assessment supersedes diagnosis of the individual, and history taking must yield to a focus on the present interaction. Diagnosis is one of the domains where family systems thinking is so very strange to clinicians practicing individual therapy. Indeed, this difference has been celebrated as an important one by the family therapy movement, legitimately for the most part, but as we go along we will see how the family systems perspective can sometimes usefully help psychoanalytically oriented clinicians clarify their objectives about the subtleties of diagnosis and initial intervention in working with individual patients.

THE IDENTIFIED PATIENT

Nothing is quite so much the hallmark of family therapy as the concept of the identified patient. The seeming flippancy with which this designation is made at any standard family therapy presentation belies the radical shift in diagnostic perspective that it represents. What is the essence of this shift? The term *identified* suggests a constituency of identifiers, which in this case is the family, nuclear or extended. The basic notion is that out of the structural misalignments and circular derailments of particular families there arises an emblematic symptomatology and a symptomatic standard-bearer. The transition to this view of symptom and symptom-bearer as representative of a collective, and not as organic to an individual, is well illustrated in the writings and tape presentations of Nathan Ackerman (Bloch and Simon, 1982). In an evocative teaching tape presentation, called "Enemy in Myself" Ackerman is called in as a consultant to a case involving 13-year-old twin boys, one of whom has recently made a suicide threat. Ackerman talks to the family throughout the session in the language of individual dynamics. That is, he provocatively asks the identified patient, Jay, whom he clearly believes is suffering from an attenuated, unresolved oedipal dilemma, whether he would want to "live with Mommy or Daddy" if his parents divorced. He sympathetically, almost paternalistically, talks to the mother about her "rage," which frightens her and which she is "projecting" onto Jay. Mother, on psychoanalytic cue, talks about her fear of rage as originating in her family of origin. The verbal text notwithstanding, however, the action of the session involves Ackerman inviting the father to hold an out-of-control Jay on his lap and then tolerating the father smacking his son on the behind, a classic example of what Minuchin was to subsequently identify as a therapeutic enactment (more on this in Chapter Nine). The son, like the son in Haley's version of the Little Hans case, thus learns that his father will contain his frightening impulses, whatever form they take in fantasy. Similarly, Ackerman openly challenges the father's presence in the family as a lifeless pillar of stone by provocatively flirting with the mother, pulling her chair closer and closer to his and asking the father if he is "man enough to do something about it." This social infraction has a somewhat shocking effect on the viewer. However, by bringing the parents "across the six inches of bed separating them" Ackerman is able to help them differentiate from their sons. The point is that Ackerman is talking to the family from the psychodynamic conceptual repertoire of his left brain and relating to them with his systemic-pattern-focused right brain.

In a sense, diagnosis and evaluation keep a paradigm honest; there is something bare-bones and exposed about the categorization process of diagnosis that reveals underlying assumptions more readily than the rambling narrative of therapeutic process. Indeed, diagnostic evaluation can evolve as so discontinuously and strikingly at odds with underlying paradigmatic assumptions that it can lead to a re-thinking of these assumptions or else to an expunging of the diagnostic category. Such a diagnostic faux pas emerged in the early work of Bateson (1956) and his cohorts when they were tracing the double-binding behavior of parents of schizophrenic offspring. The Palo Alto group originally dedicated themselves to detailing how parents double-bind their children; moreover, they conceived this double-binding as etiologically central to the development of schizophrenia. Fortunately, the flawed unidirectional causality of this explanation was caught early on, and it was caught when Bateson and colleagues realized that such behavior was neither unique to schizophrenic families nor confined to parents alone. Thenceforth, parents and children were seen as trapped in an inexorable mutual double-binding, with parents as unable as their children to leave the maddening field of irreconcilable injunctions. In fact, if family theorists had persisted in pursuing the notion that parents make their children crazy, they would have joined the psychiatric parent bashing so prevalent in the late 1950s and early 1960s, best represented by the now discarded concept of the schizophrenogenic mother.

What is the systemic view of symptomatology? From a systemic perspective, concern about symptoms can distract families from profound interpersonal dissatisfaction and anxiety. Framo (1972) wrote that "symptoms may be nonspecific attempts to introduce variability or excitement into a congealed, dead family, or they may be distress signals, dilatory tactics, games, manipulations, bribes, attempts to achieve closeness or distance, or any combination of innumerable strategic interpersonal gambits" (p. 297). But whatever specific function symptoms serve in family organization, their essence is regarded as metaphoric.

Of course, in any but the most purified biological orientation to a theory of mind, symptoms are always held to be symbolic of conflict. Even a drive theorist who contends, for example, that overly accentuated strivings for power and control likely originate in a fixation on sphincter control is still clearly thinking metaphorically about human functioning. However, from a family systems perspective, symptomatology is expressive of a family metaphor, of a pattern that involves all the family's members. The systems perspective can include the individual metaphor, but it is not confined to it. Jay Haley (1976) provided an interesting example: A patient enters therapy because he is (he knows) irrationally afraid that he will die of a heart attack. A psychodynamic therapist, according to Haley, would inquire about past traumas and would explore the metaphoric meaning of the symptom within the patient's individual history. The family therapist, however,

> will have quite a different view: he will assume that the patient's statement about his heart is analogic to his current situation. He will inquire how the client relates to his wife, about his job, about his children, and so on. . . . When he interviews husband and wife together, the therapist will take an interest in the wife's response when the husband is feeling better and when he is feeling worse. For example, he might note that she communicates depression when the husband is emphasizing the better aspects of his life and health and that she appears more involved and animated when he discusses his heart problem. The family-oriented therapist will construct a theory that the husband's communication about his heart is a way of stabilizing the marriage. The kinds of data he will seek are those that reveal how the heart analogy is built into the person's ecology, or interpersonal network [p. 91].

Note that this approach need not necessarily deter the therapist from exploring an individual's panic or fear of death; however, such an exploration is undertaken within the panorama of family-wide dynamics. In fact, balancing individual and systemic explorations is best accomplished once the therapist has been trained in the less familiar latter approach. There are interesting thematic, even symphonic, possibilities here if an ecological language can be constructed out of the individual meaning and vice versa. Thus, a patient with an incapacitating self-conscious attention to a physical anomaly on his upper torso was described in a family session as wearing the "purple heart"; this metaphor then widened into a descriptive language for the family interaction as a whole, with interpretations couched in terms of valor and sacrifice. What is paramount in the family perspective is keeping a circular loop in view. As Ackerman (1966) describes it: "Conflict between the minds of family members and conflicts within the mind of any one member stand in reciprocal relation to one another. The two levels constitute a circular feedback system. Interpersonal conflict affects intrapsychic conflict, and vice versa" (p. 75).

When do family members opt for psychiatric diagnosis as a solution to systemic dilemmas? Psychiatric diagnosis potentially serves two different dysfunctions from a systems perspective. First, it serves to reinforce a system of projection, binding and neutralizing anxieties and conflicts. Neutralizing can take various forms depending on the coloration of the collective dynamics. That is, "sick" family members can be ostracized, coddled, infantilized, or even ignored, as needed. What is important is that unstable and distressed family members can become united when a third party, here the diagnosing physician, comes into view and provides much-needed "triangulation," as Bowenian theorists would say. (Certainly, other means of triangulation are available: mothers-in-law, both loved and hated, often serve as testimony to the need to find some kind of antidote to marital tensions within the nuclear family.) It is not that family members want to gratuitously project their anxieties, but anxiety is so potentially disorganizing that once a comfortable, familiar formula is secured, the process becomes second nature. The physician who provides a diagnosis is particularly handy in this regard, being a robust, stable figure who seems to have the weight of science and society behind him or her.

The second function of diagnosis is a bit more counterintuitive. Diagnosis can serve to bolster and maintain identity and self-cohesion. A ready proof of the momentum of circularity within a family system is how tenaciously family members cling to diagnostic labels, once assigned. This applies to the individual "identified patient" as well. If attachment and devotion have been intertwined with being viewed as irrational at best, and psychotic at worse, these terms still define a loved self. The sustaining function of what Sullivan called reflected appraisals casts an interesting light on what we customarily think of as resistance. If in fact people cherish their pathologized selves, if they feel nested in the appraisals of dysfunction, they will rightfully be suspicious of anyone trying to liberate or cure them. Of this phenomenon E. A. Levenson (1991) wrote the following:

I have found it very useful to consider that in working with patients, we are trying to extract them from the family system and introduce them to a larger world. In this undertaking, we are first seen as the stranger, the enemy. The world we are trying to introduce them to is *our* world, which, for better or worse, may be over-identified with the culture. We are not—

especially in this particular cycle of psychoanalysis—very judgmental of
our own social enactments. Psychoanalysts are rarely hermits or holy
men, or even rebels. One finds more analysts in the Hamptons than in the
Himalayas. In truth, the patient has no very good reason to trust our
directions [pp. 15–16].

Reaching even beyond strict diagnostic category, family members
cling tenaciously to all kinds of self-pathologizing characteristics. Inter-
estingly, these characteristics and attributions also provide a kind of
temporal coherence, a need consistently emphasized by the self psychologists. One of the thorniest barriers to encouraging patients to
eschew inaccurate diagnostic self-attributions emerges with patients
who have been in, or are concurrently participating in, individual as
well as family therapy. For example, I saw a couple in which both
partners had extensive therapy. He, a veteran of several years of individual treatment, described himself as hopelessly "obsessional," somewhat schizoid, and particularly afraid of expressing anger. She, in
psychoanalytic treatment at the time, detailed the lineaments of her
depressive character and her special vulnerability to feeling abandoned. What was being enacted between them was recurrently crisis
producing. In an effort to gain a surer foothold in his life, or just because
she considered it acceptable, the woman would spend weekends at the
man's apartment, during which time she would move around his
furniture without asking him and wear his shirts and pajamas if hers
needed laundering. He would seethe at these intrusions but would not
yell at her; rather, he would withdraw. She would then feel abandoned
and intrude again. As long as they linked their interpersonally unacceptable behavior to their diagnoses, thereby rendering it immutable in
their eyes, they were destined to drive each other crazy.

Then, too, there is a practice of mutual and reciprocal attribution in
long-term relationships that is captured in the diagnostic idiom. I
worked with a couple whose attributions to each other were described
as features of their original attraction. One woman was impulsively
wild, the other compulsively nurturing and "holding." Ergo, a mag-
netic field arose between them. However, what was interesting was that
as the work progressed, the nurturing partner was also remembered as
severely depressed, almost suicidal, while the wild one was remembered as a "bread and potatoes" practical solution finder. Their reciprocal attributions were thus clearly more fluid than the couple originally
acknowledged—and this was likely the case in the original formulation
as well as in retrospective recollection. The more restrictive diagnoses,
by contrast, had helped organize a narrowed relationship pattern.

Diagnosis functions this way in the clinical setting more often than we choose to realize. Clearly, when we clinicians act as the professional agent of diagnosis, we are simultaneously participating in the diagnostic relationship. Our perceptions of our patients are influenced by the systemic context of our particular therapeutic relationship with them. Critical patients cause anxiety in therapists who are vulnerable to feeling sadistic, and one release for such anxiety is through the diagnostic channel. Similarly, for therapists who like to view themselves as beneficent, angry and combative personalities are probably more readily diagnosed as borderline than are needy and reality-disoriented ones. In fact, a patient personified as other than borderline often means that he or she has kept the therapist's anxiety at bay.

Working against the grain of constricted relationship patterns, family therapists often view assigned diagnoses as constituting a therapeutic opportunity. I saw a couple in which the wife exploded in bursts of rage regarding her husband's lack of consideration and his persistent disrespect. As a child, the wife had been sexually abused by an uncle to whom she was offered as victim by a disturbed mother, and she considered herself unstable. However, the husband (reciprocally) had been himself raised by a psychotic mother, and he relentlessly invoked his mother's terrifying, irrational outbursts in his maddening dealing with his wife. One could view this invocation alternatively as a repetition compulsion or as a yearning to break free of the terror of irrationality. However, as long as his wife considered herself like his mother, which she did, the husband was quite frankly locked into the despair of repetition. I asked him why he was determined to push just the right panic button in her, tumbling her into uncontrolled rage. Was it to relieve childhood trauma? Was he hoping she could save him from these terrors, if once she could stay in control? Did he yearn to be relieved of the guilt of evoking rage in women? Once his behavior was framed this way, the husband became an active partner rather than a passive victim.

I supervised the treatment of a couple in which the man was decidedly paranoid in his thinking, which he knew. It was not easy for him to contain his suspicion and rage within the treatment, but he felt it was useful to him to focus on how his wife was untrustworthy and mystifying. He knew his perceptions were skewed in a paranoid, mistrustful direction, and he felt persecuted and frightened much of the time. However, a segment of his mistrust was justified in that his wife was considerably unreliable and inconsiderate. When the wife's reciprocal provocation of the husband's mistrust was addressed in the treatment, he had an experience of reality testing that was relieving. It was worthwhile for him to tease out what was real from what was exaggerated, not in his own mind and not in reflected conversation in individual therapy but in interpersonal discourse with his wife. He was not truly psychotic and his suspiciousness was somewhat ego-dystonic but he had lost faith in his capacity to perceive others with any acuity or accuracy.

Attachment theorists have offered new and interesting research findings indicating that individuals internalize relationship schemas and likely search for partners with whom they can enact these relationship patterns (Sroufe and Fleeson, 1988). However, what is not sufficiently accounted for in the schema approach is the mutuality of relationship construction. However, the couples therapist often sees the elisions in this view. No "controlling" spouse ever truly controls another. The determined effort to do so places the controlling one at the mercy of the other's character and will, and renders the former frustrated, anxious, and dependent. Similarly, no "inadequate" person ever renounces all claim to hegemony; if the wife of an "inadequate" husband has to worry about her husband's social anxieties every time they enter a populated room, she herself is rendered socially awkward and inadequate. Sometimes looking at the elision, that is, at the illusion of enactment, offers as much possibility for change as the confirmation that individuals are living with their nemeses. In psychoanalytic therapy individuals may feel, and often are helped to recognize, that they are living out encoded historical narratives. However, as Minuchin (1985) noted, "older children and adults are veterans of multiple important subsystems, and they carry complex templates and repertoires. Attempts to know their histories or codify their internal models may unduly simplify the reality" (p. 293).

THE USES OF A SYMPTOM

There is a system of diagnosis within family systems therapy, but it is nothing that Kraepelin would recognize. First, the basic approach to diagnosis involves an assessment of the family's current context, particularly its developmental level or life stage. In interviewing a family for the first time the family therapist wonders, Is this a transitional difficulty in moving from one stage of the life cycle to another or a more chronic dysfunctional picture? P. Minuchin (1985) pointed out that "recurrent challenge and reorganization are an inevitable part of the family life cycle, and families generally negotiate these transitions on their own" (p. 290). To recap the possibilities in the interaction of symptom and developmental stage (cited by Falicov in the previous chapter) recall the case of Carlo, whose father was encouraged in a therapy session to share his middle-aged, very married, very committed worldview. Carlo was a seemingly nefarious, loud-mouthed adolescent, and his presenting symptom (fire setting in school) elicits the following questions:

1. Is the symptom a response to a particular stress, somewhat circumstantial, that drains the family of the necessary flexibility and energy to move on to the next stage? (In fact, Carlo's father had become involved in a new business venture that took him out of the country for several weeks at a time. Perhaps this absence was excessive for an adolescent who was extremely assertive and challenging. Perhaps loading the burden of discipline and control onto the mother at this time, when mother and son already had too much heated interaction between them, was what threw the family into total chaos. If the problem had been limited to this circumstantial event, discussing it this way might have normalized the crisis and might well have obviated secondary and needless elaboration of pathology.)

2. Is the problem a reflection that the family system has calcified over time and cannot adjust to developmental change? (In this particular family, the actual chronic marital disappointment could be viewed as having ultimately interrupted parental collaboration, leaving adolescent limit setting unattended. Even worse, the father colluded with Carlo in denigrating his wife as a way of retaliating for her denigration of him. Given these dynamics, it is almost certain that the symptom would have been replaced by a substitute, even if remission occurred, unless these chronic dysfunctional patterns were addressed.)

3. Is the presenting symptom a solution to a particular developmental problem? (There are instances in which a symptom homeostatically, though perhaps not optimally, stabilizes a family in transition to the next stage of the life cycle. Thus, if Carlo had developed a mild educational problem rather than a penchant for fire setting, thereby necessitating either more attention from his father or some structured collaboration between his parents, perhaps he could have traversed adolescence without too much turbulence. Such a symptom would have been stabilizing in a way the fire setting was not. In this respect, the fire setting is an example of what is cybernetically called a runaway system, a system spinning out of orbit. But here we do well to note that even runaway systems are open to change and that families, like any individual or group in crisis, are quite receptive to input while in the disequilibrated state.)

Family therapists often weight one of these perspectives in assessing the relationship of symptom to system. For example, transitional difficulties often characterize "remarried families." One clinical research project report, indeed, concluded that it takes an average of one and one-half to two years for stepfathers to form friendly relationships with their children and to attain a disciplinary role equal to their wife's (Stern, 1978, in Visher and Visher, 1984).

Similarly, there is a burgeoning literature involving the developmental difficulties of families dealing with chronic illness. Chronic illness characteristically dislodges families from their natural developmental path. In my own research work I have focused on family dynamics in cases of inflammatory bowel disease (ulcerative colitis and Crohn's disease). This is an illness that occurs in young adulthood, interrupting the launching phase of the young adult, who is often ushered into a necessary but seemingly regressive dependency. For the most part, the mother serves as the primary health manager and caretaker and the resulting cross-generational alliance between a mother and a suddenly disabled young adult can seem legitimately worrisome to a family evaluator (Gerson, 1993).

Relating symptomatology to developmental assessment is, then, the first way of conceiving of family diagnosis. Such a diachronic approach is common to the family-of-origin, existential, and structural schools of family therapy, though less so to the strategic. However, there are alternative ways of thinking about symptoms that are the particular strategies of the different schools of family therapy. Two of these approaches deserve special mention; each essentially involves a way of locating the family synchronically along a particular conceptual axis.

The Structural Perspective

Among the major categories of evaluation that have emerged in the family literature is one provided by the structural perspective, namely, the now widely cited (though often inappropriately) category of enmeshment and disengagement. First posited by Minuchin (1974) in *Families and Family Therapy,* the term *enmeshment* has become part of cocktail party parlance. Enmeshment, as Minuchin conceives of it, denotes overly rigid boundaries around the family system and a loss of autonomy and individual difference for its members. At the opposite extreme, disengaged families are characterized by diffuse boundaries; its members do not feel a deep sense of belonging, are reluctant to ask for help, and overemphasize a kind of static independence.

The concept of enmeshment was best operationalized in Minuchin, Rosman, and Baker's (1978) work on psychosomatic syndromes. The findings from this research, in fact, offer an important clarification of the differentiation between families beset by long-standing psychological dysfunction and fairly healthy families dealing with a demanding exogenous crisis that must be mastered. Minuchin and his colleagues found that in a group of families containing diabetic children there were two dysfunctional subtypes. In one, the diabetic children had behavior problems in addition to the diabetes; in the other, dubbed "psychosomatic," the children seemed to have unexplained physical exacerbations that, it turned out, dovetailed with the systemic patterning characteristic of enmeshment.

The clinical research design utilized a three-part family interaction interview that involved the following stages: (1) observation by the child, behind the one-way mirror, of the parents discussing a family problem in private; (2) the arrival in the therapy room of the interviewer, who proceeds to intensify the confrontation between the couple; (3) the inclusion of the child in the family conversation. In the families with children with unexplained exacerbations (those who were designated as psychosomatic) the discussions in Stage One were characterized by conflict avoidance. It was only these families who responded significantly to the artificially provoked confrontation exercise by becoming more combative. (The nonpsychosomatic families maintained the same level of conflict throughout.) When the psychosomatic child entered the therapy room following the provocation by the interviewer, the conversation became exclusively focused on the child as each parent attempted to elicit the child's opinions or recruit his or her support against the other parent. The child actively participated in these coalitions. The researchers noted that "the expression *involvement of the child* should always be interpreted in the passive and active voice at the same time; that is, the child is both involved *by* and involved *in* the parental conflict" (p. 43). What was unique about this study is that heparin locks (intravenous-blood-sampling units) had been inserted in the arm of each family member before the interview; these yielded laboratory data on free fatty acids (FFA), a key marker in the diabetic metabolic syndrome. Enmeshment, it turns out, is a physiological risk in juvenile diabetes. The free fatty acid production in the psychosomatic children, as opposed to the children with behavior problems, rose significantly, owing to parental conflict, and remained at a high level for a longer period of time subsequent to the interview. Moreover, though the child's FFA increased, the entrance of the child in the therapy room immediately decreased parental FFA production in parents who had an increased FFA production. This was enmeshment par excellence.

A conceptual problem is that the terms *enmeshment* and *disengagement* — but particularly the former — have been drawn into the pathologizing currents inherent in psychiatric diagnosis, with the implication that the terms themselves signify pathology. Minuchin originally proposed the idea that these terms identify the poles of a continuum on which all families can be placed and that it is only at the extremes that dysfunction can be found.

Even when it is appropriate, the designation of enmeshment is certainly subject to cultural relativism. Are Italian-American families who live in two-family homes where cross-generational child care is readily available necessarily enmeshed? Are Jewish-American families enmeshed when they interrupt each other's utterances with abandon? Historical realities have pushed some cultural groups toward one or the other pole of Minuchin's continuum. For Jews who were uprooted by scapegoating rampages, the family offered the only palpable security. However, what is culturally normative is still idiographically shaped, and highly cohesive Jewish families can represent either a stronghold or strangulation. Indeed, the enmeshed family offers interesting conundrums to psychoanalysts who treat its members and who sometimes find that their efforts to promote self-awareness and differentiation dissolve into thin air. I worked with a woman who could barely tolerate an examination of what emerged as the essentially enmeshed configuration of her family of origin. She was still agreeing with every attribution her parents had applied to each other for 20 years. Her father still straightened the tie of her highly successful brother. The enmeshment seemed to halt altogether the possibility of individual appraisal and self-examination. In retrospect, it seems to me that I should have much more gingerly approached her lack of differentiation, that is, accepted it as a given and proceeded from there. This approach would essentially have cordoned off a major segment of her character and would thus have constituted a violation of the spirit of unrestricted analytic inquiry, but sometimes it is necessary to go around the enmeshment, not over it.

The Strategic Orientation

The diagnostic axis of symmetry versus complementarity emerges from the strategic orientation. Essentially, symmetrical relationships are relationships of equality. Complementary relationships accentuate difference in a hierarchical sense, with one partner occupying the one-up position and the other the one-down position. Once again, it is the extreme and rigidified form of such a relationship that is troublesome. With most couples there is a recognition of greater and lesser talents and competencies; in a rigidly complementary relationship, one person is consistently better at everything. According to Cloe Madanes, hierarchical imbalances are the essence of dysfunction. Her position is that couples who cannot resolve power issues (the sanitized expression for this being "division of labor") use symptomatic negotiation to balance power. When depression, alcoholism, psychosomatic complaints, or any other syndrome is at issue, the power negotiations essentially cycle endlessly and irresolutely:

> Typically, the symptomatic person is in an inferior position to the other spouse, who tries to help and to change him; yet the symptomatic spouse is also in a superior position in that he refuses to be helped and to change. . . . In this way, two incongruous hierarchies are defined in the couple. In one, the person with the problem is in an inferior position because he is in need of help, and the nonsymptomatic spouse is in the superior position of helper. In the other, the symptomatic spouse will not be influenced and helped, which puts him in a superior position to the nonsymptomatic spouse, who tries unsuccessfully to influence and change him [Madanes, 1981, p. 30].

Madanes's solution, emerging organically from this nest of contradictions, is paradoxical play (covered in the next chapter).

Traditional Diagnosis and Family Treatment

Is there no place in family work for traditional, empirically developed psychiatric diagnosis? In fact, family therapists with prior individual therapy training are quite comfortable including individual diagnosis in a systems formulation. Biologically based syndromes, whether in the cognitive (e.g., dyslexia) or the affective (manic-depressive psychosis) realm, are essentially treated as individual characteristics requiring contextualization, in a way regarded like other salient biographical characteristics, such as military or immigrant experience, or like particular personality dispositions, such as creative ability in the arts. What distinguishes the systemic point of view is that diagnosis is subordinate to the systemic evaluation of the family's system of relationships. In other words, diagnosis is a building block, not a blueprint.

Slightly more controversial is the presence in the literature of diagnostic categories for whole families. This is an even more objectifying form of diagnosis because it includes several individuals under one rubric. The value of such diagnostic categories is left to the reader to decide. Several excellent texts exist describing the "alcoholic family," the "addictive family," and the family with chronic illness (although the literature edges toward the precipice of reifying diagnosis).[1] For the most part, however, systemic principles still subsume biological events. Thus, addictive substances—and medical illness in general—are typically viewed as homeostatic regulators whose interruption will cause disequilibration in the family system. In therapy with alcoholic family members the bottle is often referred to in terms of triangulation (i.e., addiction is described as a love affair of sorts). The focus is still on what purposes this kind of triangulation serves and on what will happen, for better or worse, if it is interrupted. In the family systems literature on medical illness, aggregate family meaning systems are the current focus of research. The prevailing questions are the following: What is the illness a metaphor for? Once the illness is in place, how does it organize the family? What does it come to symbolize for the family? In terms of intervention, the question is whether the illness is an opportunity for growth or a disaster representing collective tragedy.

Symptom Substitution

This overview of diagnosis should not conclude without a comment on symptom substitution, the supposed comeuppance of every renegade therapeutic model. Of course, psychoanalytic treatment does not promise, or even focus on, symptom resolution, although it is common enough for symptoms to abate or dissolve as anxiety and conflict are addressed. However, the rejection by psychoanalysts of transference cure usually includes disparagement of dramatic symptomatic improvement, the emphasis of the psychoanalytic paradigm being on depth exploration. The concern about symptom disappearance in family systems work is not about precipitousness; indeed, palpable change in behavioral symptoms of individual family members is often dramatic and rapid. The true concern is homologous to the psychoanalytic caveat; family therapists believe symptom removal should go hand in hand with meaningful shifts in family structure and communication. Otherwise, substitution will occur—often in another family member!

Family therapists basically view symptomatology metaphorically (as analysts basically do) and examine the interactional loops that wind through and around the symptom as a key to diagnosing the system. One exception to this metaphoric view of symptomatology is offered by strategic family therapists, who make quite a point about respecting the presenting request and focusing on symptoms. However, although

---

[1]Noteworthy texts include Kaufman and Kaufman (1981) and Steinglass, Bennett, Wolin, and Reiss (1987).

strategic family therapists accept responsibility for effecting symptomatic change, they still view such change as a systemic issue. Their position is that resolving what the client presents as the principal problem (while thinking of it in systemic terms) engenders cooperation with the treatment and receptivity to therapeutic suggestion. The "therapist knows best" attitude is part of the methodology, not the goal.

FAMILY ASSESSMENT

The essence of family evaluation can best be conveyed in a twofold approach. In the following pages we take a walking tour of an initial family interview. The most characteristic assessment device—the genogram—is then presented, and its relevance to initial data collection is discussed.

There are, however, issues that occur to the therapist considering a family consultation session that we must address first. Psychoanalysts are often wary of inviting a whole family in for a consultation visit, especially if the initial referral call included a vivid description of animosity or betrayal, but in many such cases a matter-of-fact request from the therapist to hear everybody's opinion of the situation often brings the whole family in. To be sure, families are legitimately concerned about having their problems exposed. If these are judged as pathological, there is virtually no retreat from the edict of failure, no "haven in a heartless world." The barrier of resistance is often traversed by emphasizing family strengths. How does the family therapist emphasize these strengths? If a child has been referred for therapy, parents generally will respond to a therapist who in the initial phone call offers support and bolsters their existing efforts to help the child. Spouses will usually respond to being invited to tell their side of the story or else to the opportunity to contribute to a solution to the marital difficulty in more constructive ways than they have managed on their own. Psychoanalysts are particularly aware that the representation a patient has of a significant other is endangered when that person joins a session. Patients are also aware that they risk exposing the "illusoriness," to borrow Sullivan's term, of the other; insofar as the self is constructed in relationships, one can empathize with patients who fear the loss in selfhood that a radically different perception of an intimate could entail. However, if the couples therapist underlines the constructive aspects of the joint clinical interview (just as a psychoanalyst does in a first consultation), the emphasis for the patient moves from loss to sustenance—or even gain—as a result of the shared meeting.

The First Interview

In listening to family members' explanations of the presenting problem the therapist attempts to regard these as definitions of an interactional issue and tries not to be seduced by a compelling individual narrative. Thus, if the presenting problem is a daughter's running away from home to escape the overbearing and overinvolved protectiveness of her father, the temptation to view the situation as either his or her resurgent oedipal dynamic gone awry is to be avoided. The family therapist, upon learning the general outline of the case, wonders first, Where is mom? In the forefront of the therapist's initial assessment will be a consideration of the issues of parental collaboration and shared responsibility for child rearing. The emphasis is on structure first and dynamics second. And structure is more accessible and offers the richest yield when the whole family is present.

The way the therapist first greets the family underscores structure. When greeting families, psychoanalysts often assume that members should be treated as equal informants; the family therapist, on the other hand, is respectful and interested in everyone's opinion but always starts with the parents and never with the "identified patient." In family systems theory there is a traditional concept of the "gatekeeper," the person who swings the gate open or closed to therapeutic engagement. In fact, an important goal in the first interview is to give the gatekeeper a systemic perspective that is meaningful, while honoring his or her special needs and sensitivities. After all, the family would not be gathered without the gatekeeper's urgings.

The best way to get a sense of family evaluation and assessment is to sit right behind a family therapist who is meeting a family for the first time. After a brief settling-in phase the therapist usually begins by inquiring about the history of the problem within the history of the family. In the first therapy sessions there is often a strong undertow, which the therapist must resist, coming from the identified patient's history and difficulties. I recently saw a family consisting of three 20-something children and their parents. One of the young adults had a psychiatric history, including a stint in a treatment facility that took him out of the family for two years. The parents experienced tremendous guilt partly because of their early pattern of denial. Before the son's residential treatment he had become frighteningly aggressive, which the parents had responded to with a kind of denying permissiveness. The family was now gathered presumably because mother was depressed, with the other two children withdrawing from her while she remained tormented about the third. There was a lot to explore with this family, but my initial efforts were devoted to recasting the "disturbed" young man as simply a son and brother. It took two sessions of tactfully interrupting his psychiatric cataloguing and assuring him that the sessions were not because of him nor for him before he relaxed and blossomed as a person. What a relief for him to feel like a member of his sibling group again! In fact, he was then able to draw upon a range of appropriate behaviors lying dormant in his repertoire.

The family therapist looks for patterning in making an initial evaluation. The traditional indices to be surveyed are the following: (1) covert and overt alliances between family members; (2) the maintenance or invasion of boundaries; (3) the range and quality of affect; and (4) shared meanings and mythologies, or what can globally be referred to as the family's "construction of reality." The history taken is largely (and as much as possible) the history of the couple or family. In couples therapy, individual recountings of childhood experience are eschewed in favor of courtship histories. "What attracted you two to each other?" is much more useful than "What was your relationship to your parents?"

The family therapist next inquires about how the problem was solved in the past (or, at least, what attempts were made to deal with it). Substituting "Why?" for "What?" Watzlawick and colleagues cited the 109th tractus of Wittgenstein: "It often happens that we only become aware of the important *facts*, if we suppress the question 'why?' and then in the course of our investigations these facts lead us to an answer" (Wittgenstein, 1958, p. 3; Watzlawick et al., 1974, p. 84). The importance of focusing on past solutions is that it elucidates much about the prevailing family belief system while opening the door for fresh intervention. An inquiry into past solutions involves noting the psychotherapy treatment history, if any, and briefly inquiring about how it was helpful, while perhaps inquiring about the relevance of that treatment experience to the current problem. A woman I saw recently remarked in the first session of couples therapy that she feared her recently terminated analysis had been a failure because she was still deeply hurting her husband. On cue, the husband then identified himself as being "in pain." When I inquired about what she had accomplished in psychoanalysis, the woman said she had worked on herself and her relationship to her parents. Tears welled up in her eyes when she talked about her father's death. It was clear that she was "in pain" as well, but she did not characterize herself as such. I pointed out to the couple that their presenting narratives included a reciprocity of husbandly feelings of injury and wifely contrition and invited them to consider this lopsided emotional balance. It then became clearer that in her prior individual

treatment this woman and her analyst had apparently intensively explored her distress but had not sufficiently addressed her husband's
difficulty with her character and style. She was essentially left holding a
bag of guilt regarding her effect on him, and one unfortunate aspect of
this guilt was to deny the residue of her own dysphoria.

What is frequently foreign to analytically oriented therapists is the
need emphasized by family therapists to "decenter" the inquiry away
from both diagnosis and history taking and to instead invite the family
to interact. There is no data like visible shared data. If the family intake
goes well at all, each member should leave with a mix of two reactions:
(1) a feeling of being unburdened of singular blame and (2) a feeling of
being more complicitous in an ongoing web of entangled dynamics.

Family therapists from different orientations have different conceptualizations as to how best to accomplish this double shift from individual diagnosis to family assessment and from history taking to *in vivo*
interaction. A particularly clear model from the strategic perspective is
provided by Haley (1976), who outlines four stages in the initial family
interview:

1. The Social Stage: The family arrives and chats. It is particularly
important for the therapist to inquire about household arrangements;
there may be a very important person (e.g., a housekeeper who is
referred to constantly) who is not present. And, of course, the therapist
observes how family members seat themselves, always a telling exercise.

2. The Problem Stage: The therapist asks the family why they have
arrived and what kind of help is being sought. Of course, family
therapists must decide whom to speak to first (generally avoiding the
identified patient). Should the therapist speak to the children first
because they are the most distressed family members? To parents
because they are in charge? To mothers because they are most involved?
Haley notes that the decision should be made in regard to the presenting problem, not according to any sociological or characterological
assumptions. Everyone in the family is asked for an opinion. There are
two aspects of this stage that typically feel different to the therapist who
is coming from a psychodynamic orientation. First, therapists who are
used to zooming in on an individual's subjective version of experience
must accustom themselves to maintaining a wide-angle focus on how
any given issue or problem exists, is created by, and is maintained by
shared action. Second, such therapists become acutely aware that by
offering family members this perspective, they are actually restructuring the family during the inquiry. There is an additional benefit to the
experience that these therapists can take back to their individual treatments: what generally happens is that they become exquisitely more

cognizant of how much the inquiry itself is mutative. This is especially true of the initial interview. Our theoretical bent and initial counter-transference reactions tend to dictate the construction of every moment of the first interview; however, we generally are not so attuned to how our patients are changing in response to our inquiry right at the beginning. This level of response is less likely to be attended to at the start of psychodynamic therapy (a most crucial time) than later in the treatment, when the therapist is more comfortable asking for responses and associations to therapeutic activity.

3. The Interaction Stage: At some point in the initial interview the family therapist is sure to have family members chat among themselves in an effort to obtain a kind of *cinéma verité* version of home life. Here the sequence of interactions becomes important to note. For example, does father become activated only when mother and children start to argue? Does mother–daughter closeness occur basically when father–daughter hostility peaks? Sometimes psychodynamic therapists have difficulty getting this stage going. Examples of easily posed invitations to family members to interact are the following: (to parents) "Talk between you about what you think is an appropriate curfew" and (to disengaged children) "Talk between you about what you think is fair for your parents to insist upon."

4. The Goal-Setting Stage: Haley considers it essential to negotiate a shared objective with the family, most notably because the consensual agreement promotes the family's participation in the treatment. His emphasis is on defining a solvable version of what the family considers is its most pressing problem. Because I do not work in the strategic model, I do not set goals in the first session. I generally tell the family at the outset that our meeting with each other will extend over two visits, with time in between to articulate questions and reservations. In the second session I state a theme (instead of "goals), often proposing a reciprocity in dynamics or a loop of meanings. For example, I might say to a husband, "If you felt you could disclose more, she wouldn't feel you were so unavailable," and to his wife I might say, "If you could feel less judgmental, you wouldn't feel he was avoiding you as much." Of course, we are already in the thicket of self-personifications here, dense and overgrown, and as in negotiating our way through any thicket, we must step carefully but firmly at the same time. Family members come to therapy thinking of themselves as being a certain kind of person. The family therapist notes that in their interpersonal actions, they behave in ways that belie their self-concept. Thus, a father who has maintained a self-satisfied image of himself as mediator between a battling wife and daughter is exposed to the systems-focused family therapist as a

troublemaker who refuses to establish an allegiance to his daughter that is qualitatively different from his allegiance to his spouse. This observation is not stated baldly in the first session, but nudging questions to illuminate this undercover operation generally begin the work of articulating and then challenging this pattern.

For example, the Gerber family was referred to me because of the long-standing anorexia–bulimia syndrome of the older daughter, Roberta, aged 35. She had been severely anorectic in the past, though she never required hospitalization. Now she was merely quite slim, but she engaged in at least one bulimic episode every evening and had been doing so for about five years. Gertrude and Gerry Gerber had a younger daughter, Barbara, age 33, who was psychiatrically asymptomatic. The referral came from Roberta's current individual therapist, whom she had been seeing twice weekly for about two years (following a three-year period of individual therapy with someone else). The treatment was psychodynamic, but it included behavioral work in a group setting around the bulimic behavior. There had been one failed antidepressant medication trial and a recommended hospitalization, which had been refused. Roberta had stopped vomiting for eight months during the previous year's treatment but had then felt somehow inexplicably coerced into resuming this behavior. Her individual therapist reported that Roberta said she consistently felt "dead" in therapy but that she nevertheless seemed more committed to the work recently. Three years earlier the family as a whole had been in therapy for about eight months, which had not been helpful.

Needless to say, this was a very challenging case. The basic structural family perspective on eating disorders focuses on boundary disturbance; the working assumption is that the family with an eating-disordered member is generally dysfunctionally enmeshed and allows its members too little individual space and opportunity for self-determination.

I noticed in the first session that the Gerbers were a considerably enmeshed and conflict-avoidant family. Like many enmeshed families, they made one more place for their therapist; I felt as if I were squeezing onto a warm couch in their living room for a chat. There were two active members of the family, Roberta and Gertrude, and two rather passive members, Barbara and Gerry. There was an almost nonexistent boundary separating Roberta and her mother. Roberta needed only to flash the family a rageful look, and Gertrude would start talking about how upset she was about Roberta's "condition." If one were to draw a diagram of the energy in the session, all arrows would emanate from and circle around Gertrude and Roberta. In this family gestalt there was practically no contact between mother and father and little evidence of a sibling bond.[2]

I concentrated much more on interaction than on symptomatology, since I wanted to contextualize Roberta's symptomatology in the nest of family relationships. From a diagnostic standpoint, I initially referred to the eating behavior as "strange" and agreed to call it "self-destructive" only under pressure, making a point that this was a descriptive, not a dynamic, assignation. Some of my work in the initial session with this family illustrates the principles of intervention and will be covered in the next chapter. Here I will focus on our initial meetings. I felt that I had to present the family with an alternative perspective early in the work since this was a family somewhat jaded about the effectiveness of psychotherapy.

I took down genogram information in the first session. In recording Roberta's data I asked for a history of the bulimia; otherwise, the genogram taken was a simple one. The genogram information is as follows: Gerry's father, aged 85, had been a liquor store owner, a "real operator"; his mother had died ten years earlier. Gerry had a sister who died of cancer when he was 28 and she was 25. Gertrude's mother had died eight years earlier, and her father had died when she was 28; Gertrude was an only child. Gerry, aged 65, was an ear, nose, and throat specialist; Gertrude was 63 and a homemaker. They married when he was 22 and she was 20. Lacking emotional input from extended family members, the Gerbers had only their own emotional resources. Enmeshment within the family, especially intense between mother and Roberta, had been part of their response to this situation.

My first-session goal was to recast Roberta's symptomatology and to loosen the stricture around Roberta and mother. In the first session I called Roberta and her mother "the infantry" (because they did all the work for the family). I suggested that Barbara should thank Roberta for taking on mother, who was a generally agitated woman and needed a focus for her concern and energy, and I suggested that Gerry thank Gertrude for battling with the "kids" (as the parents referred to their grown daughters). Lastly, I suggested that Roberta really liked having center-stage "stardom" in the family, and I challenged Barbara to give her some competition.

In the second session my effort to link Roberta and Barbara took shape; proximity bred contempt, and the sisters argued and bickered at

---

[2]An interesting complementary perspective on bulimia is one that views it as a transgenerational problem emerging from a long history of overvaluing success and appearance (see Roberto, 1986).

the beginning of the session. The parents looked embarrassed and distressed. The energy flow had shifted. Father rushed to Roberta's aid, concerned that she felt "intimidated" by Barbara. Mother lamented that Roberta was "sick" and worried that the fight with Barbara would be upsetting for her. I asked Barbara whether she felt neglected. What a disturbing question for them all! They saw themselves as such a loving family that the notion of neglect was unacceptable. Besides, the prevailing family assumption dictated that Roberta was the needy one. Continuing the work on "depathologizing," I encouraged the sisters to explore their sore points but to do it while avoiding "shrink talk," as it was called in this family. I encouraged their father, who had been concerned that Roberta felt intimidated by her sister, to devotedly protect her whenever the daughters were together during the week. With these interventions I was hoping Gerry might intrude upon and loosen the overly tight coalition between Roberta and her mother as well as help challenge Roberta's supposed impotency. In the following transcript excerpt, five to ten minutes into the third session, social chitchat had begun to develop an edge between mother and daughters and father now jumps in:

> *Father:* Well, last week I didn't have an opportunity to stop anybody from intimidating Roberta. That was my job. I couldn't do it.
> *Roberta:* You did. In the car.
> *Father:* I did? I did my job?
> *Roberta:* You don't remember?
> *Father:* I remember the effect.
> *Mother:* I had the week off.
> *Therapist:* Wait a minute. I want to know . . .
> *Father:* I don't know. Someone said something.
> *Roberta:* I remember. I was talking with Barbara about something at work. I said something. You said, "Don't let her." I said I love her, but I don't want her to use me, and you said, "Don't let her."
> *Therapist (rises and shakes father's hand):* You did it!

Here I acknowledged and "punctuated" father's commitment to the task and to Roberta. I then focused on the sibling subsystem, which was characterized by a kind of childlike bickering. I challenged Roberta's perceived sickness and her potential for redefinition.

> *Therapist:* You appreciated it?
> *Roberta:* Yes, I did.
> *Therapist:* You didn't thank him?

Roberta: It never occurred to me. Well, yes. I think I said thank you.

Therapist: Now the goal of this session is to prevent Roberta from being intimidated.

Father: Someone try to intimidate Roberta, so I will have the opportunity to protect her.

Therapist (to the sisters): How did you two do? In cutting back on your attack–defense style?

Barbara: I don't know. We hardly talked this week.

Roberta: On Monday you wanted me to ask Bill about the show, and I didn't want to.

Barbara: You didn't say so.

Roberta: I did so!

Barbara: Not right away. I had to ask you.

Roberta: I did too. I said, "You'll have to do it yourself. I don't want to do it."

Barbara: Well, you gave me a look, and . . .

Roberta: What's the big deal? I said, "I don't want to." Then you said, "You're my sister."

Barbara: I said that?

Roberta: What does it matter? The fact is that you are using me. The word *sister*—I mean, what's the difference who I am? If I'm a friend or something? I don't want to do it! You use the word *sister*—it's like I have to do it.

Barbara: You always say—it's gotten to the point where I ask you—if I ask you something, it's like I'm using you, I'm exploiting you—where are your boundaries?

Therapist: Oh, no! Back to that. Psychologizing? I'm going to have to arrange a honorary degree for you? Just tell her!

Barbara: I thought I was.

Therapist: On the contrary. You were therapizing her.

Barbara: I was?

Therapist (to Roberta): Do you want her to be your therapist?

Roberta: No.

Therapist (to Barbara): She doesn't want you to be a therapist.

Barbara: I'm not trying to be! It pisses me off. I ask you something—it's like it's the wrong thing to ask or I'm asking too much.

Therapist: You are still therapizing. Can you talk to your sister without analyzing her dynamics?

Barbara: It's not her dynamics, it's our dynamics.

Therapist: No. You're saying, "I ask you things and it means this to you, and you personalize it . . ." What irritated you here?

Barbara: That you wouldn't ask Bill a simple question for me!
Therapist: Congratulations.

The therapeutic point here is that Roberta had discussed, in individual therapy, the complex dynamics that determined and currently sustained her bulimia—with minimal success. Certainly, any respectable exploration of an eating disorder would include a thorough family inquiry, but it is unlikely that Roberta's autobiographical narrative would have included the relevance of the enmeshed sibling bickering, which reassured the parents of the childlike innocence of their "girls" and which distressed them only when it reached a pitch that challenged their happy family imago. A detailed historical inquiry was irrelevant, moreover, to the salience of this subsystemic oddity of two grown women acting like little girls. Roberta certainly knew that her parents infantilized her, but how she participated in this dynamic eluded her. Why? Because her participation also involved her sister's participation and her parents' propensity for distortion. This complex scenario exceeds the limitations of dyadic transference exploration and enactment.

How effective was the family treatment in ameliorating Roberta's bulimic symptom? There was some reduction in the frequency of bulimic episodes during the latter phase of our work, her individual therapist told me, and an up-and-down course shortly afterward. Then an interesting confluence of therapeutic and real-life events occurred. The group I was working with in consultation with Salvador Minuchin became interested in follow-up interviews. I called the Gerbers approximately six months after therapy ended, and they said they were interested in seeing me to talk about gains in the therapy. There was one dramatic change: Gerry had been killed in a hit-and-run accident approximately two months earlier. In the follow-up session, mother and daughters agreed that the most dramatic effect of family therapy had been a noticeably intensified and pleasurable closeness between husband and wife, accompanied by more casual relating to the two daughters. In what Minuchin described as a mourning or *shiva* (in the Jewish religion) session, each family member described what the loss of Gerry meant to her. Roberta said that she had noticed, when sorting through her father's possessions, how disturbingly similar she was to him. She also said that she had felt safer in the family when he was there; "He could say things for me and then they'd hear them," she explained.

We did not discuss bulimia in that session, but Roberta's individual therapist reported to me that after the father's death her symptomatology ceased altogether. How do we explain the disappearance of the symptom? Our heads spin with hypotheses regarding boundary re-alignments and tolerable and intolerable levels of enmeshment, all circling the question, Why was Roberta's dysfunction no longer relevant in a family constellation minus her father? An equal panoply of psychoanalytic hypotheses could be generated. In fact, there is no way of tracing the link between the family treatment, Roberta's individual treatment, and the interaction effects between these two therapies in explaining this highly desirable outcome. What I did know was that it seemed very appropriate to me that this family entered therapy together and that, once there, my approach moved along ordinary and expectable systemic guideposts.

The Genogram

The most fundamental assessment tool of the family therapist is the genogram. It is a relatively easy instrument to master and provides an experience of looking at relationships across people. Sometimes it is remarkably valuable as a heuristic; at other times it is only mildly useful in suggesting initial clinical hypotheses. The genogram data of the Gerber family was not very revealing, except insofar as it highlighted the context of their enmeshment, namely, their isolation as a very small unit with practically no immediate extended family members available for attachment or support.

There are universal symbols for genogram construction, some of the most basic of which (male, female, death) are noted in Figure 8-1. Note that for every generation, the oldest is placed on the left of the sub-system lineup.

I generally take down information on three generations of family history—the siblings of the patient, the parents (with their siblings), and the grandparents—sometimes with a sketch of their sibling number and position.

I ask for the cause of death of deceased relatives. Other dates that are important are those for divorce and separation. There are some basic texts that can orient the psychodynamic therapist to genogram construction and usage (Marlin, 1989). A key variable is whether the genogram is executed in the first session or in the second or third. If in the first session, I generally take fairly bare-bones information, which is nevertheless quite useful. If I do the genogram in a later session, I will sometimes focus it on a theme, such as marital satisfaction across the generations or male insensitivity—that is, on something that captures the concerns and patterning of the presenting problem. Wachtel (1982) recognized that the genogram often allows constricted individuals,

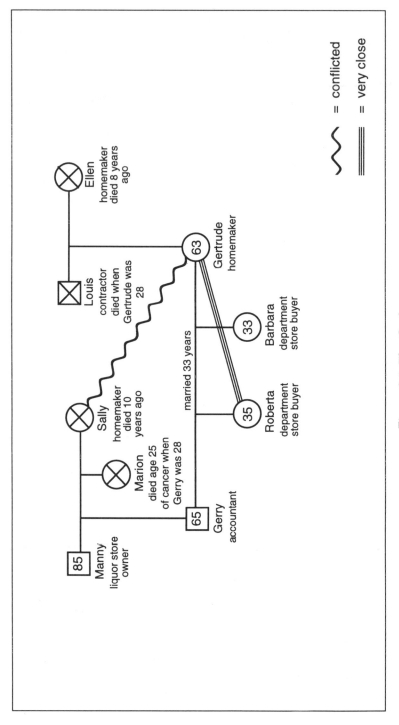

Figure 8-1. The Gerbers.

who become absorbed in the task of supplying factual data, to become uncharacteristically self-revealing and that, paradoxically, it allows overresponsive and angry individuals to calm down by talking about history. She pointed out that in the process of supplying information for the genogram patients' unconscious longings may be expressed through affective tone and word choice and through the incidental information they choose to share with the therapist at this time.

For me, the genogram functions as a form of inquiry and is particularly suited to what E. A. Levenson (1988) calls the "pursuit of the particular." The attention to detail that goes with genogram construction, like any carefully conducted factual inquiry, potentially deconstructs the known and the defensively palatable, revealing loose threads or even threadbare areas of experience. It is quite astonishing how just-out-of-awareness experience bubbles up during certain genogram constructions in a way that invites psychoanalytic explanation. (One such incident occurred when a student welled up with tears after simply mentioning the funeral of his mother's first husband. He was shocked at his own response since this death occurred fifteen years ago and was rarely mentioned. Somehow, however, this loss and its meaning had permeated his consciousness.)

Then, too, genogram information can be very usefully conscripted into interventions for family members who will entertain the need for change only if it is couched in historical terms. A couple whose treatment I came to supervise in its second year were locked into a rigid pattern of wifely psychopathologizing of the husband. Their application for therapy, in fact, looked like a case report filled out by her. Many, many approaches to expanding this system had been tried in the previous year to no avail. The therapist finally succeeded by grounding the opportunity for change in past identifications: The therapist proposed to the husband that he invite his wife to control him because he was afraid of defining his own identity owing to his father's embarrassing failure in life and his mother's fear of self-definition. In a symmetrical proposal the therapist suggested to the wife that she control her husband because she was truly familiar with being "parentified child"—note here the use of a diagnostic label to satisfy a diagnosis-hungry individual—having rescued the care of her younger brother from a psychotically disturbed mother during his adolescence. Is this kind of identification-linking a necessary approach to individuals who in fact are overly loyal to their family of origin? Do we understand why some identifications are locked in vises and others are loosely hinged? Not really.

Jumping ahead for the moment to the topic of intervention (the subject of Chapter Nine), I should point out that the presentation to the couple of this formulation was done formally and seriously, though the therapist described it to them as a proposition derived from supervision. In this case we drew on the "mystique" of the genogram, as identified by Wachtel. The iconic genogram is like a Rosetta stone that cries out for continued decoding, which a free-flowing history taking does not.

Genogram execution always functions as a kind of boundary-refurbishing exercise for family members. I insist that the family *remain absolutely silent* while members each report on their family of origin. At the end of each member's presentation the others can then ask questions or comment on anything that seems to them to be a glaring omission. I like to punctuate that individuals own their own lives even if they do not own their present relationship realities.

In meeting a family for an initial interview, one indexes in a sense all the major systemic factors thus far addressed in this text (including information that goes beyond the genogram). The following is a list of the major variables affecting family functioning, particularly with regard to symptomatology.[3]

1. Ethnicity
2. Social class
3. Family ecology (support systems, such as extended family or religious group)
4. Family configuration or shape (nuclear, extended, or "blended," i.e., remarried)
5. Family life cycle position and individual life cycle positions
6. Family structure (boundaries, coalitions, and hierarchies within and across subsystems; symmetrical, complementary, enmeshed, or disengaged structure)

Family Health

Before leaving the area of diagnosis from a family systems perspective, we should talk about family health. Not surprisingly, when a family is initially presented in a continuing case seminar, evidence of family strength and sustenance is often submerged beneath a wave of worrisome psychopathological signs and symptoms. Accustomed to thinking of assessment as diagnosis in the medical model tradition, we tend to focus on invading or destructive forces rather than on the resilient host. (Here let me identify the strengths of the Gerber family:

---

[3] I am indebted to Ema Genijovich (1995), who presented the initial outline of this diagnostic profile.

warmth, humor, and dependability. These are not throw-away characteristics in a postmodern era.)

What, indeed, is family health? In fact, an important index of countertransference is how one poses oneself to answer this question. Beyond that, one's personal therapeutic signature can be identified from the domain selected. Differentiation as well as closeness, open expression of feelings, clarity of expectations instead of mystification—these are some of the responses frequently offered by beginning family therapists.

As one would imagine, each orientation within family therapy emphasizes a different aspect of well-being. For example, structural family therapists emphasize permeable membranes encasing the healthy tissues of subsystems. Strategic family therapist, the most problem-oriented of all the schools, define health in the negative; that is, when hierarchies are imbalanced in families, or are arbitrarily inserted into a marriage, family health is threatened. For Bowenians, tolerance of anxiety and maintenance of equanimity in the face of irrational affect is crucial to well-being.

It is the existential school, as personified by Whitaker, whose concept of family health is potentially most familiar to the psychoanalyst. For Whitaker, health is ultimately flexibility in all domains and all directions. Thus, recognizing that alliances are inevitable in human affairs, Whitaker posited that a flux of alliances (e.g., mom and sis against dad and brother on Monday and both parents battling kids on Tuesday) is both honest and robust. Similarly, Whitaker emphasized the need for families to dip into "craziness" together, a kind of collective regression in the service of the ego. These characteristics of health are in fact the most apt response to the need for a living organism to maintain its steady state in a larger context of ebbing and flowing life forces.

My own personal view is that what emerges as a key indicator of health from a systems perspective is the ability to view self in context, as organized by others. It is interesting to scan our individual diagnostic categories and consider which of them lend themselves to this new perspective and which do not. Are hysterics more able than obsessives in this regard? What does a hyperinvestment in autonomy really signify? Cushman (1991) noted that "those who 'own' the self control our world" (p. 218). Health from a family systems perspective ultimately resides in an ability to flexibly imagine new configurations of relationships. In psychoanalysis we imagine new selves; in family therapy we imagine new relationships. The creativity required to foster these different kinds of changes may draw on different characterological repertoires in the clinician no less than in the designated patient.

chapter nine

Interventions in Family Therapy

Illusions have reality; they are real illusions.
T. S. Eliot

The creativity of family therapy lies in its interventions. Representative interventions include straightforward task assignment, focused use of metaphor, dramatic techniques, rituals, and verbal reframing of dynamics. Although a consideration of the underlying rationale of the family intervention repertoire takes us to some of the finer points of contemporary analytic debate, family interventions cannot be explained or encompassed by the analytic model and have to be appreciated in terms of family systems theory.

Family therapy interventions often appear alien to the traditionally trained psychodynamic therapist. They seem to embody an unrestrained, nonreflective abandon and, even worse, sometimes appear arbitrary and authoritarian. Why? For the psychoanalyst, meaning is embodied in language; the quintessence of psychoanalytic practice is the interpretation. Yet there is much more that the psychoanalyst brings to the clinical encounter than the ability to capture dynamics in a focused interpretation. Other significant aspects of the analyst's presence identified in the literature include a faith in the restorative function of empathy (Atwood and Stolorow, 1984), containment of the patient's projections and anxieties (Bion, 1962; Winnicott, 1975), and a commitment to honestly examine how participation is shared in reenacting the patient's disowned experience (I. Z. Hoffman, 1991).

Within a broadened and elaborated perspective on psychoanalytic treatment, interpretation nevertheless remains preeminent. In psychoanalytic treatment the critical point of most intense and mutative contact is when the analyst reflects back to the patient what he or she thinks is happening therapeutically. As E. A. Levenson notes, "psychoanalysis is what is said about what is done."

The family therapist, however, is not focused on capturing dynamics in a well-honed, symbolically drenched verbal communication, as the analyst is. Rather, family or couples therapists wedge themselves into the relationship system of the family and like a symbiote, attempt to alter it from within.

Though interpretation has a rich and variegated history in psychoanalysis, its essence has remained relatively constant; it is a delicate blend of developmental experience, extratransference relationship, and, most crucially, transference phenomena. A bedrock definition of interpretation is offered by Laplanche and Pontalis (1973): "a procedure which, by means of analytic investigation, brings out the latent meaning in what the subject says and does" (p. 227). Yet the latent often remains ineffable, and as Spence (1982) notes, "an interpretation, we might say, provides a useful gloss on something that is, by definition indescribable" (p. 63). Exactly what the interpretation offers the analysand has been viewed differently in different quarters at different times. Mitchell and Greenberg (1983) deftly summarized the gradient in the evolution of our understanding: to wit, for Strachey (1934), interpretation offers a moment of sharp distinction between early-in-life relationships and the analyst as a new object; for Racker (1968), the distinction is offered in a way that becomes more explicitly caring and restitutive. We know that Winnicottian interpretations are meant to create a sense of holding and that through their interpretations Kohutians attempt to provide empathic mirroring.

In contemporary psychoanalytic practice the participation of the analyst in making an interpretation is being carefully reassessed. Analysts have become more introspective about why they choose interpreting over inquiring or remaining silent (Greenberg, 1995) and are aware that interpretation embodies meaning beyond its specific content, that, for example, it can indicate the "analyst's willingness to be with the patient in the dangerous transference moment" (Greenberg, 1995, p. 12).

From the perspective of the new constructivist appraisal, analysts have begun examining the margin of interaction between patient and therapist that is not intended but that nonetheless may be both potent and often helpful. The risk, which is perhaps felt more deeply in some quarters than in others, is that this trend will lead analysts to underemphasize the unique contribution of interpretive activity. Most analysts would agree that we should be wary of obscuring the difference between what we intend and how we behave. Gill (1993) made a simple but necessary distinction: "An interpretation is usually conceived of as a witting, explicit statement by the therapist. An interaction may be performed wittingly or unwittingly" (p. 115).

Whatever our particular reconfiguration of interpretative activity is, we analysts map the constellation of our therapeutic effectiveness largely by pinpointing moments of interaction in which we offer what we hope is illuminating commentary on the subjective experience of our patients. Out of the clutter of dissociated memory and wish the patient, with the help of the interpretation, may actually perceive self and therapist in a new way. This can be viewed as a systemic effect; the gestalt is changed. However, one might propose, also from a systemic perspective, that the shift in gestalt remains a two-person event, limited to dyadic realities.

By contrast, family therapists are involved in creating new gestalts between people who are multifariously cued to each other. The essence of family therapy is the converse of the psychoanalytic in its simplest form; it involves what is done about what is said. In order for anything to get done in the sense of offering new experience to a family, the family's endlessly repetitive interactions must be interrupted; the "threshold of redundancy," as Minuchin calls it, must be crossed. Certainly, psychoanalysts are interested in crossing the threshold of redundancy of personal neurosis and constriction; we encourage an overelaboration of text, a kind of saturation of the manifest content to the point of dissolution. However, the practice of family therapy, even when multiple narratives are encouraged, is focused on disrupting redundancy more directly, almost surgically. The analyst believes that the power of the unconscious—if an ally and an unlatched gate are offered—will deconstruct falsehood.[1] The family therapist believes that the survival of a rigidly organized family, like a highly organized battalion, will not deconstruct without subversive action. The problem in such a family is that any one member who contemplates rebellion will be surrounded by the friendly faces of unwitting Vichyites. The therapist is outnumbered, even by those who yearn for a change.

In this chapter the texture of intervention in family therapy is illustrated through the examination of case material. To be sure, describing

---

[1]Hirsch and Roth (1995) have provided a useful schema of current psychoanalytic conceptions of the unconscious. They describe the classical position as identifying the mental contents of the unconscious in terms of drive derivatives and defenses against drives, both of which emerge in transference projects. The developmental arrest model assigns "inborn potentials" to the unconscious (Bollas or Winnicott), potentials that the analyst helps nurture to emergence. Lastly, the interpersonal (Sullivan) and relational conflict models (Mitchell) view the unconscious as reflecting "internalized interpersonal relationships and identifications" (Hirsch and Roth, p. 264), which are inevitably dyadically enacted in the transference and countertransference matrix and are reflected upon and subsequently analyzed.

a single case offers a very limited sampling of the work in any clinical arena, but it does provide an opportunity for other clinicians to create alternative hypotheses and think of other approaches, close at hand.

PARENTHOOD AND PARENTS

My work with Lionel (age 33) and Andrea (age 29) spanned one and a half years. Lionel was Andrea's boss in her first job in a creative profession; she was attracted to him from the start. Andrea had a fairly active dating and sexual life. Lionel had always been bisexual; Andrea was the only woman he had been seriously involved with. They had been married for three years.

The genogram (Figure 9-1) illustrates the following historical data: Lionel's Italian-American family was fairly problem ridden. His mother was chronically depressed, hypochondriacal, and somewhat agora-phobic and had turned to Lionel, her second son, for daytime compan-ionship and diversion. Lionel's older brother, Joseph, still lived at home, only marginally self-supporting at age 36. His father played the traditional role of the good provider who is relatively absent from the emotional life of the home (Lionel's feeling was that he was "dropped" by his mother when his father returned home in the evening). Andrea was the older of two children; her younger brother was a kind of ne'er-do-well, who was coddled in his irresponsibility by both parents. Her family was a matriarchal one; her Irish-American father was in the background while her Italian-American mother occupied center stage. Andrea was her mother's glamorous protégé.

Lionel's previous therapeutic experience had been extensive. He saw a child therapist at age nine; a college counselor for one year; another therapist for a year shortly after that; and a therapist once or twice a week for the past seven years, with one year of concomitant group therapy. Andrea had a more restricted exposure: five years before appearing at my office she had gone to a clinic for a brief stint of therapy and five months before seeing me she saw a therapist once every other week for a while in order to discuss her marital difficulties.

Lionel and Andrea were in considerable distress when I first saw them. After losing twins in a miscarriage the year before, Andrea had suffered another miscarriage within the past six months; during both losses she felt that Lionel was not only dispassionate and uncaring but cruelly critical of her. Lionel felt restless and empty in the marriage, as though he were living with a shadowy figure who barely articulated her needs, her wishes, and her thoughts. Their successful business part-

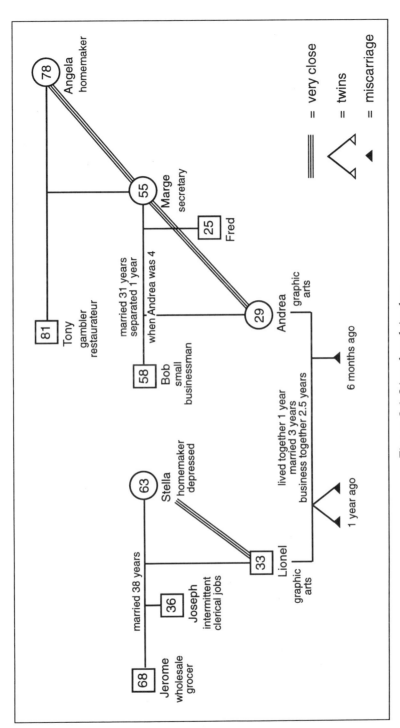

Figure 9-1. Lionel and Andrea.

nership provided a kind of tense connection, though their sexual relationship had become bankrupt. They began to reconnect erotically
early in couples treatment, and three months after they began therapy
Andrea became pregnant. In spite of their marital difficulties, there was
no question for either of them about continuing the pregnancy. It was a
difficult pregnancy; it involved medical complications and periods of
mandated bed rest.

Since I had done considerable research and writing on why people
want to have children, focusing on individual dynamics concerning
gender differences in parenthood motivation and issues of parental
identification and competition (Gerson, 1980, 1986, 1989), during treatment sessions with Andrea and Lionel individual hypotheses and
considerations popped into my head like blinking Christmas tree lights:
Was Lionel ambivalent about fatherhood because he had internalized
so little that was positive in his identification with each of his parents?
Might Andrea be partially compensating for her compromised self-
esteem by wanting to conceive a child in the face of their relationship
difficulties? However, I was committed to maintaining a systemic
frame, and for this particular life cycle transition that meant a focus on
boundary definitions. From working with couples who cannot decide
whether or not to have children, it seems to me that the issue of
boundary permeability is paramount. The boundary ensconcing the
couple has to be sufficiently permeable so that the dyadic unit is capable
of stretching triadically to include a child, but it must also be sufficiently
robust so that the spouses each feel shielded from the emotional failures
in their family of origin.

Overall, my work with Lionel and Andrea was very pleasurable.
Because they were flexible and unconventional, there was really no
family therapy intervention that was off-limits, and I had the experience
of coconstructing a "liminal space" with them. Let me digress briefly to
define liminality, since it captures the essence of family therapy praxis
for me. Victor Turner, an anthropologist, introduced the concept of
liminality into cultural studies. Liminal time is the space–time suspen-
sion in ritual when transformation occurs, that is, when boys become
men, when social class inferiors best their superiors, when decorum
erupts into abandon. Turner (1977) described liminality as follows:

> "Being-on-a-threshold" means a state or process which is betwixt-and-
> between the normal, day-to-day cultural and social states and processes of
> getting and spending, preserving law and order, and registering structural
> status. Since liminal time is not controlled by the clock, it is a time of
> enchantment when anything *might*, even should, happen. . . . There may

be a play of ideas, a play of words, a play of symbols, a play of metaphors. In it, play's the thing. Liminality is not confined in its expression to ritual and the performative arts. Scientific hypotheses and experiments and philosophical speculation are also forms of play [p. 33].

Family therapy interventions are often performance pieces designed to accentuate and heighten liminal experience. The family is the social fabric that is deconstructed. Lionel and Andrea were each capable of losing themselves in the flow of liminal experience. In reality, of course, while they were deconstructing their accustomed relationship in therapy, they were also biologically reconstructing it in pregnancy and plans for future parenthood. Neither Lionel nor Andrea was in individual treatment at the time. However, though I felt that Lionel was more anxious about impending parenthood, I felt that his prior experience in analytically oriented therapy had provided him with the ability to tolerate psychic distress and with a general hopefulness about treatment outcome. Most of all, the reality of Andrea's advancing pregnancy (a palpable reminder that their family configuration was inexorably changing) focused me on the here-and-now patterning in their relationship and its possibilities for change.

Task Assignment

Task assignment is the most straightforward of the family therapy interventions; it is highly recommended in work with nonrigid families experiencing transitional difficulties. However, tasks potentially offer interesting possibilities to all families at various stages of treatment. In the beginning stage of treatment, response to a task is a good indicator of therapeutic resistance; in couples therapy, for example, partners who are unwilling to try something new together are in for a longer trip. Toward the end of treatment, tasks can reinforce a new configuration of a family system, acting like a fixative on a painting that seals in the color with a protective coating.

There is no manual for or catalog of task assignments in the family therapy literature. Nevertheless the family literature provides a ready reservoir of practical—and sometimes deliberately impractical—possibilities. In fact, to the experienced therapist task assignment feels the most pedestrian of all the family therapy interventions. Because there is a modicum of irony and ambiguity in task assignment relative to other interventions, this approach comes to approximate telling people what to do. The psychoanalytic practitioner may be especially wary of task assignment; after all, it is precisely the lack

of utility in telling people what to do that launched the entire psychoanalytic movement, with its focus on what is out of, rather than
in, awareness.

There are two ways to think of task assignment: First, one can think
of tasks as probes, as a dramatic form of inquiry. The hope is that when
the family returns for the next session, the therapist and the family will
have learned something important. If, for example, a daughter is sleep-
ing in her parents' bed every night and it is dad who has heretofore
been the one who has tried to remove her, it is informative to ask mom
to help him take on this particular responsibility. One could learn a
great deal about secret coalitions and the architecture of triangulation in
this family. Moreover, even as inquiry, the task has restructuring potential. Thus, for example, this particular task posits mom as a helpmate,
thereby eliminating a comfortable rationale for father's chronic resentment toward her. More fundamentally, if a therapist assigns the family
this task, he or she will enter further into their web of reciprocal
relationships and will see at closer range how they are sustained. If
mom succeeds or fails or if daughter is relieved or outraged or if father is
pleased or blasé, the therapist will have learned more than a sustained
verbal inquiry in the office could possibly have produced. Task assignment can be viewed as the equivalent of anthropological fieldwork; the
purpose is to secure "local," or subjugated, knowledge, as Foucault
would have it.

Secondarily, as Minuchin (1965) pointed out, tasks increase self-
consciousness. If we accept the fact that it is quite difficult to participate
and observe oneself simultaneously (the epitome of therapeutic talent),
then tasks enable individuals to heighten this dual awareness. The task
becomes a performance piece, and ordinary interactions are spot-
lighted in the artificially heightened stage setting.

How does one prescribe a task? Playfully, soberly, even mournfully,
depending on one's personal style and the mood and organization of
the family. One thing is certain: It is a waste of one's own and the
family's therapeutic time for the therapist not to follow through on task
assignment. If one chooses to create performance art, one should care
enough to see it produced. Otherwise, the frame of intervention is
broken. The family might conclude that the therapist is as hopeless as
they are about changing anything. A family's seeming to ignore a task
assignment is quite the equivalent of an interaction in which an analyst
renders a carefully shaped interpretation only to have the patient
abruptly change the subject. The analyst would certainly inquire. The
same applies in family treatment. If the task is ignored, the therapist
"interprets" the resistance to the family in terms of whatever organiz-

ing dynamic they are currently working with and then generally reassigns it.

Lionel and Andrea were business partners, which naturally made for a particularly intricate web of interlocking dynamics. Their marital complaints about each other were recast in the workplace. However, the context of the workplace had its own special rules and cast of characters and its own special rewards and gratifications. Sometimes their work situation served to rationalize their difficulties, sometimes to intensify them, and sometimes simply to mask them. Thus, their professional relationship and the marital relationship were tangled in a complex knot of discord. It was a systemic mess, and it was important both for our therapeutic clarity and for an enhancement of the spouses good-will toward each other to cordon off work from home. Thus, I assigned Lionel and Andrea the simple task of completely avoiding business talk at home for one week. They complied. They were surprised. What unfolded, paradoxically, was a new perspective on their work relationship, which they decided was considerably more sterotypically gender based than they had imagined. Andrea acted rather like a mother hen in the business, shepherding the work of the female staff while Lionel stomped around shouting directives.

Having more clearly differentiated her role as wife from her role as business partner, Andrea began to grow more discontent with her business role; she also began sensing an opening for self-definition in other areas. Now, in principle, we could have talked at length about the relationship of work and love, and I could have investigated this couple's particular conflicts and resistances on an individual basis. But the discontinuity of arbitrarily separating these domains of interaction provided more ready access for self-awareness. Moreover, by assigning the task to Lionel and Andrea as a couple, Lionel's participation was assured even though the result reverberated more clearly in Andrea's favor. If they had only talked about the issues in my office, Lionel would likely have squelched Andrea's nascent rebellion outside the office through guilt, power, or whatever overlearned gender responses were available. What is more, without the limits set by the task the focus of their discussion might have spread too readily to motherhood, daughterhood, and sundry other relationship systems, with the possibility of a new relationship diffusing like a faint vapor in a dense atmosphere.

Tasks serve as probes that uncover assumptions about relationship reciprocity. It is not that tasks themselves are a healing elixir but, rather, that they release other interactional possibilities in the family's repertoire. Tasks can also serve to maintain an in-session change throughout a longer time frame and are thus a form of intensity building. For

Minuchin (Minuchin and Fishman, 1981), intensity is necessary for the family to hear the therapist's message:

> Cognitive constructions *per se* are rarely powerful enough to spark family change. Nonetheless, therapists are frequently satisfied that a message has been received just because it has been sent. But a therapeutic message must be "recognized" by family members, meaning it needs to be received in such a way that it encourages them to experience things in new ways. Therapists must learn to go beyond the truth of an interpretation to its effectiveness. They can do so by actual observation of the feedback from family members, indicating whether the message has had a therapeutic impact [p. 117].

Intensity can be increased by repeating the same therapeutic message, by describing different interactions with the same therapeutic formulation, and by changing the ordinary and expectable duration of a key interaction (e.g., by making an interaction, either a negative or a positive one, last longer than usual). The injunction to Lionel and Andrea to resist talking at home about business for the seven days between therapy sessions was designed to provide a temporal bulwark for increased intimacy.

The Milan group has evolved a style of task prescription that is ritualistic in nature (Selvini Palazzoli et al., 1978). After identifying a pattern or sequence that is maladaptive, they enjoin the couple to change it—but only on odd-numbered days. Needless to say, this brings the ordinary interaction under the most self-conscious scrutiny and renders the even-day experience somewhat familiarly absurd. In this vein, I might have asked Lionel and Andrea to huddle together at the kitchen table and pore over spreadsheets and designs only on Monday, Wednesday, and Friday nights, hoping that candlelit dinners would have interspersed these self-consciously dreary evenings. Analysts will likely recognize the Janus-like mask of ambivalence here and will wonder at a therapeutic effort arbitrarily designed to separate pleasure and displeasure. However, because couples and family work involve more than one person, ambivalence becomes a shared and complicated matter. Suppose Lionel had thrown caution to the wind and expressed his need for comforting from Andrea, suspending his opposing tendency to oppressively control her responsiveness. Sadly enough, since his ambivalence has now been coded into a shared relationship, Andrea could very likely interpret his genuine risk taking as a new form of interpersonal control seeking. If he sensed this interpretation of his behavior from her, he would likely instantaneously resort to oppressive measures. The wiring between his ambivalence and hers would keep short-circuiting; it might well be impossible for a therapist—even in a treatment session—to keep the circuitry clear. What seems most vital is to provide an arena in which a fresher, dissociated knowledge ("subjugated knowledge" in a Foucaultian sense) can be experienced. Wheelis (1950), writing from a psychodynamic perspective, posited that personality change cannot occur in the absence of action, which he differentiated, somewhat controversially, from thought:

> There is also a qualitative difference between thought and action, although it is not to be found in the nature of the energy involved but in the outcome. Action usually has definite environmental or interpersonal consequences, some of which are irreversible; thought is largely confined within one's self, and—in and of itself—has no external consequences. By thought one can stage an action in miniature, rehearse it, revise it, change the ending. If it suits one, he may then enact it in reality; if it does not, he may discard it without paying the penalties that an unwise action would entail [p. 145].

In the real life of family relationships, thought pales and is often dominated or severely constrained by reiterative action.

It is important to note that task assignment almost always follows an exploration of interactional issues. When it precedes exploration, it is authoritarian; when it follows, it is emboldening or sustaining. From an analytic perspective one would assume that task assignment evokes transference reactions, which might run the gamut of issues—submissiveness versus rebelliousness, delight versus resentment, and so on. However, from a systems perspective one assumes that the emotional traction intensified between the couple is more gripping than the transference response to the therapist. Nevertheless, task assignment does sharpen a sense of therapeutic presence. Optimally, that presence conveys both a belief that experimentation is more valuable than redundancy and a willingness to enter empathically into the life of the couple and imagine alternative realities.

Thematic and Metaphoric Play

> *The Heart has narrow Banks*
> *It measures like the Sea*
> *In mighty—unremitting Bass*
> *and Blue Monotony.*
> Emily Dickinson

Emily Dickinson's metaphoric constructions, which collapse disparate identities into evocative likeness, are often uncannily penetrating in their effect.

> In metaphor, one sign is *substituted* for another because it is somehow similar to it. . . . What happens in poetry, however, is that we pay attention to "equivalences" in the process of *combining* words which are semantically or rhythmically or phonetically or in some other way equivalent [Eagleton, 1983, p. 99].

Metaphoric language weaves throughout much of therapeutic conversation, sometimes undiscernibly and sometimes unintentionally. Family therapists, like poets, use metaphor self-consciously and evocatively. Peggy Papp (1982) noted that "metaphors provide a complete gestalt in which dissociated facts and events can be seen in relation to one another. Explanatory language tends to isolate and fragment, to describe one event followed by another in a linear fashion. Figurative language tends to synthesize and combine" (p. 455).

Metaphor is garnering an important place in psychoanalytic practice. One of the key emphases of the hermeneutic perspective is on grasping the idiosyncratic motifs of a patient's life. Thus, Pizer (1994) noted that in his analytic work he

> found that metaphor is a particularly useful analytic instrument for maintaining the area of illusion, and for bridging the paradoxes of subjectivity and objectivity that govern the perspectives of analyst and patient. The aptness and the utility of a metaphor—one coined by either analyst or patient, but accepted by both as currency within that analysis—reflects the negotiation of approximate meaning that gives each party room to move, to feel recognized but not "had," and which is, in itself, pleasurable as the symbolic range of potential space is conceived in "the marriage of true minds" (an intimate union allowable to both parties in that intermediate area within the constraints of an analytic framework) [pp. 8–9].

Pizer's definition can aptly be applied to work with family members, who also need to feel "recognized but not 'had.' " Metaphor liberates the redundant attributions that a couple or family assume are their lot in relationship life.

Then wherein lies the difference between the analytic and systems theory conceptions of metaphor? First, there is a quantitative difference in the preeminence granted metaphoric imagery in family therapy. Metaphor pervades the family therapy literature like a leavening agent, easing and lightening interventions and the focused, parsimonious pacing of the work. This recurrence of metaphoric imagery and phrasing is not simply decorative. Rather, metaphor is deliberately and strategically invoked to weld interlocking dynamics. As Papp (1982) said of her work in couples choreography, "metaphors are projected into concrete forms and staged so that perceptions, behavior, and interaction are linked simultaneously" (p. 455). Thematic play is an extension of metaphoric work. Rather than let the session meander with the implicit frame being transference and countertransference exploration, family therapists often identify—in fact, organize—an entire session around a particular thematic emphasis. The metaphor serves both to focus the accustomed redundancy and to imaginatively release new interpersonal experience.

In their first year of treatment with me, Lionel and Andrea were encouraged to focus one session entirely on the theme of Mother's Day. Drawing on the calendar event of Mother's Day because it had provoked extended-family conflict, I drenched one session in the permutations, conflicts, and elaborations of motherhood. This session reflected a domain of activity identified by Turner as "liminoid." Liminoid phenomena are the postindustrial equivalent of liminal ritual celebrations or forms in tribal societies. Drama, art, poetry, scientific procedures are all categories of experience that carry us into and through a transitional moment toward redefinition. However, liminoid (as opposed to liminal) experiences are elective, not obligatory, and they are generally idiosyncratic as well as collective. In this session the couple and I were playing with layers of liminoid phenomena: (1) a calendar event, our posttechnological celebration of fertility known as Mother's Day; (2) Lionel and Andrea's current extended family relationships, which reflect timeless anxieties and rites of passage concerning procreation; (3) Lionel and Andrea's specific relationship, with its behavior pattern of Lionel's dominance and Andrea's submission covering an underlying need structure of Lionel as longing and dependent and Andrea as removed and attached to her own mother.

At this time Andrea was seven months pregnant; amniocentesis had indicated that the baby was a girl. With my encouragement, she had been thinking about the matrilineal tradition of her family of origin. She was still extremely solicitous of her mother's feelings; she considered it unthinkable to criticize her and tried to accommodate most of her requests. Lionel was afraid Andrea and her mother would parent their little girl when she arrived and that he would be excluded. We had been talking about Lionel's fear of neglect and Andrea's difficulty in making him number one in her life. Andrea's efforts in this direction, and ironically even more so her success, had uncovered other issues for her husband. Lionel clearly was experiencing anxiety because of the more secure emotional berth and the increased importance his wife was giving him in her life. Could he fill these shoes for her? This anxiety informed Lionel's narrative regarding the celebration of Mother's Day. Or at least that was how I heard the narrative.

What was the narrative? Lionel had the idea of inviting his parents and brother to the apartment to help Andrea celebrate Mother's Day for the first time. His wish reflected a still fragile beginning to both nest building and individuation (in a generational sense) on his part. He was met with multiple resistances by his family of origin: His brother was disinclined to accept the invitation, his mother was unable owing to illness, his father was willing but unsure. Lionel erupted in rage and told them to forget it; he would celebrate Mother's Day alone with his wife.

In the transcript excerpt that follows, the major relationship themes being framed are mutual exclusivity (i.e., that choosing one mother means the rejection of another) and a more variegated context in which multiple loyalties and identifications might coexist. The therapist encourages them to consider the issue of exclusivity. Lionel resists this invitation whereas Andrea embraces it.

> *Andrea:* When you called your father back, that was more out of anger and stubbornness. It was "Forget it! I don't want to have anything to do with it right now!" So right now you are kind of saying there can't be two mothers on Mother's Day. Which is what I wish it didn't have to be. Because it wasn't the concept for Sunday.
> *Lionel:* So making the choice means there can't be two?
> *Therapist:* It has that feeling to me, and as you talk about it, and I think to Andrea even more so. As you decide . . .
> *Andrea:* Yes, a little bit.
> *Lionel:* But I have no problem with *her* mother coming.

The therapist then encourages Andrea to respond to Lionel's resistance, that is, his shift of focus to her mother. Inviting partners to engage intensely with each other in order to expand their ordinary or constricted perceptions and experience is a natural approach in structural family therapy. Here Andrea, not the therapist, can pose the most resonant challenge for expansion; she is both wife and emergent mother, a palpable integrative presence for Lionel. When the therapist encourages increased interaction between the couple, she is also supporting the boundary around their relationship. Though the dynamic text is rivalry and exclusivity, the structural text is boundary resiliency.

Lionel remains somewhat committed to rejecting his family of origin. He shifts his focus to his father and brother, but the therapist brings him back to his mother. His shift seems likely motivated by anxiety, and the therapist senses that the crucible of maintaining shared versus split loyalties lies in his dual attachment to his wife and to his mother.

> *Lionel:* Well, it's interesting. Because I'm sure my mother had a lot to do with this, but I have no anger at my mother about this. It's at my father and my brother.
> *Therapist:* You just said you were not going to be a son anymore. That includes your mother.
> (*A brief discussion concerning Lionel's relationship to his mother follows.*
> *Lionel:* Primary importance. Yes. Is there anything to the fact that it has been so painful being her son, so now I have a better option, why not go for it?
> *Therapist:* I think you are making Andrea nervous.
> *Andrea:* No, not nervous. Whenever he says things like that it doesn't make me nervous. It makes me sad.
> *Therapist:* You know, you did say, "I am her mother." Your baby's. But there was a way you said it before, that I thought . . .
> *Andrea:* In that sense, sure. I can't replace his mother. I think she is such an important . . .
> *Therapist:* Can't you try?
> *Andrea:* Sure. A little bit.
> *Lionel:* No. No!
> *Andrea:* Yes! You always say I remind you of her, anyway, so I'm halfway there. I can try. *(turns to therapist)* I do try, in some ways, to be his mother. In sort of stereotypically maternal ways. *(to husband)* Just like hugging you and holding you. Things like that, that I don't think you got enough of. Like this morning I was holding you in bed. *(to therapist)* But I am not his mother.

In this segment the therapist playfully teases Andrea to collapse her role of mother and wife. Instead, Andrea affirms her identity as a woman in a matrilineal context; that is, she says that she is the mother of their child, just as her husband is the child of his mother. In this way she supports a three-generational familial structure with defined subsystems while talking with Lionel about psychic disruption (i.e., the pain of being a son and the fantasy of renouncing his mother). The therapist does not directly connect to Lionel's distress, and in this sense the work is unbalanced or unsymmetrical. However, the therapist's leaning on one member of a couple sometimes releases redundancy and constriction.

As the session continues, the therapist focuses on intensifying and restating the theme, reworking it like a composer who plays a musical theme in other keys with other instruments. Ultimately, the theme of Mother's Day and the whole symphony of maternal rights and obligations is played back and forth and through each family relationship unit, highlighting old patterns and creating new motifs.

Therapist: To them [Lionel's family] this Mother's Day, this pregnancy, really represents the loss of their son. They may have exactly the same mixed feelings you have. To be in a room with your wife, who is producing a child. They are envisioning exactly the separate, independent family that you are, and maybe they can't take it. They don't want to lose you.

Lionel: Do you think so?

Therapist: I'm not sure. You would have to check it out. Andrea, what do you think?

Andrea: I think there is a bit of that. I think there is probably more of it in his mom than his father. I also think it's just part of her personality. I have never taken it personally, that she wasn't as warm as I would like in a mother, or mother-in-law, whatever you call her.

Therapist: Because you are a son snatcher! He is smirking. (*to Lionel*) You like that.

Lionel: I have exactly the opposite feeling.

Andrea: You are so important to your mother. It's only normal to me for her to have a little bit of that . . .

Lionel: But if I am so important to my mother, my father wasn't so important. I think that my father is extremely threatened by this whole deal.

Therapist: The baby?

Lionel: I think by me in general.

Andrea: Well, that may be true. Because you were in competition with your father. And your mother may be a little bit threatened by me.

Therapist: Maybe he is not used to being a husband. If you really took hold, and went on to be someone else's father, won't there be new demands made on him?

Lionel: I am getting confused.

Therapist: Well, let's stay with your mother. Andrea thinks she took you away to some degree, and that hurt. You don't think so?

Lionel: I think probably.

Therapist: Can you be enough for two women? Soon to be three?

Lionel: I am not sure I was ever loved by the first one. There is that.

Therapist: Andrea, do you think so? You thought you caused her some grief.

Andrea: Yes. I took away her best friend. Her son. I'm sure my mother is going to go through this with her daughter-in-law. You were really an awful lot of things to your mom. Yes, they were happy you were going out with me *(laughs)*, and they liked me at first, and all those nice things. But—maybe that's why they don't celebrate our anniversary.

Lionel: That's true. They've never given us anything for our anniversary.

Therapist: We have complicated your life. You came in with nice, clean anger . . .

Lionel: I still have it.

Therapist: Yes, but now you have some sadness, too.

Lionel: Oh, I was very sad about the whole thing. *(to therapist)* Happy Mother's Day.

In this session I used the theme of the coming Mother's Day celebration as a cultural designation, a lodestone, for exploring the interlocking meanings of motherhood for the couple. What was my overall therapeutic focus in this session? I was thinking, as always, about strengthening the boundary around the couple. Here was a couple about to have a child; they were traveling together to a new stage of the life cycle. It seemed that Lionel's concerns about having more emotional valence for Andrea and thereby overshadowing the importance of her mother in her life was increasing his anxiety and leading to the formation of a maladaptive security operation. He seemed to be trying to contain his anxiety by foreclosing his connection with his own family of origin. He felt that he could not be both a father and a son. But if this magical solution of cutting off his family of origin had transpired, it would have left him feeling not only more bereft and then likely angrier at Andrea but also, quite possibly, even more troubled by his identification with his family of origin and less prepared for fatherhood on his own.[2] In playing with the Mother's Day theme, I attempted to spin with this couple a web of relationships, each one recursively defining the other. The dynamic themes of loss, rivalry, and exclusivity are familiar enough registers for psychoanalysts. However, the therapeutic approach here was active and intentional and thus quite different. I did not, in Bion's terms, enter this session without memory or desire.

To be sure, the session reflected analytic thinking, particularly the shifting and reversing of roles. In the twinkling of an analytic eye, a husband metamorphoses from a son into a father. More problematic

---

[2]Bowenian family therapists have written extensively about the dangers of patients' cutting themselves off from their family of origin, which, it is posited, results in restricted self-awareness and individuation (see Kerr and Bowen, 1988).

from an analytic perspective is the lack of exploration of the transference issues. In fact, Lionel came to the next session alone, and these issues became quite salient (and will be discussed in the next chapter). Suffice it to say here, if I had seen Lionel in psychoanalytic treatment, I would have assumed that his relationship with me would be the site of enactment and transformation; themes of exclusivity and rivalry would have implicated my presence and my participation, and if and when these issues had become clearer with me (as a mother/father/sister figure), I would have assumed that the rest of his character gestalt would shift as well. However, in couples treatment Andrea was present, a real mother-to-be and a maternal transference figure in her own right. The attempt was to obliquely rotate the transference and focus a spotlight on Andrea as helper.

To be sure, there were several troublesome aspects to the session's process, and here I am referring only to what emerged from conscious reflection, not what went unattended. Was Andrea inducted as a therapeutic assistant because she is a woman, that is, the relationship caretaker? Was she submitting to my urgings as she submitted to her mother's demands, thus remaining in a powerless position? Had Lionel's fatherhood transition become paramount as the "real" issue, rendering motherhood the imaginary one? An enactment such as the one I fostered necessarily entails a concretization of something multifaceted in human experience, and not all those facets within it can be attended to equally. On balance, it seemed to me most essential to focus on the integrity of the marital relationship, which was now threatened by the long-standing imbalances in it; by the intrapsychic stress each partner felt; and, most currently, by the extended-family disruption and possible cutoff. Within that frame it was Andrea who could most convincingly and most enduringly bring Lionel back from the brink of relationship fragmentation.

Rituals as Thematic Foci

Perhaps the sharpest lens for focusing thematic interventions is through the use of ritual forms within the therapy process itself. In contemporary modernist—and even more so in postmodernist—culture we are rapidly effacing ritual. Yet the loss of ritual means the loss of the essence of liminal experiences, of a heretofore essential category of human experience, a category that enables us to transcend our own mortality, our own existential sense of meaninglessness, and our isolation. Family therapists who work on the edge of liminality have regularly been moved to comment on the significance of cultural rituals in relation to family therapy process. Thus, Imber-Black, Roberts, and Whiting (1988), in *Rituals in Families and Family Therapy*, identify some of the functions of ritual in culture: marking and making transitions, incorporating contradictions, providing an enactment of roles and relationships connecting past and present and individuals and communities. Might there be a basic need for ritual?

> Admittedly, there still exist rituals, such as the Brazilian carnival, but many have become empty vessels, such as its European counterpart, the *Fasching*, or modern marriage ceremonies. Ritual has largely been forced into the underground and thus . . . threatens the reasonable order of the world by the dark, orphic violence which is typical of the repressed. How many people would find it easier and less painful to overcome the breakdown of their marriage if the banal signing of the divorce papers were embedded into some modern ritual? [P. Watzlawick, 1978, p. 155].

Family therapists early on became interested in ritual as technique. For one thing, the stories families tell about their lives often involve references to rituals. Ceremonial events such as baptisms, anniversaries, and bar mitzvahs, supposedly signifying redemption and continuity, often serve as mirrors to family members that reflect fractures and dysfunction. Particularly poignant in therapy—and this includes analytic as well as family therapy—is the contrast between ritual as renewal and ritualized behavior representing imprisoning redundancy. It was from observing the deadening culture of families living with constricting, ritualized rule systems that Selvini Palazzoli (1974) first conceived of creating new rituals for families as a therapeutic intervention. She wrote:

> The "invention" of a family ritual invariably calls for a great creative effort on the part of the therapist . . . if only because a ritual that has proved effective in one family is unlikely to prove equally effective in another. This is because every family follows special *rules* and plays special games. In particular a [prescribed] ritual is not a form of metacommunication about these rules, let alone about these games; rather, it is a kind of countergame, which, once played, destroys the original game. In other words, it leads to the replacement of an unhealthy and epistemologically false rite (for example, the anorexic symptom) by one that is healthy and epistemologically sound [p. 102].

A colleague reports a ritual intervention that she used while working with a Jamaican mother and daughter a few years ago. The mother centered her life around the daughter, and she seemingly had all the more reason to do so once the daughter became involved with a young man in prison, whom she surreptitiously visited. Each visit brought the mother into closer surveillance of the daughter. The lack of separation between mother and daughter was multiply determined: by the mother's own history with her abandoning mother, by cultural factors, and by interpersonal isolation of both mother and daughter in their particular neighborhood. Thus, the daughter's differentiation had been considerably delayed, and her prison romance was a transparently awkward and halfhearted first step away from a kind of psychological imprisonment. After two months of therapy, the daughter decided to move out of her mother's home, causing much alarm. The therapist decided to create a ritual separation ceremony for them. She asked each to pack a personally designed case or box with specific items. The daughter was asked to pack what was left of her childhood artifacts (i.e., clothes, mementos, and books) so that her mother could keep these as memories for her. Mothers, the therapist posited, serve as the historians of their children's past. The mother was asked to assemble the articles she felt a young woman needed most in setting out on her own (i.e., household items, family treasures, etc.). The mother resisted performing her part of the ritual; she packed a few things but never proffered them. The daughter, however, did her part very thoughtfully and carefully and enclosed a letter she wrote (with the therapist serving as consultant) expressing her wish to stay close to her mother in a new but comfortable way. The therapist saw the daughter just a couple of times afterward, and she reported that following the completion of her part of the ritual she had experienced an uncomfortable coolness between herself and her mother. However, she was able to tolerate this, her mind being generally occupied with the demands of a new training program she had started. Miraculously, her mother, who had absolutely no social life for the previous ten years, had started dating a man! The potential for change had been likely activated by the ritual. Turner (1986) noted the following:

> Those rites we call "life-crisis ceremonies," particularly those of puberty, marriage, and death, themselves indicate a sort of breach in the customary order of group life, after which many relationships among group members must change drastically, involving much potential and even actual conflict and competition. . . . Life crisis rituals (and seasonal rituals, too, for that matter) may be called "prophylactic" [p. 41].

According to Watzlawick, Beavin, and Jackson (1967), what hangs between the digital and the analogic is canonized in ritual.

We are so identified with the rituals of psychoanalytic treatment that sometimes we fail to consider all that is suspended and captured in our analytic ritual: closeness and yet separateness, penetration yet secrecy, submission plus defiance. In fact, the major parameters of our analytic work, especially when they are considered ordinary operating procedure (i.e., optimal frequency of hours, resting position of the analysand, the length of the termination process), can serve to mask the essence of the reciprocal relationship between any particular patient and psychoanalyst. Sometimes a slight elaboration of an accepted analytic ritual can signal redundancy rather than a guiding parameter. In the last vein, an analytic colleague who was committed to working with a patient in the self-psychological model because he believed the patient needed empathic mirroring reported that he had begun to notice an odd ritual that was being transacted between them. At the end of every session, even if the time had run over, the patient stood up, took time putting his coat on, and shook the therapist's hand. The repetitiousness of this highly ritualized interaction was out of the therapist's awareness for a long time. Once he became conscious of it, he realized that he had been suppressing awareness because the ritual made him feel submissive to the patient and controlled by him. He had rationalized maintaining the ritual to avoid challenging the patient, whom he had considered disorganized and wounded. Attending to it, he reorganized his sense of the man's character structure and, actually, his potency.

Reframing

Reframing is probably the most widely practiced family therapy technique, as familiar to the seasoned family therapist as the inquiry is to the interpersonal analyst and as mirroring is to the self psychologist. Watzlawick, Weakland, and Fisch (1974) define reframing as follows:

> To reframe, then, means to change the conceptual and/or emotional setting or viewpoint in relation to which a situation is experienced and to place it in another frame which fits the "facts" of the same concrete situation equally well or even better, and thereby changes its entire meaning. . . . Reframing operates on the level of *meta*reality, where . . . change can take place even if the objective circumstances of a situation are quite beyond human control [pp. 95–97].

The action of reframing is drawn from Russell and Whitehead's logical typing theory; once class membership is changed, membership in the new class becomes the new reality. The quintessential example of reframing is the wearing of the Star of David for the Nazis by the king of Denmark, whereby Jewishness was strategically deconstructed.

When I first met Lionel and Andrea, he bitterly complained about her wishy-washy vagueness and his sense of emptiness living with her. She was distressed by his relentless criticism and rejection. In the first treatment session with this couple I introduced a reframing of their complementarity. They were, needless to say, rooted in their own individual perspectives, convinced that their surrounding environment was not providing the nutrients they required for sustenance. I suggested to them that Andrea was rendering Lionel desperate with her evasiveness and that Lionel's nasty attacks were his only way to reach her. This certainly reversed their complementarity; it gave her a modicum of dignity and relieved his sense of impotence. The element of surprise implicitly bespoke a radical proposition, namely, that things could be different.

Reframing follows a conceptual sequence for the experienced clinician. The first step calls for a disavowal of familiar and accepted explanations. Thus, for these two veterans of individual treatment I was not going to interpret Lionel's lack of empathy in terms of narcissism nor Andrea's tolerance in terms of masochism. One then asks the question, What is a novel way to connect the raw data of interpersonal complaints without relying on the customary hypotheses? Reframing, though seemingly disingenuous, becomes viable insofar as it accesses subtextual realities. It is a way of harnessing these, of integrating ambivalence and complexity. Lionel was both expressing his narcissistic needs and desperate for Andrea's interpersonal presence. Andrea was, in fact, self-effacing and self-denying, but this was in the service of avoiding a commitment to Lionel. The activity of reframing accepts *a priori* that there is another way to view the relationship; it is the couple's and the therapist's task to find it.

The effects of reframing range across a continuum. Sometimes it serves mostly as an abrasive, clearing off the crust of overcertainty and allowing one or more of the family members to associate to new thoughts and possibilities; indeed, sometimes the new possibilities are only peripherally related to the reframed perspective. At other times family members become absorbed by the reframe and elaborate on it until the circuitry of their relationship is coiled around it. Often, the therapist has to reinforce a reframing in various ways—by literally repeating it; by buttressing it with other examples from the couple's repertoire; by drawing analogies to it; and by supporting it with historical multigenerational data, if available. Sometimes one member of the couple or family can be singularly taken by the reframed proposition, leaving the others nonplussed. However, receptivity by anyone in the family incorporates it into the therapeutic relationship. Lionel was more taken by the suggested reframe than was Andrea. It was easier for him to relieve himself of the guilt of hurting her than it was for her to think of herself as an active perpetrator. Reframings can be gentle and stroking, or they can sting. In the latter vein, a colleague who specializes in treating psychoanalysts in couples treatment reports an expectable difficulty: too often the analyst couple is generally overinvolved in reading each other's mind. Where this dynamic has become routinized and unbalanced, the reframing he adopts is to ask the dominant partner, "When did you decide to take your spouse on as a patient?"

An important distinction to be made is the difference between reframing and relabeling. Relabeling is content oriented; it maintains the patterning by calling a rose by another name. Relabeling would have been to call Lionel "demanding"; this would have rendered him a tad kinder than "cruelly attacking" but would still have kept him in a dominant position. A true change in reciprocal experience occurred only when Lionel had the opportunity to see himself as dependent and Andrea as powerfully depriving.

Drama and Action Techniques

Psychotherapy of any form can be read as dramatic text. Both therapist and patient assume roles, imagined and real. Schechner (1986) noted:

> Performances . . . are strictly framed by rules—sometimes labeled ritual, sometimes labeled aesthetic convention—so that spectator-participants can be reassured concerning what is "actual" and what is "feigned"— though each society has its own often shifting definitions of these terms. I would say that everything imaginable has been, or can be, experienced as actual by means of performance. And that, as Turner said, it is by imagining—by playing and performing—that new actualities are brought into existence. Which is to say, there is no fiction, only unrealized actuality [p. 363].

There are many resonances between drama as an art form and family therapy. Many family therapists use role play in supervisory groups for this reason. It has happened more than once that a supervisee has reported being able to empathize with a member of a family for the first time while enacting that person's role during role play. When I teach family therapy to clinical psychology students, I ask them to role-play a family (with a defined problem but not much more forethought). They report that the role play takes on a life of its own. E. M. Forster, for one, noted that characters in novels take on their own lives, beyond the direction of the novelist. So it is with identificatory enactments. In a kind of reversal of this process Sherry Glaser, the author of *Family Secrets,* a play in which she plays four different women in her family, describes the genesis of that work: "I felt myself getting this familiar tense feeling brought on by my mother's craziness, her angry need to control. And I thought, 'Instead of fighting this, I should really become her' " (McGee, 1993).

Role-playing can be particularly useful in couples work. A particularly interesting dramatic intervention has been developed by Chasin, Roth, and Bograd (1989). Each partner in a couple enacts three dramatizations: (1) a desired relationship scene with the other in which the other must perform as the partner wishes (this may require several practice role reversals until the scene is fully realized); (2) a painful past experience, usually from childhood and with the therapist playing the hurtful other; and (3) a revision of the painful scene with the partner playing the previously hurtful other as a healing person. This is a method to use with people fairly grounded in consensual reality, but it is a very interesting technique in which time frames and rigid notions of self expand and deconstruct.

Minuchin (Minuchin and Fishman, 1981), in refining the praxis of structural family therapy, has been particularly interested in dramatic forms and techniques. For example, he emphasizes the dimension of intensity, which addresses the difference between a family cognitively *listening* to a well-formulated interpretation and actually *hearing* a therapeutic message and feeling a pressing and emergent need for change. He recommends several techniques for increasing intensity, one of which is to repeat the same therapeutic hypothesis in several different forms and to apply this hypothesis to different family members. Another technique is to invite family members to continue an interaction after they have mutually signaled each other that the discomfort point has been reached.

Clearly, Minuchin's concept of enactment is dramatically inspired. The enactment begins with the family engaged in a customary and dysfunctional pattern of relating, which Minuchin silently observes and makes no effort to discourage. He then highlights the interactional difficulties and invites change. The family rarely succeeds in resolving the difficulty, which results in Minuchin entering the "third movement" of the enactment, a movement in which he cocreates a family drama with alternative patterning and which ends in a finale in which success is recognized or "punctuated" by Minuchin as different from the ordinary. Therapeutic enactments generate and affirm new possibilities of experience. Of the similarity between theater and family therapy, E. H. Friedman (1984) stated, "Both represent a revolt against the normal use of discourse, and understanding of the natural limits of rhetoric and a recognition that communication is at least as much an emotional phenomenon as a linguistic one" (p. 24).

The use of enactment in family work makes an interesting comparison to the psychoanalytic concept of enactment recently highlighted in the literature. Many analysts are now valuing the dramatization of conflict and the influence of therapeutic action, even when these processes occur beyond language and conscious reflection. In a case discussion Eagle (1993) even went so far as to state, "It seems . . . that this case suggests that positive therapeutic outcome can occur through transference enactments rather than always requiring direct interpretation and analysis of the transference" (p. 104). However, though psychoanalytic enactments are inevitable, in most instances they still function as grist for the mill. Inevitably, psychoanalytic treatment returns to the dense and intense verbal examination of dyadic participation. What is unique about the psychoanalytic treatment relationship is its recursive self-examination, at times playful and at times piercing, and in optimal circumstances always ongoing.

In contrast to psychoanalytic enactments, enactments in family therapy are choreographed. There is less possibility for continuing recursive examination since the domain of relatedness is simply too extensive. Thus, family therapy enactments, rather than serving as the topic for another exegesis, are themselves the intended therapeutic process, providing verbal and kinesthetic awareness. The intention is to fuse verbal and nonverbal, pretend and real, in a form that releases new patterns of relating. This is not to say that nonverbal experience—encoded and reenacted—has not been thought about in the psychoanalytic domain. Bollas (1982), in developing his concept of the "unthought known," stated:

> As in all of our relations with people, we somatically register our sense of a person; we "carry" their effect on our psyche-soma, and this constitutes a form of somatic knowledge, which again is not thought. I am sure that psychoanalysts could learn a great deal about this form of knowing from modern dance where the dancer expresses the unthought known through body language [p. 282].

Bonamo (1990), in fact, has attempted to construct a schema of representation that includes kinesthetic modes and verbal representation in an effort to understand psychoanalytic process. His schema derives from Bruner's developmental observation and includes enactive representation (memories of motor actions), imagistic representation (qualitative data based on input from sensory systems), and conceptual representation (verbal encoding). Translation among the three modes can and does occur at times (e.g., gestural movements may awaken verbal storage). However, Bonamo emphasizes that a boundary can exist between representational modes not necessarily because of the active process of repression but because, for example, aspects of the content were selectively unattended to at the time of encoding. In that case the representation of the event in each mode is preconsciously available but the connections among them may be weakly held, thus preventing real reexperiencing. Bonamo (1990) proposes the specific use of therapeutic metaphor as allowing "for the expression of . . . imagistic and enactive contents" (p. 467). However, the use of dramatic forms in family therapy sessions can release and integrate imagistic and enactive contents far more intensively than can the use of verbal metaphor.

Sculpting (described in Chapter Six) is really a form of dramatic technique. Let us return to our sample clinical case. Over the course of Andrea's pregnancy I did several sculptings with her and Lionel, mostly depicting the anxieties of parenthood. Andrea had a healthy baby girl, and some of the scenarios Lionel had feared came to pass: Andrea became somewhat more involved with her mother than she had been just prior to the delivery. Lionel, feeling displaced, resumed some of the acidic criticism that characterized the couple's relationship when I first saw them, and Andrea was beginning to settle back into her too comfortable one-down but avoidant position with him. (In a session Andrea attended alone I inquired about her professional work. For the first time, I learned that her training had been equivalent to Lionel's. Since he was the boss at work, I had mistakenly assumed that his position was meritoriously based.) At their next visit Lionel was on a critical rampage. He had recently staged a dramatically successful work event and described himself as a "balloon" that Andrea was obstructively keeping tied to the ground. I tried to reframe Andrea's action as "grounding," but it was contemptuously rejected. At the same time, I was aware that Andrea was, as ever, veiling her own talent and competency. At the start of the next session, when the balloon imagery surfaced again, I seized an opportunity to explore themes of ambition and success:

> *Therapist:* What is success to you, Andrea?
> *Andrea:* I have a lot of what I want.

(Andrea's subsequent remarks emphasize recognition from others.)

Therapist: So it's recognition? When you think about personal success?

Andrea: Yes. It's dependent on recognition, what other people think.

Therapist: Actually, if you wanted to create an image like Lionel's balloon, what would be your image of your success?

Andrea: It definitely wouldn't be something solo. I would need support. If it was something up in the air, it would have to be something like a 747 with lots of other people on it.

Lionel: Are you the plane? Or are you just on it?

Andrea: I would probably be the pilot. I would be in charge, but I would have other people.

Therapist: A lot of people?

Andrea: Yes. As I say, it would probably be a 747, and there would be a lot of other people for their support.

Note that Andrea's image of success is an ambiguous amalgam of traditionally feminine affiliativeness carried aloft in a powerful masculine vehicle. Since the former had been her dominant text in our therapy, it seemed to me that her assertive, larger-than-life aspirations might well be subtextually elaborated.

Therapist: Let's just follow it. Where are you flying to?

Andrea: I don't have a destination. I'm just going up.

Therapist: Seven forty-sevens go very fast, very quickly. So what's the destination?

Andrea: There wasn't one.

Therapist: Make one. Play with it. It's interesting.

Andrea: Well, Mars. Not on earth. No place realistic.

Therapist (probing for more elaboration): Try to make it more realistic. Make it someplace you would be recognized.

Andrea: Maybe I would circle La Guardia and come back here. If I wanted recognition, I would want it here, where home is.

(Therapist encourages couple to continue discussing Andrea's imagery.)

Lionel: You are piloting a plane full of people. It means you are the boss, which is pretty grandiose. But then it sounds like you got scared, so you said, "We won't go anywhere." I think there is a part of you that wants to be much bigger than me. I think you want to be queen of the world. Probably that's why you are jealous of me . . .

Therapist: Let's play with this. Let's do one of those sculptings. Do a sculpting of your own personal success, and put your partner in the position he or she would take if you had that kind of success. Fix it in your mind, so whoever goes first doesn't influence the other person.

Andrea: Get down.
(Lionel starts to ask questions.)
Therapist: (to Lionel) No talking. *(to Andrea)* Just choose a position for him.
(Lionel sits on the floor. Andrea raises his hands so he is like an animal sitting up and begging.)
Therapist: Where are you?
Andrea: I'm above. I am higher.
Therapist: Okay. Fix the experience.
Therapist (to Lionel): Now you can do your success.
(Lionel walks to Andrea, puts his arm around her, and stands holding her close.)
Andrea: You did the opposite of what I experienced.
Lionel: The begging was a nice touch.
Andrea: It wasn't so much begging. I was a little jealous. Maybe it was begging, but it was also scratching.
Therapist: What would you do if he scratched?
Andrea: Probably nothing.

Andrea had moved from a general desire for recognition from others — which doesn't travel very far—to a stinging sense of what recognition meant to her with Lionel. Note that Andrea was able to articulate aspects of her suppressed wishes and ambitions when the approach ensures reciprocity, that is, when Lionel was actually available for her to plastically model and when she could remain in total control of the medium. One is reminded here of Benjamin's (1988) discussion of the vicissitudes of mutuality in which she emphasizes the intersubjective need for recognition as an essential corrective to an illusory ideal of autonomy. A corruption of mutuality is the need to dominate the other, to deny dependence on the other as the source of recognition. Andrea seemed caught in this dilemma. Suppressed and conflicted for so long about seeking recognition, she could fantasize about it in Lionel's presence but only when she could dominate him. However, she was likely attuned to his ambivalence about her attaining success—though he stated otherwise—and thus her wish to control him included control over feared retaliation. Unfortunately, her fantasies, though released, were transient. She was always at the cusp of retraction.

In the following transcript excerpt the therapist encourages an expansion and intensification of the sculpted imagery:

Therapist: Sometimes it's helpful to sculpt what is, and then sculpt the ideal.

Lionel: I could sculpt what is!

(He takes Andrea to the wall and turns her to face it. Then he climbs onto a hassock and stands teetering on half of it and motions to the half left empty. They sit back down.)

Therapist (to Andrea): Say what you felt and see if it matches with what he wanted you to feel.

Andrea: I felt stupid with my face to the wall.

Therapist (to Lionel): Do you understand? You can ask her. You can interview her about your sculpting.

Lionel: Do you feel like a dunce?

Andrea: I felt stupid. Not like a dunce in the corner, but maybe opportunity's here and I am not taking it.

Therapist: Why don't you?

Andrea: Scared? I don't know if it really is there for me. I don't know if I'm scared to take it, or I don't feel I deserve it, or . . .

Therapist (to Lionel): So why don't you tell her what you were trying to convey . . .

Lionel: She's very right. Andrea's place was there, but Andrea was in the corner, ignoring it, punishing herself.

Therapist: For what?

Lionel: That's the problem.

Therapist: I am going to push you because this is something sculpting can help with. For what?

Lionel: Because she is angry. Because she doesn't deserve it. Andrea doesn't want to be the less famous one. She wants to be the famous one.

Therapist: She wants you on your knees.

(The therapist proceeds to play with all the imagery of the session, mixing visual and narrative representations.)

Therapist: The 747's flying to Paris, and the famous artist gets out. And the money's coming in, and you're earning it and supporting your family . . . as a woman, can you be good in that way?

Andrea: Yes. I think I am capable of that.

Therapist: And getting the recognition that he would?

Andrea: No. I am not capable of getting the same kind of recognition.

Therapist: Why not? *(gestures that Andrea should talk to Lionel)*

Andrea: I don't know. Scared? I want it. But I am afraid.

Therapist: We have to figure out what's scary. You see, you sculpted something scary. It's there, and we shouldn't deny it. You are afraid that if you got it, he would scratch your eyes out. It is a metaphor, it's a fantasy. But it's very powerful.

Andrea: Sure.

Therapist: Okay. Why don't you talk to him about it?
Andrea: I feel like I just hurt him—made you *(to Lionel)* feel bad—and I don't want to do that. Because I know I should be able to ask for what I want, and I can't.

Later in the session, Lionel's image of the balloon is again discussed:

Therapist: If you don't have someone holding you down, you'll go out of control.
Lionel: That's what employees are for, to hold you down.
Therapist: Maybe. Maybe. Maybe he is changing your job description.
Lionel: That's actually something we've been trying to figure out how to do.
Therapist: You are scared, Andrea. Do you want to think about it?
Andrea: Yes.
Therapist: Why not talk about this together. I want you to talk about it this week, without threats. Can you do that for a week?
Lionel: Without talking about divorce?
Therapist and Andrea: Yes.
Therapist: Without any suggestion of dissolution or ending, for just one more week. Because this feels tame here, but I think it could get hotter. And if it gets hotter, I want it to be without explosion.
Lionel: I don't see why you feel this is such a hot issue!
Therapist: Your wife is very frightened about this.
Lionel: Why? What is so frightening?
Therapist: Because she experiences you—and she is a perceptive woman—as the kind of figure who could pounce and scratch.
Lionel: But I am not! The fact is that—like, I have an assistant I have launched into his own business. I encourage everyone to do all the good things they can. So when you are looking at me and feeling that—who am I? I am so frustrated! Whose resonances am I giving you?
Andrea: I don't think it is coming from you. I mean, trying to be good . . . I don't know whether this is childhood or background stuff, or putting it on you . . .
Therapist: I think it is always both. But I think you should focus on the two of you.

For me the impact of this session was that aspects of Lionel and Andrea's relationship became articulated for the first time. The imagery slid across a "chain of signifiers," as Derrida would have it. Clearly, the images were spontaneous and perhaps evanescent, but they were public, to husband and wife and therapist. Once Andrea's suppressed wishes to be recognized and desired were identified, they became the basis for a kaleidoscope of reciprocal perceptions. Andrea became less elusive, and she was able to identify Lionel's grasping competitiveness. Lionel became intrigued by her challenge. However, it is important to note that though the issue of Andrea's suppressed ambition and feared retaliation from Lionel was dealt with effectively through this intervention, other marital issues required attention and resolution in the months that followed. Though family therapy interventions are compelling within one session, interventions generally act by accretion as we have seen in the work with this couple. Each intervention was directed at a particular area of dysfunction at the same time the effect of the intervention diffused throughout the general patterning and context of the relationship.

Summary

The therapeutic engagements delineated in this chapter offer considerable contrast to our customary psychoanalytic experience. The family therapeutic stance is active, intentional, and often explicitly experimental and playful. In their office family therapists face a group whose meaning systems are coded in multiple channels across individual subjectivities. This multiple coding and multiperson participation makes these meaning systems inaccessible to ordinary inquiry and interpretation. However, for the clinician comfortable in both modalities the interventions that are characteristic of family therapy practice can in many instances be enriched and understood by appropriately indexing psychoanalytic theory. The nature of interventions in family treatment potentially offer a new perspective on our accustomed psychoanalytic assumptions about the process of change. Here we turn to a perspective on liminality introduced into the family therapy literature by Kobak and Waters (1984), who proposed that the experience of family therapy itself replicates the structure of ritual, of which liminality is the middle phase. They stated, "We believe the notion of rites of passage lends an overall coherence to the development of the therapeutic setting. Therapy in our view can act as a rite through which a family system passes and emerges in a new state" (p. 99). In this connection Turner cited the folklorist Van Gennep (1909), who divided the ritual process into three phases: a separation phase (withdrawal from the ordinary social world), a liminal phase (play, flow, and antistructure), and a reaggregation phase (the return to ordinary life). Psychoanalytic treatment can be viewed similarly. Are not the heated debates within psychoanalysis regarding frequency of sessions, recumbent or upright positions, and membership in privileged societies but evidence of its ceremonial structure? This is in no way pejorative. The psychoanalytic experience is framed and deepened by a division of the sacred from the profane and by the timelessness of the analytic hour. Certainly, Freud, with his profound sympathy for the mythic and the occult, helped imbue the psychoanalytic enterprise with this liminal ethos. However, for a multiplicity of sociological and cultural reasons, the psychoanalytic ritual experience reflects solemnity more than play or abandon. In fact, the rigidification of psychoanalytic ritual has been most pronounced in America, a fundamentally puritanical culture and one that is largely devoid of deeply rooted endemic ritual structures. It may be that psychotherapeutic work in a more playful, experimental modality, which nonetheless at times can offer moments of transformation, may lead psychoanalysts to reconsider what have been considered givens in our tradition.

In our current postmodern context, psychoanalysts arguably have become as concerned about the suppression of passion as about its dangerous release. In an electronically organized society we are as concerned with the mechanization and objectification of the self as with its disruption. Perhaps permitting more ritual, liminal unruliness in our process – in whatever form we choose – might offer a deeper experience of renewal and transformation to our patients.

chapter ten

The Therapeutic Relationship

There is a right size for every idea.
Henry Moore

Working with families feels totally different to analysts. The exploration of unconscious material becomes more diffuse in family therapy. Of course, unconscious derivatives and representations are ever present, but because these representations span several psyches of several family members, they cannot be easily decoded. For similar reasons, transference and countertransference, the heart of dyadic analytic work, moves from figure to supportive groundwork in family therapy. More compelling than an exploration of transference to the family therapist is a systemic grasp of the relationships between family members. And more essential than open-ended countertransferential awareness is the task of following one's experience of participation while staying focused on active and somewhat experimental intervention.

For the analyst, the issues that arise in making this shift include everything from soup to nuts in the psychoanalytic canon. The contours of the treatment relationship are different, issues of neutrality and engagement take on different parameters, the tracking of transference and countertransference diminishes radically, and the inevitability of enactment in treatment takes on an entirely different coloration.

Of these shifts the diminishment in attention to the transference and countertransference, the conceptual anchors of the psychoanalytic relationship, is the most unsettling to the psychoanalyst. One of the most compelling narratives in psychoanalysis is that of Freud's coming to terms with the inevitability and resistant strength of transference. Freud had to abandon his belief that the power of his patients' attachment to him would vitiate their neuroses. Moreover, he had to recognize that it was in fact the fervor of their attachment that was blinding them to the possibility of renunciation and change and that only by offering himself "in effigy" for unrequited longings could irrational bonds be dissolved (L. Friedman, 1988). The paradoxes inherent in Freud's original discovery have seeded multiple dilemmas and controversies in our working use of this concept. In fact, Freud continued to rely on what he considered positive transference, converted by some into a concept of the working alliance or, currently, into the notion of holding the patient through the tortured labyrinth of transference qua resistance exploration. Schimek (1983) questioned this approach and stated that "this facilitating transference is just as much a transference, just as much a repetition, a reenactment rather than a memory of the past, as the resistance transference is; it has the same origin, in childhood libidinal wishes and conflicts" (p. 439). The most radically intensive transference focus was proposed by Gill, who believed that analysts must remain vigilant to the most oblique reference to their person.

The idea of countertransference developed as a by-product of transference and was originally thought of as a necessary evil demanding recognition and subjugation. When Freud first introduced the concept in 1910, he admonished the analyst to "recognize his countertransference in himself and overcome it" (p. 144). However, Tansey and Burke (1989) have asked, "Did he mean eliminate the countertransference response, which is to be regarded *only* as an impediment deriving solely from the analyst's unresolved conflicts; or did he mean attempt to analyze and understand the experience, thereby reducing its intensity?" (p. 11). This question frames what Tansey and Burke rightly identified as the current countertransference dialectic in psychoanalytic theory, namely, the opposition between the classical position that countertransference is obstructing and the "totalist" position that all the feelings evoked in the analyst are both inevitable and informative.[1]

Today countertransference has become a vital component of psychoanalytic treatment. When the heart or gut quickens to a countertransference reaction (which often only occurs after the fact, in the analyst's dreams or as an embarrassing faux pas), the analyst feels most engaged and most in the thrall of transformation. Friedman (1988) noted:

> His most important datum is the *impact* he feels, and impact means that the therapist's own wishes and attitudes are affected. The therapist would like

[1]Whatever our specific conceptions of transference and countertransference, it is clear to analysts of all persuasions today that what we perceive regarding transference material and what we allow ourselves to know about our countertransference is informed by these very conceptualizations. Interpersonalists do not see envy in the transference as often as do Kleinians, and Fairbairnians do not experience themselves as aggressive as often as classical analysts do. As Schimek (1983) noted, "Strictly speaking, there is no such thing as transference, only transference interpretations, that is, patient behaviors which are selectively perceived, labeled, and interpreted as transference" (p. 452).

to have the most general, objective attitudes, but if he did not have particular attitudes he would not feel an impact, and he would have no receptors for the patient's meaning. He must keep particular dramatic attitudes alive within himself even though they pull him away from abstract, objective theory of the mind. A therapist who could not be put on the spot would probably never know what is happening [p. 529].

There is a straightforward rationale for rendering transference and countertransference as background, not foreground, in couples and family work: there is not enough time. Psychoanalytic theory today embraces a two-person psychology; its basic unit of investigation is the dyad (Ghent, 1989). Yet transference is hard enough to get hold of in a dyadic field. After all, transference is essentially an expression of unconscious longings (the reason they are "transferred" is because they are dissociated). Transference is not a single snapshot but, rather, a slowly emerging collage, and the collage components simply do not and cannot get adequately identified in family therapy. Attitudes toward or reactions to the therapist, yes, but the amalgams of unconscious and conscious percepts that we think of as transference constructions, no. If transference could be adequately identified in family therapy, all of psychodynamic psychotherapy and psychoanalysis would indeed be very brief.

Moreover, from an operational standpoint the presence of one or more significant others in a therapy session influences the transference experience and its communication. Thus, exploring in a family therapy session the transference reactions of a husband necessitates taking into account the fact that everything he says about himself or the therapist is uttered with his wife as witness. The data are implicitly organized by the here-and-now relationship context. The same operational constraints affect other psychoanalytic concepts, such as resistance. What is resistance in a couple? Shared between them but how? How do you combine individual meaning systems without being facile or heavy-handed? These questions invite contemplation, to be sure, but only when one has the time and the space for it.

Consider George and Martha, the couple from Edward Albee's (1962) *Who's Afraid of Virginia Woolf?* Let us remind ourselves what they are like. The following is a sample:

Martha: (armed again): Well, maybe you're right baby, SNAP! It went snap tonight at Daddy's party. (Dripping contempt, but there is fury and loss under it) I sat there at Daddy's party, and I watched you. . . . Watched you sitting there, and I watched the younger men around you, the men who were going to go somewhere. And I sat

there and I watched you, and *you* weren't *there!* And it snapped! It
finally snapped! And I'm going to howl it out, and I'm not going to
give a damn what I do, and I'm going to make the dammed biggest
explosion you ever heard.
George: (Very pointedly): You try it and I'll beat you at your own
game.
Martha: (Hopefully): Is that a threat, George. Hunh?
George: That's a threat, Martha.
Martha: (Fake-spits at him): You're going to get it, baby.
George: Be careful, Martha . . . I'll rip you to pieces.
Martha: You aren't man enough . . . you haven't got the guts.
George: Total war?
Martha: Total. (Silence. They both seem relieved . . . elated) [p. 75].

Where would a couples therapist start with them? What inquiry would
unlock this vise of sadomasochistic behavior? Would a transference
enactment be anything more than gladiator fare or one of their playful
interludes of triangulation, more neutralized, one would hope, than
"hump the host"? Martha and George's reciprocity, circularity, and
complementarity are particularly invariant and particularly grisly in
content. However, the form of it (i.e., the interlocking and endlessly
redundant process) is, unfortunately, what much of matrimony is made
of. What can we draw on to rechoreograph this duel to the death?
Sander (1979) wrote an interesting exegesis of this play from a systems
and largely classical psychoanalytic perspective, with particular reference to the issue of childlessness and the family life cycle. Whatever
transference (individual and/or shared) these two people form toward
their therapist will undoubtedly have to do with their individual histories and dynamics, reflected, of course, in a shared choice of fantasied
rather than real parenthood. However, how is one to hear those complex thematic notes above the booming rhythms of their hostility? As
for the analyst's countertransference, would it be to them as individuals, to them as a couple, or both? One is indeed put on the spot, in
Friedman's terms, but in a very different way.

THE THERAPEUTIC ALLIANCE

Obviously, how one approaches work with any patient is defined by
what one considers to be the outlines of the therapeutic relationship.
This is a deceptively simple expectation. To begin with, there is a
growing body of research on psychotherapy effectiveness that cites the

quality of the therapist–patient relationship (i.e., the patient's experience of affirmation, helping, and protecting) as a crucial variable in predicting therapeutic outcome (Henry, Schact, and Strupp, 1986). Relationship factors press on psychoanalysts in a very complicated way. We assist, as midwives in self-discovery, but we know that we cannot will its moment nor fashion its features. We rely, most of all, on a belief in a certain process, a frame for our moment-to-moment clinical encounters. All of therapy is a game in the best sense of the word, noted Bateson (1972), requiring a frame of expectations. In this vein, E. A. Levenson (1992) noted:

> Without a container for the therapy, the therapist would be overwhelmed, lost in a chaotic "real-life" participation. So, in addition to a doctrinaire position, analysts require a carefully contrived and maintained psychoanalytic frame which defines, in advance and somewhat arbitrarily, all those condition of therapy which may be considered as superordinate to the content [p. 558].

If we collapse our frame, we get lost in a constructivist morass. Nonetheless, there is a growing trend in psychoanalysis today to be less interested in parameters and technique, the girders of the psychoanalytic frame. Because of their heightened interest in regressive experience, object relations theorists, such as Winnicott and Guntrip, loosened the strictures of traditional technical approaches. Ferenczi and Fromm daringly experimented with these parameters. Today it is probably more difficult than ever to distinguish between a countertransferential rejection of a frame constituent because it seems too arbitrary and a wish to enact something going beyond the frame because it offers fulfillment of a self-serving need. The current trend, for the most part, has been to worry less about frame violation and more about relationship enhancement. However, is it not true that our helpfulness, our relationship quality, lies precisely in how self-aware we are in working within our chosen therapeutic frame? Should we not be able to psychically relax into our methodology if we believe in its integrity and usefulness? The frame in this sense sustains the therapeutic relationship. Blum (1992) correctly noted that "interpretation involves a corrective analytic experience, as does the analytic alliance and the continued analytic experience of acceptance, interest, and empathy—of understanding and being understood" (p. 259).

When psychoanalysts first begin working with couples and families, they feel caught in a kind of briar patch of conflicting frame directives. Without shifting to a systemic focus, an analyst can feel unduly concerned about unleashed expressions of aggression or interpersonal accusations of hurt and betrayal among participants in family sessions. Garden-variety sadomasochism like George and Martha's can be seen as an emotional time bomb. The circularity or redundancy of the interaction, overshadowed by its cruelty, is often unattended to. In an effort to be helpful without rooting in a systemic frame and to avoid feeling uncomfortably vulnerable to treatment failure, analysts reenter the analytic frame and often make individual assessments and prematurely recommend individual therapy. There is a pull to feel more sympathetic toward the more self-reflective, self-expressive (though not necessarily the more systemically virtuous) partner in a couple. In contrast, working within a frame of systemic thinking, of interlocking dynamics, helps bolster therapeutic stamina and vitality.

A NEW NEUTRALITY

Neutrality is a fundamental psychoanalytic tenet, albeit defined and redefined by every major psychoanalytic theorist. Adopting a systemic view when working with a couple or family enhances one's ability to stay both balanced and noncollusive with whatever dysfunction is present in the room. On the other hand, analysts who try to grasp individual psychologies and individual transferences often feel uncomfortably lopsided in their working alliances. Neutrality might come easily in working with George and Martha. Their viciousness is executed with such parity that one is hardly drawn to a lopsided sympathy reaction. In fact, the ever-escalating and symmetrical vitriol almost masks the individual texture of their dynamics. However, remaining balanced becomes considerably more difficult when presented, for example, with a couple in which the husband seems self-involved and unreliable because of his overextended schedule and the wife appears distraught and helpless. If the husband rages defensively, there is a therapeutic undertow to challenge his self-absorption. However, viewing the wife's distress as accusatory (and it likely would be in his experience) balances the undertow. One could speculate about whether the wife's distress makes the husband feel lonely or sadistic, and one could raise these as therapeutic questions. Once one works with concepts of complementarity and symmetry, of the seesaw of power and hierarchy, attention to the relationship configuration largely replaces attention to individual data. Systemic balancing potentially gives one a subjective sense of lightness. Nonetheless, the experiential reality is that a relatively strong pull to one person's dynamics is often present, at least transiently, a pull to which family therapists refer when they speak of "discharging linear hypotheses." Sometimes supervisors will encourage a whole group to give voice to a passionate individual assessment, or rather invective, such as, "How can she put up with a creep like that?" The sentiment is qualified by the command function: this is only half a relationship circle.

By noting reciprocity in dynamics the therapist is able to initiate therapeutic action that highlights previously unattended provocations. For example, it can feel uncomfortable to a trained analyst to somewhat peremptorily stop a family member from detailing suffering at the hands of a significant other. We are accustomed to giving space to the pain our patients feel. In couples work, however, personal suffering at a content level is generally accompanied at a pragmatic level by denunciation of the significant other as a perpetrator. This generally makes the perpetrator either angrier and more attacking or more humiliated and withdrawn. Thus, not much therapeutic use is served from hearing out the testimony, however heartfelt the need to recount it. Empathy is frequently overridden in family therapy in the service of loosening rigidity.

STANDING OUTSIDE THE CIRCLE OF INTIMACY

Analysts ordinarily work in intense emotional proximity to their patients. When one moves to a more systemic position, it is as if one moves to a more temperate climate. The couples or family therapist is now standing outside, not inside, the circle of intimacy.[2] This new emotional stance is not easy. Stegner (1989) divided all of psychoanalytic theory and practice into two versions, or "visions," of reality: the classical and the romantic. The essence of the classical position is that we must overcome our wayward impulses and strive toward a compromised satisfaction in life. The essence of the romantic vision (embodied by Winnicott and Kohut) is that our birthright grants us the potential for ongoing joyful vitality and meaningfulness. Though Stegner has captured an interesting bifurcation within psychoanalytic theory, it would seem that the essence of psychoanalytic engagement is inherently romantic, being a commitment to restore vitality and meaning to lives rendered inauthentic, constricted, or false. In fact, psychoanalysts are probably among the last romantics in a detached, ironic postmodern

[2]The therapist creates interventions that burrow into the accustomed and the redundant within family interactions, but these are crafted from the position of outsider to the circle of intimacy the family inhabits.

era. Are we not drawn to the work because of its interpersonal intensity? Moreover, for some or all of us, this valence may be partly compensatory, giving us an opportunity to experience an intimate relating that was inadequately available developmentally or is not sufficiently accessible in our current relationships. But even if it is not partly compensatory in nature, it is hard to imagine a person being drawn to analytic work who does not have a certain characterologic relish for intimacy.

Thus, standing outside the essential circle of intimacy is not easy for psychoanalysts. What one must develop is an empathic response to a relationship system, not to the individuals within it. What compensates for the loss in dyadic intimacy in family treatment? Its obverse: the pleasure of experiencing emotional intensity at close range without feeling central to it or responsible for it. In the case of George and Martha a therapist would be grateful for an opportunity to observe rather than participate and would want to have some idea of how to avoid even the most subtle indication of support for one spouse over the other. Of course, a new and encompassing circle of intimacy is formed when the therapist offers a glimpse of his or her perspective through an intervention. Therapist and family then stand within a newly formed arena of participation. However, a large part of what the couples therapist treating George and Martha would feel would be a heat- and energy-emanating intensity radiating outward from their duel-to-the-death circle of intimacy.

If there is a unique sphere of countertransference experience in couples and family therapy, it is likely within the domain of "outsider experience," with whatever meaning that holds for the therapist. From an analytic perspective, this is the relatively uncharted domain of countertransference. I suppose that in thinking about the experience of exclusion, classical theorists would index the feelings accompanying oedipal exclusion. Interpersonalists might consider juvenile or preadolescent experiences as templates (being excluded from the game can be more difficult than being implicated in it). Relational theorists might invoke some vital lack of connectedness in early childhood (such as Andre Green described in relation to a child's confrontation with "the dead mother," i.e., one who is literally alive but emotionally absent). But however one indexes outsider experience theoretically, it is likely to be something that the analyst is accustomed to empathizing with in a patient, not feeling in himself or herself. It is a relatively rare patient whose self-preoccupations can be relentlessly enough expressed in interpersonal pressure to make the analyst in the room feel like an outsider. But families can do this much more readily; indeed, excluding outsiders is part of how families function. Thus, the therapist must come to terms with the role of outsider to be effective.

At first glance, it may seem reasonable for analysts who are newly involved in family work to index their countertransference as a way of potentially getting a sense of what the family may be putting out by way of "shared transference." However, appreciating shared transference does not automatically bring us affectively closer to family members. To be sure, a couple or family may present with a shared relationship style, and it is in these instances that explication of something we can call a "shared transference" can be useful. But the therapeutic trajectory, like a boomerang, should return to the circle of intimacy. Working with a couple who, for example, are equally inconsiderate of the therapist (e.g., leaving food wrappers behind in the office or paying bills late) should evoke the pertinent *intra*relationship question "What does this kind of shared disrespect distract them from within the relationship? Sensing a transference dynamic of dependence toward the therapist shared across family members leads one to similarly reflect on intrafamily dissociation. The question becomes, What would happen if these people faced how much they needed each other? Partially, this is simply a matter of conceptual economy. To consider separate individual dynamics about frustrated dependence on the part of two parents plus two children—or even one husband and one wife—leads to a kind of unsolvable algebra of relationships in which there are too many variables and not enough formulas. Beyond this, the therapist must bear in mind that it is the family's job to solve the equations—or to find new ones.

Sometimes the intracouple issue is stated in couples therapy, but its impact is registered only when it is replicated in the therapeutic relationship and enlivened by the therapist's participation. If there is an important dynamic of secrecy within the life of a couple, then secrets might well be kept from the therapist. For example, clinical work with one couple in which the husband cross-dressed seemed to revolve around a principle of mutual exclusivity. The key meaning of his cross-dressing was that his wife felt excluded from being a woman. Gradually, it became apparent that the couple kept important secrets from their therapist regarding their commitment and payment. It seemed they could only feel like a couple with a therapist if they actively excluded the therapist as a trustworthy agent of change.[3] Once the therapist was able to raise this relationship issue with them, it emerged that implicit in it was a shared phobia regarding ambiguity. It was in discussing that phobia as a therapeutic issue that the couple finally took

---

[3]Let us distinguish this kind of exclusion from the ordinary resistance that any couple will show.

hold of their anxiety. But here we should note that while the therapist's participation allowed the intracouple dynamic of exclusion as a defense against anxiety to be mobilized in a way that allowed for its examination, this is a far different process than what would be entailed in tracking their individual transferences. Working with and trying to merge both spouses' representations of their parents into something integral and coherent would strain even the most nimble psychoanalytic imagination.

TRACKING COUNTERTRANSFERENCE

An important part of Gill and Hoffman's (1982; Hoffman, 1983) landmark contribution to the understanding of the matrix of transference and countertransference is their emphasis on the legitimacy of the patient's noticing the idiosyncratic in the analyst's behavior. The patient thereby has a window into the analyst's character, but, as Gill and Hoffman note, the view through this window is often clouded. A patient may accurately perceive an aspect of the analyst's behavior, but patient and analyst may radically differ about the meaning attributed to this behavior. A patient may accurately perceive that the analyst is uncomfortable in presenting a bill for missed sessions; what the patient believes is embarrassment about unfair business practices might be "owned" by the analyst as fear of retaliation for acquisitiveness. The possibility of having a therapeutic effect lies in the negotiation of these attributional differences.

Patients notice—and certainly on occasion take exception to—the behavior of family therapists as well. How one incorporates this material is, once again, complicated by the fact that though one member of the couple or family may raise the issue, the relationship context includes significant others. The most parsimonious approach is to view the issue systemically. For example, a wife in couples therapy began a session by rebuking me sharply for overemphasizing her anger the week before and for generally faulting her more than her husband for psychological deficits. In a flash I checked out the countertransferential reality that the woman did indeed anger me because of her accusatory style, which had made me feel abused by her on occasion. However, I did not think I had found greater fault with her than with her husband. (The husband irritated me because he remained enragingly rational and disengaged, no matter how much his wife tried to invoke his recognition and sympathy—albeit often in a provocative fashion.) Thus, I thought she was right about my response to her but inaccurate in comparing my responses to her with those to her husband. Responding to her challenge, I first expressed appreciation for her being direct with me and acknowledged that I may have spoken too sharply. From an intervention perspective, I challenged her husband for failing to respond to her: How could he have turned a deaf ear to her distress? Why hadn't he taken it seriously when she brought it up with him during the week? Why did he compulsively treat her responsivity as explosive and irrational? Her sense of being attacked by me reflected an ongoing experience that her emotional responsivity was always ridiculed or dismissed. This dynamic characterized her childhood experience, but it was being disturbingly enacted in her marriage. I think it would have been wrong not to acknowledge my own irritated response to her, but her accusation about my behavior was posed with her husband present. Since that was the case, I chose to shift her challenge back into the circle of intimacy rather than be a stand-in for a member of it.

Overall, because their therapeutic eye is focused on reciprocal family dynamics, family therapists (even when psychoanalytically trained) inquire less about observations and reactions by family members than they do in individual treatment. The analysis of "mutual influence," as Aron (1991) designated it, is encouraged between family members, not from them. One generally avoids drawing therapeutic energy away from the partner or family member as an agent of renewal and hope.

Mother's Day Revisited

Let us return to Lionel and Andrea as a case example. The signature of my work with this couple was a determined distance taking from each spouse's individual dynamics. Why? They were a couple facing a real event—pregnancy. Transference configurations did not provide the fulcrum of awareness concerning conflicts about motherhood or fatherhood. These conflicts were literally expanding and dilating in the couple's relationship. However, from an analytic perspective, one knows that therapists are magnets for transference constructions; the task in family therapy becomes that of staying aware of these constructions without becoming focused on them in the sessions. In the following transcript material the reader can track just how the inevitable evocation of transference feelings interpenetrated a deliberate focus on the couple's relationship.

This excerpt is from the transcript of the session following Mother's Day. Lionel arrived alone because Andrea had suffered an obstetrical crisis that required bed rest. I remembered my thematic emphasis and activity from the session before, and I remembered its coda—Lionel saying to me, "Happy Mother's Day." For a while in the treatment I felt that Lionel regarded me as more than a good-enough mother, and most of the time I felt like one! In this session Lionel reported that he was very depressed and had been obsessed with physical ailments all week, fearing that he would die. His parents never materialized for Mother's Day. In a brief Mother's Day greeting on the phone Lionel found his mother noticeably "cool" and disturbingly insistent that he had intended to exclude his brother from the family festivities.

Lionel: It's exactly the way they would treat a stranger. It's as if they were invited to a stranger's house for the first time who they didn't know well enough to ask, "Is Joseph invited?"

Therapist: You mean you're the stranger and he's the insider? So when I asked you last session, "Can there be two mothers on Mother's Day?"—You remember that was kind of our theme—the focus shifted to you and Joseph.

Lionel: Maybe it became "Can there be two sons on Mother's Day?" But why not? Really, what is a son? Do sons ever leave?

Therapist: Maybe they become strangers.

Lionel: It's like being cast out. I don't think I did anything to warrant it. I've done everything that is good.

Therapist: You worked; you got married; you're having a child. Maybe that's the last straw.

Lionel: It's so painful for me to be cast out. I've been cast out my entire life. In the first part of it it was because of their manipulation. They didn't want me to have friends, and they dressed me differently. Now I fit in but I'm still cast out.

Therapist: It's like you're cast in *and* cast out. But you're still attached to them, and why shouldn't you be to your parents? I think you're trying to make a new boundary, a new perimeter which includes everyone else *and* them, where you can live. Do you have a design?

Lionel: It's like I have to die to do it. They're really sick.

Therapist: That's a big price.

Lionel: It's pretty painful not having a family.

Therapist: But to die to have one? It's one thing for Jesus to do so . . . but

Lionel: I'm *so* glad you said that. I had two dreams this week-end . . .

Lionel recounted two dreams. The first had occurred the night after our Mother's Day session:

I am in some dark area of a cathedral, and there are crucifixes of Jesus hanging everywhere. There are paintings cramming the walls with details of hands with nails in them. Someone is telling me that I have to die and I'm saying, "No, no way." Then I was crying and lying on the floor with my arms stretched out.

The second dream occurred two days later, on the evening before Mother's Day:

I dreamt I was having lunch with Barbara Bush—she's the first lady! It was a Mother's Day dream!

(*Dream One seemed to be a stunning tapestry of oedipal and masochistic iconography. I wondered about Barbara Bush. Lionel's associations clarified both.*)

Therapist: So what do you make of them?
Lionel: The first one was like this incredible empathy for Jesus, having to sacrifice yourself—having to die because your father said so. But all will be saved. It is a noble cause.
Therapist: You felt that in your dream?
Lionel: Twelve years of Catholic school. (*laughs*)
Therapist: Jesus felt his father forsook him and he had to submit to his will. But you know his mother adored him.
Lionel: I am in sort of a weird spot these days.
Therapist: What do you mean?
Lionel: I feel so bad.
Therapist: The other thing about the dreams is you are in very important positions in both. On Mother's Day the only person who is going to have lunch with Barbara Bush is the President and the first family. Do you like Barbara Bush?
Lionel: Yes. I think she is pretty cool. There's a lot to like about her.
Therapist: What do you like?
Lionel: She seems really grounded. There is a real earthiness about her.

Typically, when I talk about dreams with family members I do not move deeper and deeper into the subjective imagery. Rather, I treat dreams as fanciful narratives about family themes we have been elaborating. In this session I was definitely not interested in having the dream exploration intensify Lionel's transference relationship to me. Instead, I wanted to redirect his attention to the multiple family relations that had been the focus of our work to date. I was not pursuing a master narrative that would envelop the dream imagery and Lionel's developmental history within the contours of our transference–countertransference relationship. Rather, I was working with multiple narratives prismatically, hoping each narrative facet would locate Lionel in his relationship context with surer footing. In fact, the archetypal quality of the dream material and the associations of this session created a stained glass representation, luminous and fractured, depicting Lionel's conflicting attachments and wishes. Thematically, I tried to elaborate and play with Lionel around the imagery of the Holy Family, hoping to multiply his narrative perspectives. Thus, later in the session excerpted here I asked Lionel about the impact on him of his mother's adoration and whether it balanced his father's demandingness. Then I asked him about his refusal to be crucified in the dream. What did it signify about his own self-protection? I was trying to evoke Lionel's interest in his own web of family relationships. My comment about his occupying "very important positions" in both dreams was meant only to note his pervasive focus on his self-image (which was addressed in the sculpting exercise described in Chapter Nine). I did not seek to contextualize that focus in his relationship with me.

The heart of dream interpretation for the contemporary interpersonal analyst often resides in reading the margins of the manifest content, as opposed to digging under for latent meaning. The dreams in this session decidedly evaded one margin—its inevitably coded transference message. My thoughts went to Mary, the compelling though silent protagonist in the crucifixion drama. There was no mother figure present in Lionel's crucifixion dream. However, the dream followed our Mother's Day session, and we had focused in that session on the multiple triangular relationships in which Lionel was nested. Grotstein (1994) has proposed that a pietà is an iconic representation of therapeutic healing, that the heart of psychotherapy is the therapist's willingness to serve as container for the suffering of the patient until the patient becomes individuated enough to "resume the responsibilities of bearing his/her own pain *and* for redeeming him/herself of putative pain (s)he caused the parents to bear" (p. 712). Was Lionel pleading for me as the therapist to bear his suffering? In another vein altogether, might I have been for him the mother whose beatification depended on his crucifixion? Was I, in a countertransferential and unwarranted manner, intruding myself as a mother figure into a father–son drama? Perhaps Mary's absence in his dream indicated that Lionel was not experiencing acute conflict regarding his mother or me. I wondered whether Barbara Bush's secular "groundedness" was a different form of reassurance in the second dream. Was Lionel's juxtaposition of her to Mary his idiosyncratic way of comparing the Madonna and the good-enough mother or of representing that polarity? Did I represent this polarity for him? This is just the kind of associative process, the hallmark of psychoanalytic therapy, that one has no time to really explore in family therapy sessions. There is so much data to attend to between family members and their relationship patterning!

As the session progressed, Lionel talked about his unborn child, whom he considered the "perfect offering" for his parents.

Lionel: But I have created the perfect offering. I have a child coming. How could they not want it?

Therapist: But this is the time they seem to be casting you out more. So how do you explain that?

Lionel: I keep thinking that they are afraid of me.

Therapist: Because of what?

Lionel: I have broken free of this kind of thing. I was stuck in a whirlpool. If I get too close, I could get sucked in again.

Therapist: And if they get too close to you, they can get sucked out. They're afraid of you because you're out.

Lionel: But parents are all-powerful. If I'm out, they can punish me.

Therapist: Your parents are afraid of the world you've entered. Children are unpredictable that way. Do you think you can make that world less fearsome?

Once again, my focus was on helping Lionel and Andrea establish a healthy boundary around their parenting. When I asked Lionel if he could conceive of another expression of attachment to his parents, a solution that involved connection rather than forced separation, I was directing the material toward contextual realignment rather than subjective exploration. Intellectually, this suggestion emerged from a systemic understanding that cutoff relationships fester and become toxic; however, the suggestion felt like it emerged organically from a sense of who Lionel was and where he was in the family life cycle. My therapeutic language stayed close to his subjectivity; the exploration of my participation did not.

This was not an easy session for me. As an interpersonal analyst, I am comfortable working intensely with the data of the treatment relationship, but I have enough respect for its complexity to be conservative about entering into its exploration on a piecemeal or one-shot effort. Perhaps I should have inquired more than I did about Lionel's feelings toward me, instead of becoming almost phobic about the intensity of the latent transference I sensed. However, I felt that there was so much in the therapeutic discourse already—pregnancy and a potential cutoff from his family of origin (not to mention ordinary marital difficulties)— that another focus of inquiry would implode or derail the discourse rather than clarify the data.

FAMILY THERAPY ENACTMENTS

Sometimes therapists must address their participation directly. Ideally, this should happen when the therapist has a clear idea as to what an enactment was about, as opposed to the transient hunches that result from the continuous scanning that is characteristic of analytic work. Today, enactment is the psychoanalytic rage, allowing analysts of many persuasions to relax into the participant observer position that interpersonalists have always accepted, namely, accepting that we inevitably become protagonists in our patients' dramas. But that is still not the same thing as trying to initiate an enactment; since Franz Alexander's time this initiation has been taboo for the individual therapist, and the ban on it still stands. In contrast, as Aponte (1992) pointed out, "the structural family therapist is on the lookout for the enactment, and when it does not present spontaneously, *fosters* its appearance. The structuralist treats family transactions as the behavior to change, assuming that a change in their interactional patterns in the office will lead to change at home" (pp. 270–271). The kind of corrective emotional experience that the family therapist tries to offer differs from what Alexander had in mind in that the therapist is not playing a part but, rather, trying to get family members to do so and to do so "for real." Otherwise, the similarities are striking. Accordingly, the term *enactment* refers to quite different things in the two modalities. Still, there is a kind of enactment that draws on both traditions, namely, the inadvertent but undeniable countertransferential participation that, once recognized, unbolts a relationship system.

Case Example

Carol came to see me because of unresolved rage toward her father, which she felt was spilling over into her relationship with her husband, Bill, with whom she had frequent and explosive confrontations. Bill was in treatment; Carol had undergone intensive psychoanalytic therapy in the past. They had seen Bill's therapist for couples treatment during the previous year, an experience they both felt had yielded them little relief from dissension. Carol wondered whether she should now consider individual treatment or whether couples treatment was more to the point. It seemed to me that couples treatment was more appropriate. Carol had already spent five years in individual therapy, which she felt had been very illuminating, but it had left her mystified by her tendency toward rageful reactions. When I did a family genogram and inquired about fighting in Carol's family of origin, I found it hard to grasp the genesis of Carol's explosive style. In contrast, Bill grew up fairly fright-ened of an irrationally angry mother and older sister. My hypothesis was that he had likely chosen a hotheaded wife as a chance to master his developmental trauma. I raised my hypothesis about Bill first. He found it only mildly interesting. He was extraordinarily upset by the marital arguments, and mastery was nowhere in view.

The treatment of this couple moved forward in fits and starts. Nasty arguments were a weekly fare. My task assignments went generally unheeded, and my reframings of the marital relationship seemed to briefly bloom and then rapidly wilt. Carol and Bill were mistrustful of playful experimentation.

Over time and through inquiry into Carol's family of origin, I learned about her mother's highly intense but disguised competitiveness as well as her total submission to her husband's financial domination, and the imprinting of Carol's explosive character style in terms of her family of origin became clearer. I also learned that Carol had fought with her father on behalf of her mother and that she had been conscripted to do so. Her mother sent Carol in as the infantry, Carol got bloodied, and her mother still kept the spoils—Dad. It occurred to me that Carol might see my participation in the treatment as similar to her mother's. I had been challenging Bill's lack of sensitivity and irritating rigidity. Yet somehow he and I had avoided sharp confrontation. Carol, however, continually and angrily challenged my interpretations and interventions. Thus, she was fighting with me while I maintained a somewhat unflappable and beneficent relationship with Bill. It occurred to me that I was offering the interpersonal resolution for Bill that Carol needed to provide—the presence of a strong woman he could tolerate. However, to Carol I had perniciously become the infuriatingly betraying mother she had de-scribed. In an unplanned but useful session alone with her I raised her objection to my therapeutic approach, her complaints about my easy "seduction" (her words) by Bill, and her general discouragement about the treatment. I asked her if she felt I was selling out her interests, as her mother had done. She was struck by my question. The marital fights diminished but, unfortunately, not dramatically.

Then, what I consider an important—and somewhat compensatory—therapeutic enactment occurred. Bill had been particularly infuriating to Carol the night before this particular therapy session. It occurred to me in the session that I should be wary of my hands-off policy toward him, and I became much more challenging of him. I asked him why he was determined to play dumb about his provocations. "Does your therapist know you play dumb?" I asked. I simultaneously tried to remain aware of Carol's rage about having to be responsible for any and all family negotiations, and when Carol got anxious and started interrupting my conversations with Bill, I asked her why she was trying to take over my role as therapist. They both left disgusted with me – and I cannot say I was altogether pleased with myself.

Yet this was a pivotal session with this couple. In the following meeting Bill reported that he had talked to his therapist and that the individual session had two effects: his decision to show Carol he could listen to her angry complaints even if he might not agree with them and his realization that he was truly committed to her. For the first time in the course of therapy with me, Carol talked vulnerably and openly about the irrational anxiety she felt when provoked. She reported that during the week she realized that in her family vulnerability had to be efficiently "fixed" and dispatched and that anger was the suit she had chosen. Grotstein (1994) has described the process of externalization in psychoanalytic treatment in terms of "psychoanalytic 'plays' in which a repressed traumatic situation can be dramaturgically externalized and enacted so that its clarity is obvious" (p. 727). Clearly, something like this had happened between me and Bill and Carol, though even now it is difficult to track what exactly I managed to become transformed into vis-à-vis each of them in terms of their developmental histories.

Simply recognizing that this kind of enactment can and does occur in family work raises more questions than it answers. Which couples and families evoke a developmental enactment that seems essential to the expansion or loosening of the system? Is the enactment necessitated by so clear a fit of reciprocal dynamics between the partners that the therapist must be introduced as dramatic leverage? Was the enactment successful with this couple because my behavior as "reasonable" therapist had to be deconstructed by Carol because of her idiosyncratic family history? Did I in fact encourage her sparring because she was an easier partner for me than I thought her husband would be? In terms of my participation, might she and I have been enacting gender-coded cultural as well familial assignments? And how does an unplanned drama relate to the planned dramatic enactments we stage as intervention with families?

These kinds of questions, which invite analytic contemplation, are relatively new to the family literature. In the first flush of the family therapy movement, there was a minimum of discussion regarding therapist participation in family structure and dysfunction. The goal of experiential expansion in the face of the robust redundancy of the family's system seized the day. However, it eventually became unavoidable to consider family therapists and families as shaping therapeutic systems together. Nowhere does this need become clearer than in family therapy training centers where therapists-in-training work on a time-limited basis. As a trainee therapist takes over a case, one often witnesses a radical transformation in mood, disclosure, and motivation for change on the part of family members. Obviously, the family and therapist of the prior year were locked in a homeostatic, overly accommodated relationship structure, a relationship that was difficult to see at the time despite intensive supervision.

How do family systems therapists reflect upon their participation? Traditional approaches include questioning whether one is standing in for a missing member of the family (e.g., a cut-off member), displacing a family member, or representing a crucial but dissociated family dimension (e.g., forbidden affect). In structural family approaches the search for ellipses in the data caused by the therapist's participation is active and intervention oriented:

> It seems evident that the therapist, himself, introduces new information by becoming the third party to a dyadic relationship. Alternately observing what occurs in a relationship, and then establishing dyadic ties, first with one participant and then the other, while the third person takes the observer's position, in our opinion, constitutes one of the structural elements of the therapy [Andolfi and Angelo, 1988, p. 242].

In all schools of family work there is significant concern about "induction into the system," which is essentially worry about the therapist being swept off the reef and washed into the family's customary tidal patterning. How does one recognize induction? One indicator is when one has stopped thinking systemically. Another indicator is that the family's relationship patterning stays exactly the same or becomes even more redundant. Most commonly, systems therapists are concerned about triangulation, about the therapist working as an anxiety rudder that keeps the family's relationships temporarily stabilized. If the couples therapist, for example, simply oscillates between inquiring about her experience and then inquiring about his, the core of the couple's parataxic distortions, which typically occur only in the heat of the moment of their engagement, will really not be challenged.

Family therapists of the Bowenian school have used intensive work with the therapist's family of origin to search for unexamined biases. Therapists are enjoined to research their family and to trace central themes such as success inhibition or the conflict of work and pleasure. However, this knowledge, which is conscious and programmatic, is not the same as knowledge of unconscious or dissociated types of relationship patterns.

After all, how does a dissociated representation of the therapist's mother become a filter for what is apprehended in a family therapy session? Does one project the dissociation onto a mother figure who is very similar? Or totally different? Does one try to force into the family's relationship system the reciprocal experience of being dependent on such a mother? How could one do any or all of this in the face of the multiple stimulation afforded by the other family members? There is certainly a great deal to be gained in terms of knowledge of one's own parataxic distortions from a personal analysis. But the knowledge gained has to be reconsidered in terms of how it might emerge in a systems context, and here we are in relatively uncharted territory. We entered the quandary of autobiographical narrative in Chapter Six when we considered developmental schemas, particularly as they related to clinical assessment and intervention. Now we face these same thorny issues in considering our own therapeutic participation. The self-awareness we develop in our own treatment is necessary, but is it sufficient to understand our out-of awareness participation in family relationship systems?

We talk in psychoanalysis today about allowing ourselves postmodern multiple perspectives and a kind of fragmentation in the service of the ego. However, we do not really remember to talk about reconstruction this way. The rainbow reportedly sighted at the end of the long haul of psychoanalysis is usually a coherent narrative of dynamics (e.g., "My mother narcissistically used me, and my inept, dependent father barely noticed"). I think we are all subject to dominant or colonizing narratives. The narrative may have been cocreated in an intensive analysis, but then it is copyrighted. Moreover, we therapists probably spend little time in an ordinary psychoanalytic treatment reflecting on the systemic patterning of our own families. To return to George and Martha once more, any therapist would have a multileveled and overdetermined countertransference response to Martha. She is desperate and yet demonic. Particular characterologic issues regarding rescuing and destroying would be likely activated in us. And of course there would be a corresponding gamut of responses to George, so trod upon and yet so talionic in his revenge. However, less articulated in an ordinary expectable psychoanalytic exploration might be the yin–yang fit and the extraordinary traction of George and Martha's dynamics. Suppose we imagine their unborn imaginary child as an analysand. Wouldn't the focus in his analysis be on his parents as separate developmental figures? Less accessed and perhaps more mystifying and disturbing might be his observation of the delight in which they pierced each other's vulnerabilities. How to recapture and understand this cyclical and archaic domestic bloodletting ceremony? Even more disturbing might be the eerie and dissociated sense of George and Martha's true devotion to each other, a phenomenon impossible to reconcile with the sadism in a child's mind. The impact of these overarching relationship configurations are, for the most part, somewhat understated psychoanalytically.

The real problem is that our response to a family system can travel along several different channels. Thus, if a therapist had been a general mediator and peacemaker in his or her family of origin, a fighting, raucous family session might (depending on the degree of self-monitoring) stimulate that very response. Bowenian self-examination should account for this tendency. However, if one had been frequently subjected at a more unconscious level to acute guilt and then anger during particular interactions with one's siblings, then these emotions might be simultaneously evoked by a similar encounter between the children in a family therapy session. Would the unconscious experience of guilt and anger synergistically reinforce the impulse to make peace, or would these unavailable feelings derail it? What is the genetic relationship between the dissociated emotions and the role response of peacemaker? In the face of this kind of complexity, the examined psyche does become something of a life raft in systemic work.

SUMMARY

Analysts who move into family systems work have a kind of phantom limb experience: something crucial is both accessible and yet absent. The limb is the centrality of transference and countertransference exploration, which moves from figure to background in systems work. Analysts will always bring to family therapy a dedication to observing the quality of the treatment relationship and the effect of their participation, but in family work this becomes just one of several assets the analyst brings. Just as important are a honed talent for inquiring, a comfort with the irrational, and a familiarity with recognizing slippages in awareness to evoke new interactions between family members and transformations within relationship systems.

In fact, psychoanalysts first working with couples and families from an explicit systems perspective often experience an uneasy sense of freedom, as though illicitly untied from their respectable moorings. This freedom is generally accompanied by a more disquieting loss of pride as the analyst witnesses the unexpected power of healing and transformation that family members can offer each other. Most of all, once they enter the systemic view, analysts are invariably drawn to reexamine fundamental psychoanalytic concepts about the self and about changing the self. The upshot need not be a withered commitment to psychoanalysis. Paradoxically, working systemically can renew the analyst's sense of wonder about the unique, dyadic, intense, symbolic journey that is psychoanalytic treatment.

On the other side of the ledger, analytically trained clinicians potentially have a contribution to make to current debates within the family literature. As we have seen, the guiding concern in family therapy has traditionally been about the influence of therapist participation on the pragmatic goal of bringing about family change, that is, the relationship of participation to efficacy. Real (1990) summarized this emphasis on efficacy:

> Guiding the therapist's use of self is the principle of "usefulness" (Glaserfeld, 1984). What is the feedback to the position one takes? . . . Is the conversation opening up into greater variety and experimentation; or is it constricting, moving deeper into rigidity and monologue? (Anderson and Goolishian, 1988) [p. 270].

As discussed in Chapter Four, there has recently arisen a strong countermovement within family therapy, Foucaultian in derivation, that challenges the "colonization" tendencies of the therapist. However, the newer family systems theoretical work in social constructionism and narratology does not resolve the most fundamental problem of therapist participation. Though White and Epston (1990) talk about sensitivity to the dominant culture, I think it is mystifying and misleading to pretend that therapists, with considerable expertise (and fees to prove it), are not "experts" (and thus in possession of dominant narratives). Deconstructing language does not deconstruct culture.

There is no doubt that from a psychoanalytic perspective there is too little attention to therapist influence and participation in family therapy. Indeed, one could make an argument that each orientation of family therapy was constructed out of the basic personality and character structure of its founder, just as the major psychoanalytic orientations were. Is it not true that Minuchin, for example, challenges families because he feels most comfortable in an intense relationship?

There is a potential cover-up in the intervention focus of family systems literature; being efficient and parsimonious can cover a multitude of unconscious therapeutic actions that are potentially all the more colonizing because they exist out of awareness. There are present dangers for family therapists, humanistic and quasi-ethical, that a psychoanalytic exploration can potentially illuminate.

chapter eleven

Playfulness, Authoritativeness, and Honesty

It would be a great help if the word serious *could be eliminated from the vocabulary. It must have been invented by critics not too sure of themselves, condemning all of the most exciting and profound works that have been produced through the ages.*

Man Ray

Beyond the broad scope of transference exploration, there are three specific domains of treatment that invite comparison across the two modalities of family systems theory and psychoanalysis: the domain of playfulness, the issue of authoritative versus authoritarian practices, and the axis of therapeutic honesty. These three areas can serve as compass points orienting the therapist to the basic shifts in paradigmatic assumptions as one moves from one modality to the other.

PLAYFULNESS

One analyst reported that when she first began working with families, she felt more spontaneous, her sense of humor seemed to be an asset, and she experienced overall a sense of pleasurable freedom. This is actually a common, though not universal, reaction to the work, and it reflects a praxis phenomenon emphasized in this text. Experimental playfulness feels comfortable in relation to systemic, not personal, vulnerabilities. When the therapist is confronted with systemic redundancy, inviting people to experiment with alternatives can be done playfully and without the same sense of risk of inflicting inadvertent hurt. Playfulness is important in family therapy because it offers a positive, nonthreatening way to try out new patterns of relating.

Playfulness in the psychoanalytic canon has an aura of potential regression about it. The emphasis on developmental unfolding tends to both explicitly and implicitly locate play in childhood experience. Mit-

chell (1984) addressed this bias in his comments on a case example of
Balint's that described Balint spontaneously inviting a young woman to
perform a somersault in the middle of a treatment session. The young
woman had, metaphorically, always kept her feet drearily on the
ground. Mitchell objected to Balint's characterization of this acrobatic
act as "regressive": "Is the behavior itself so 'childish' and 'primitive'?
Adults are not supposed to make spontaneous physical gestures, to
play in this way?" (p. 486).

Winnicott's *Playing and Reality* (1971) is probably quoted as much as
any psychoanalytic text when psychoanalysts admit to having become
self-consciously playful. In it Winnicott states:

> Psychotherapy has to do with two people playing together. The corollary
> of this is that where playing is not possible then the work done by the
> therapist is directed towards bringing the patient from a state of not being
> able to play into a state of being able to play [p. 38].

Good playing in the Winnicottian tradition emerges from a prototype
of maternal "holding" and nonimpingement and becomes the model for
psychoanalytic treatment. Yet Winnicott's discussion of play is decidedly serious. This is because playing, for Winnicott, is the site where
developmental trauma can best be addressed; his constructs of object
usage and survival shift the coloration of play and illusion to necessarily
darker tonalities. Playing involves the annihilation of the mother and
the rediscovery of her survival. He notes that play is at once serious,
sincere, and fragile:

> The thing about playing is always the precariousness of the interplay of
> personal psychic reality and the experience of control of actual objects.
> This is the precariousness of magic itself, magic that arises in intimacy, in a
> relationship that is being found to be reliable. To be reliable the relation-
> ship is necessarily motivated by the mother's love, or her love-hate, or her
> object-relating, not by reaction-formations [p. 47].

In this context, Winnicott introduces a distinction between play and the
structured, concerted activity of games. He states, "Games and their
organization must be looked upon as part of an attempt to forestall the
frightening aspect of playing" (p. 50). Above all, in the Winnicottian
tradition the prototype for therapeutic playing is dyadic play within the
mother and child relationship recaptured in the psychoanalytic space.

Ehrenberg (1992) has contrasted Winnicott to Bateson, who was more
egalitarian in his concept of play and, in the bargain, disinclined to

exclude games from it. Bateson's (1972) position with regard to analytic play assumes a degree of self-conscious equality between partners:

> As we see it, the process of psychotherapy is a framed interaction between two persons in which the rules are implicit but subject to change. . . . It is this combination of logical types within the single meaningful act that gives to therapy the character not of a rigid game like canasta, but instead that of an evolving system of interaction [p. 192].

Thus, while for Winnicott the essence of play is its open-ended and/or restorative function, for Bateson the essence of play is the experience of interdependence. Once we move to a conceptualization of play as "framed interaction," we are open to considering that frame from a broad cultural perspective. For Turner (1982), play is a necessary activity toward creating liminal experience: "In Vedic India . . . the gods play. The rise, duration and destruction of the world is their game. Ritual is both earnest and playful" (pp. 34–35). In his discussion Turner quotes an anthropological investigation of play by Csikszenthmihalyi and Bennett (1971). These investigators culled their definition of play from analyses of games of childhood and adulthood as well as from preindustrial ritualized playing; in their view the essence of play is that it offers the player an opportunity for total self-absorption without self-referential thinking. Playing in all three primordial forms of games—chance, strategy, and skill—collapses in a suspended moment in time the age-old conflict between the individual and the social group. Players are egotistical and equal as they pursue a preordained, socially defined process and goal. Csikszentmihalyi and Bennett described the phenomenology of playing as follows:

> Play . . . is what happens after all the decisions are made—when "let's go" is the last thing one remembers. Play is action generating action: a unified experience flowing from one moment to the next in contradistinction to our otherwise disjointed "everyday" experiences [p. 45].

The invitation to family members to play together in a circumscribed arena is in the service of attempting to evoke exactly this experience of flow, of possibility, and of personal intensity without self-examination. Quietly implicit in the emphasis on playing in systemic work is a view of the self as organized by interpersonal processes. In a paradoxical mode, the aim is to liberate individual experience through prescribing collective experimentation. Family therapists embrace all forms of playing and gaming. For the family therapist, game playing does not carry a pejorative connotation, though anyone—therapist or not—would agree with Winnicott that playing stops when coercion begins. And there are persecutory games, such as the fun and games between George and Martha of Albee's *Who's Afraid of Virginia Woolf?* — which can be viewed as a marital perversion of a game of strategy. Thus, for family therapists there are good games and there are bad games, though interactional rules are present in both.

The Playful Therapist in Psychoanalytic and Family Treatment

To explore the difference between psychoanalytic and family systems playing, let us return to Ehrenberg's (1992) discussion. As an inclusive definition of play she opts for "the mutual experience of fun and pleasure" (p. 118), and she provides us with a clinical taxonomy of analytic play. Like Winnicott, Ehrenberg warns us about the potential dangers of playfulness in the analytic relationship. She locates these not in the patient but in the therapist, as she speaks of the dangers of "seduction, manipulation, even coercion" and of "what Stern (1985) calls 'misattunement' and 'emotional theft' " (p. 121). However, one might wonder if there is really more reason to worry about these negative relationship experiences in playful, rather than serious, therapeutic moments. Two issues are at stake here; the first is an issue that emerges from the frame that is inherent in the clinical methodology of psychoanalysis, namely, the avoidance of too active a therapeutic presence — in any form. Even if free association is only free insofar as it conforms to the analyst's narrative constructions, as Spence (1982) pointed out, the analyst nevertheless tries to maintain an even-hovering, nonobtrusive attention. No matter how much one may embrace a two-person psychology in theory, the analytic stage is set for the unfolding of a soliloquy. The analyst has the delicate task of being present enough so that the patient will continue to disclose while remaining contained enough so that the discourse has wide berth. The danger with analytic playfulness in this context is that it may disrupt the patient's unfolding or, worse still, become a vehicle for mobilizing the analyst's countertransferential blind spots. In family therapy the therapist is less concerned about unfolding; rather, the task is to challenge an entrenched system. Though remaining focused on systemic expansion, family therapists range freely in fashioning the content of their interventions, which encompass, willy-nilly, primary and secondary process, prototaxis, and parataxis. To do this playfully does not involve the same sort of risk to the therapeutic frame that might exist in psychoanalysis.

The second factor behind the difference in attitude toward play in the psychoanalytic and family systems approaches is related to the fundamental difference in the therapeutic role we assume within the two praxes. Whether it should be so or not, psychoanalysts feel parental. We assume that the fulcrum of transference is toward parental imagos. The work is generally serious, protective, and quite steady. As evocatively described by Winnicott, the analyst sits quietly at the side of the patient, who playfully discovers and rediscovers truer experience. Yet an important feature of playing is deconstruction of the old order—if only in an abstracted and artificially framed space-time—and deconstruction raises the question of how intimate relationship systems are structured to begin with. The psychoanalytic view has been dubbed the "socialization" model in the family systems literature; the belief is that who we are is largely due to past shaping. This is contrasted to the "social constructivist" model, characterized as a second-chance approach in which spouses weld their separate histories into a shared marital identity. In this model, personal history is viewed as a work in progress, with the partners reworking and reconstructing past memories to be congruent with a new shared life script (Wamboldt and Reiss, 1989). Thus, the deconstruction of the old order in psychoanalysis will likely have important transferential implications; what gets deconstructed in personal history gets reconstructed with the analyst as participant. In family therapy new narratives can be formed more fluidly; there is so much more data floating through a multiperson system, especially when they are all present.

The stance of the family therapist is, accordingly, considerably less parental, and such playfulness as occurs is less likely to be molded in the therapist's mind along the lines of a child playing alone with the mother. The play is at once more interactive—more likely to find some structure as a game—and more egalitarian. In its egalitarian mode it can at times feel more like play between preadolescent chums than between adults. Nor is that necessarily regressive. According to James Youniss, a developmental psychologist, the Sullivanian style of chumship is a crucial stage of postlatency development not only for the experience of intimacy it affords but because of the implicit challenge it provides to parental rule systems. Through intensive interviews with preadolescent boys, Youniss uncovered what he considered a crucial complementary relationship between peer intimacy and child-to-parent intimacy. The chumship stage thus initiates a kind of democratization of social knowledge structure. Preadolescents view their parents as having become less omniscient, according to Youniss, but readily forgive them for this deficit because they begin to create their own shared views of the world.

Of course, in a sense transference enactments are all a form of playing. The patient plays with a surrogate parent, self, or lover in the person of the analyst. This is a drama of mistaken identity, in which both patient and analyst play sleuth as they puzzle their way toward a solution that can be agreed upon. But transference play is also the work of psychoanalysis:

> The analysis of a transference neurosis takes place in an interaction that has the formal qualities of a state of play—a "ludic" context. The rest of the analytic work, equally significant, takes place in a "non-ludic" context. Following Huizinga (1944), the adjective "ludic," derived from the Latin *ludere,* to play, is used to emphasize a special non-serious quality of the interactional context of a transference neurosis [London, 1981, p. 8].

The balancing of work and play in the analysis of the transference is a delicate matter for analyst and patient, but the playful aspect is largely the patient's to initiate and the analyst's to respond to.

Play in family therapy, by contrast, is suggested and organized by the therapist. The family members are the players; the position of the therapist is somewhat ambiguous. Hierarchically ensconced as game-master yet simultaneously a coparticipant playmate, the therapist enters into a liminal space with family members, who live a real life together, in order to play with other possibilities of personification and relationship. What is real and what is play remains for the family to decide. My most vivid experience of play with a family occurred when I brought Roberta Gerber and her family in for a consultation with Salvador Minuchin. Recall that the Gerbers were a particularly en-meshed family (albeit lovingly so). Time has stopped for the Gerbers, and they still referred to their 30-something daughters as "the girls." At one point in the session I suggested that the two daughters and I sit on the floor in the cozy consultation room while the parents discussed some important matter at hand. To my chagrin, neither the girls nor their parents seemed to find this odd!

Play takes many forms. With couples where one member is aggressively verbal and the other cannot find protective verbiage adequately or rapidly enough, the verbal behavior can be reframed as "anxiety ridden" and the aggressor can be invited to go mute and to use only hand signals to communicate. Or play can be exclusively verbal: I spent one session with Lionel and Andrea inquiring, teasing, and joking about madonnas versus whores.

Every clinician should heed Winnicott's warning about the dangers of play: Play can be hazardous. As in William Golding's depiction in *Lord of the Flies,* what starts as play can give license to sadistic impulses. It is incumbent on any therapist to be acutely mindful of the relationship—nay, difference—between playful metaphor and trauma-tic reexperience. One cannot mindlessly touch, even in an affectionate handshake, a sexually abused patient. Similarly, there are games that must not be played with certain families. There is often a crucial therapeutic line of protection that has to be guarded.

AUTHORITATIVE VERSUS AUTHORITARIAN APPROACHES

Once one has become accustomed to them, strategic techniques, from reframing to paradox, start to seem quite playful, yet these are the same approaches that most frequently repel psychodynamic therapists be-cause they seem dishonest and authoritarian. The family therapist acts with apparent certainty, generally tempered with irony, when present-ing an essentially invented reframe or a system-twisting paradoxical injunction. This disjunction in perception relates to the unfamiliar, seemingly authoritarian, posture of the family therapist, particularly in regard to paradoxical suggestion.

Authoritativeness has to be distinguished from authoritarianism. Thus Singer (1969) distinguished between therapeutic *irrational author-ity*, which stems from a desire for power, and *rational authority*, which is rooted in competence. In fact, the four family therapy orientations can be characterized by the position of the therapist along the axis of authoritativeness. Bowenian therapists are always central as expert; their role is that of a cerebral investigator linking influences across generations. Strategic therapists, as delineated by Haley and main-tained in the Milan orientation, also almost always operate from the expert authority position; tasks or injunctions are delivered with executive crispness. Carl Whitaker, by contrast, offers a very complex persona as a therapist: He almost intentionally mystifies the family with his disavowal of expertise (e.g., "I've forgotten how to raise kids altogether") and he provides a steady stream of consciousness in reporting his dreams and "crazy thoughts," as if to demonstrate his lack of expertise. However, the demystification of his role as expert is cou-pled with his singular choreographic control over the session. Min-uchin (Minuchin and Fishman, 1981), with arguably the most complex view on the authoritativeness of the therapist, differentiates three posi-tions for the therapist to assume: In the *close position* the therapist joins and affiliates with family members, even entering into coalitions with them; it is in this position that the therapist can most readily be in-ducted into the rules of the family system. The *median position*, most familiar to psychoanalysts, is that of attentive listener. In the *disengaged position* the therapist functions more as a director of the process, as an expert. In the close position the therapist can respond affectively to family process; in the disengaged position the therapist's affective experience is channeled into a well-crafted intervention. Clearly, the choreography of these positions reflects an adaptation of the participant-observer model Minuchin worked with analytically earlier in his career.

But granting that expert knowledge does carry with it a degree of authoritativeness does not automatically absolve an endeavor from all possible taint of authoritarianism. And this applies equally to psychoanalysis and to family therapy. In a highly provocative article on psychoanalytic transference Haley (1963) delineates what he believes is the highly authoritarian, albeit useful, structure of psychoanalytic treatment. In what he feels is a deconstructive reading of transference, Haley posits first that the psychoanalytic situation demands regression and infantile ideation owing to its basic structure (i.e., inequality, recumbent position, etc.). Then, according to Haley, psychoanalysts "interpret" this regression as privileged data. He argues that the analytic treatment system is constructed from a series of basic paradoxes; for example, treatment participation is voluntary, but if a patient is late or misses a session, this behavior is discussed as if attendance were compulsory. Haley grudgingly admits that the procedure is therapeutic, but in his view the patient is cured through paradoxical injunctions whereby old behavior becomes inoperative. For Haley, the actual content of subjectivity, of self-understanding, merely "provides a subject for patient and analyst to talk about; a *modus operandi* for dealing with each other" (p. 370). Haley's view of transference is narrow but piquant. His emphasis on paradox harnessed into a therapeutic bind is partially echoed by those in the psychoanalytic literature who view paradox as rather integral to the therapeutic bond.[1]

Relevant to the issue of authoritarianism is the current focus within the psychoanalytic literature on the axis of asymmetry versus mutuality in the therapeutic relationship (Burke, 1992). Important questions have emerged from this discussion: (1) Are we psychoanalytically determined to maintain an essential quotient of asymmetry by our relatively

---

[1]One vision of paradox in the psychoanalytic literature denotes an individual intrapsychic struggle based on the mutual contradiction of human strivings. Ghent (1992) noted that such "dark forces as envy, greed, hatred" may yet be "heralding the (re)vitalization of some genuine need" (p. 143). Thus, psychic conflict is inherently paradoxical for Ghent, with growth, like a Janus face, emerging from the fiercest resistance, and this paradox inevitably informs the treatment relationship.

conservative position on therapeutic self-disclosure (Aron, 1991)? (2) How much psychoanalytic flexibility in moving from asymmetry to mutuality is helpful to patients? (3) Do we mystify and confuse patients by shifting inexplicably from an intimate (mutual) to a more distal (asymmetrical) position (I. Z. Hoffman, 1991)? (4) Is the therapist–patient role relationship inevitably asymmetrical due to the fact that the patient is paying the therapist?

These kinds of questions actually expose what has been neglected in the analytic literature — a social systemic view of the treatment relationship. Newton (1989) has addressed the issue of the dyadic analytic relationship as social system. He points out that there is a wide divergence on technical emphasis within psychoanalysis and cites a recent poll conducted by Lichtenberg and Galler (1987) in which respondents were divided in their responses, with half citing analysis of resistance and the other half the facilitation of a cooperative atmosphere as the technical focus of treatment. There is thus a demonstrable empirical divergence in how practicing analysts construct their ideal relationship to the patient, let alone their actual relationship in the therapy room. Newton views this as evidence justifying the necessity for analysts to examine their social systemic context. He states:

> The clinician is asked to shift the focus, at least initially, from the patient to the enterprise, to ask first, not how the personality system, but how the treatment system, is structured. . . . The personality system of the patient strongly colors the social system of his or her treatment, and the latter is organized in such a way as to effect change in the personality of the patient. To say that the two realms are interrelated is not, however, to say that one is reducible to the other, nor that either may be ignored [p. 33].

Interestingly, Newton remarks that authority, in both the patient's and the therapist's mind, tends to be associated with parental role behavior and with "irrational superego imagos," particularly in post-Enlightenment Western societies. However, he calls for a more functional distinction between authority as personified in family experience and authority that is task oriented.

Newton organizes his presentation around the technique of free association, which he feels should be an explicit and consistent expectation of treatment participation. His point is that bending the parameters (for the most part to suit the needs of developmentally disadvantaged patients) can become a form of "parent knows best" patronization. Analysts, in being flexible at their own clinical whim, are thereby encouraging dependence on irrational, albeit kindly, authority in the service of loosening this dependency.

These issues are perhaps particularly thorny for interpersonal analysts who sometimes eschew technique and emphasize authentic engagement. Then again, it is reasonable to argue that authenticity ought to include honesty about treatment expectations and acceptable working conditions. Certainly, all analysts, even the most egalitarian interpersonalist, believe in certain treatment caveats, such as, for example, that consciously withholding information from the analyst is counterproductive. This means that there is necessarily a degree of authoritativeness in the analytic contract, whether we are particularly mindful of it or not; it is hoped that, in practice, this can be kept distinct from the kind of authoritarianism we and our patient coconstruct in the process of battling the old parental imagos.

As for authoritarianism in family treatment, here I would like to give my personal view. As an analyst, I do find that strategic interventions such as paradoxical injunctions seem a bit too explicitly authoritative, particularly when I design and deliver them as part of a deliberately selected treatment approach. However, they do not feel authoritarian to me. For one thing, I enter the strategic realm only when all else fails. Moreover, what adds to my sense of functioning in a distal expert position is my sense of the inherent absurdity in relationships. One can feel rather Gulliverian about absurdity—it is larger than all of us. This may well be a logical marriage of strategic thinking and psychoanalytic experience. Psychoanalysts are most at home with irrationality. Entering the circle of redundant absurdity via a paradoxical intervention can initiate a clear sense of intimacy with a family's experience.

Much of strategic work is executed with a very noticeable and characteristic wink. And it is quite remarkable how affect-rich and alive the effect of strategic work can be. For example, a supervisee was asked to direct a woman to actually rate her husband's competency every other evening for one week. Both husband and wife had entered treatment agreeing that he was inept and that she was relentlessly harsh in her criticism; this was a marital arrangement calling for strategic input to highlight the collusive complementarity. The therapist entered the session with a husband-rating scale for the wife to complete. The wife was put off but agreed to take the scale home on trial. Although she was even more inflamed in the next session, her outrage marked the beginning of a change and was a heightened last defense of a just-about-to-be-atrophied personification (a Sullivanian term) of the self. What was interesting here was that the wife depended on her husband's resentful collusion to maintain the seeming appropriateness of her abusiveness. When the intervention rendered him an "object," the game was over. She never rated him, never completed the task, but she grew softer. The therapist had felt empathetically disturbed by the wife's chronic fury and the husband's compulsive cowering in the face of it. Paradoxically, however, the therapist got even closer to their desperation through the use of the strategic absurdity.

In the videotape "Who's Depressed?" family therapist Olga Silverstein in three sessions creates an airtight construction for a family in which the parents cannot and really must not "desert" their seemingly dependent 33-year-old daughter. The parents are described as people who dare not go on with their own lives. As if she were operating a hand-held loom, Silverstein tightly weaves a family-of-origin design from the husband's desertion in an orphanage by his mother and the wife's parentified child status in precociously caring for her dysfunctional brothers. Silverstein tells the wife that because she is such an experienced caretaker, she has made sure that her husband will not have his early traumatic history repeated (i.e., his daughters will in no way be deserted). The therapeutic moment is dispassionate and almost arbitrary (this is Silverstein's style and method), yet the mother begins to cry, poignantly and gratefully. Why? It cannot be because of the open acknowledgment of her devotion; she has made this all too apparent in the family already. Is it because Silverstein as a mother figure is offering her affirmation (i.e., a passing illustration of curative transference)? Does the acknowledgment of the mother's sacrifice offer her a deeper awareness of her sadness and lifelong sense of deprivation? Most radically, is there something about the focused linking of all the family protagonists that creates a kind of hyper-real moment of connection, a connection they have all been desperately seeking and yet compulsively disavowing? Paradoxical prescriptions typically are only effective in families whose members are densely interconnected (i.e., enmeshed), albeit at times the depth of the bondedness may be covert. There must be a strong underlying attachment in order for the radically new perspective to seem startling or gripping. Disengaged families tend to move in the direction of the thrust and offer no resistance; their redundancy exists in rigid dismissal and disengagement, and the paradoxical challenge dissolves in their midst.

THERAPEUTIC AUTHENTICITY: THE HONEST THERAPIST

There is yet a third domain to be considered in comparing modalities: therapeutic honesty. We are not talking about self-disclosure here but about a basic expectation on the part of the patient that the therapist will "tell it as it is," without misrepresentation and without unnecessary elaboration. In other words, patients expect therapists to be trustworthy. Haley's strategic view of treatment offers an interesting comment on our dedication to self-awareness and therapeutic authenticity in psychodynamic treatment. His concern about therapeutic "forthrightness" involves something besides the more obvious constraints on authenticity arising from therapist dissociation or lack of awareness as well as from the fact that dynamic therapists must select one percept or connection from a multitude swarming in hovering attention. Haley's question is, Are there instances in which a dedication to honesty results in obtuseness?

> If a wife is "depressed" and one notes that her depression occurs whenever her husband avoids her sexually, it is naive to assume that she and her husband do not know the depression is related to the marriage.
>
> Along with the interpersonal explanation of symptoms has come the idea *in family therapy* that people do not have problems because of ignorance but because of their social situations. If a therapist conceals information from a client, he is usually concealing what the client already knows. The therapist is showing both courtesy and respect by that concealment [Haley, 1976, p. 213; italics added].

Of course, Haley is genuflecting in the direction of the psychoanalytic community in making this point, since he otherwise is quite clear that psychoanalysts are committed minimalists in terms of therapeutic commentary and description.

The issue of authenticity in therapy is a complicated one. In a sense, whenever an analyst is deliberately trying to "hold" or "structure" or "build," he or she is being as instrumental as any family therapist who is reframing motivation (perhaps more so because the instrumentality is laced through the therapeutic relationship without being explicit). As Oscar Wilde noted, "Being natural is only a pose." The "deceptiveness" of paradoxical reframing (e.g., prescribing a symptom) gives me, as an interpersonally oriented therapist, pause but does not produce avoidance. Even more basically, when I work analytically, I try not to do anything in particular with patients except inquire for more data and make our relationship open to examination. My reassurance in family work is that paradoxical prescription yields new data and often facilitates decoding the relationship between family members.

As noted earlier, there is a unique kind of inquiry that occurs in the process of family therapy. The tasks assigned and the directives issued function as probes for further understanding the family's worldview and relationship assumptions. The inquiry simply takes the form of a show-and-tell exercise rather than a conversation. For example, a therapist enjoins a husband to reassure his wife about his commitment to the marriage by actively criticizing her. The husband has spent most of his married life in constricted, avoidant silence, which recently erupted in an episode of marital infidelity. He must now overcome his fear of confrontation and retaliation if he is to stay and not stray again. The pairing of commitment and criticism in the therapist's directive to the husband is an odd reframe of the couple's previous requests from each other, but it seems to be one way of relieving the chronic smoldering paralysis of their relationship. However, task prescription is also a probe; how will the husband access and express aggression? What is the wife's repertoire for tolerating faultfinding? What is the scope of her insecurity? The hope is that the task prescription results in honest inquiry, not a dishonest manipulation.

Family therapists are not the only ones who can inquire via an active intervention. Analysts can risk doing the same on occasion. Analysts might even indulge in that most taboo of transgressions—advice giving—as long as it is followed by a transference–countertransference exploration. In the crucible of feeling one's patient is at risk one can say, for example, "Safe sex is not just a slogan," and then inquire about the effect of this participation.

Once working with systemic ideas becomes part of one's experiential therapeutic repertoire, one is probably never the same analyst again. Issues of complementarity versus symmetry within the psychoanalytic relationship become sharper. The redundancy of process, its particular patterning, becomes a more recognizable phenomenon. In general, the commitment to more than one psychotherapy paradigm makes one less of a believer and more of a sportive participant—but, then again, that is only if one enjoys playing.

chapter twelve

Referrals: Who? When? Where?

To exist is to co-exist.
Gabriel Marcel

Referrals are the bread and butter of clinical practice. Henry Kissinger once said, "The absence of alternative clears the mind marvelously." Practitioners who never consider alternative modalities might subjectively feel clearest about their clinical work. What leads a practitioner to consider making a referral? How is it executed and tracked? What are the best parameters for deciding *when* to refer? What are the working assumptions of the referral relationship? What is the most heuristic schema for exchange of information between the therapists involved? What are the guidelines for the ordering and/or combining of family versus psychodynamically oriented therapy? The answers to these questions offer one of the cleanest mirrors to the clinician's working theory. However, to reasonably limit this exploration, the focus in this chapter is on referrals to family therapists, rather than the reverse.[1]

There are two basic questions that underlie the decision to refer across treatment paradigms. There is first the question of therapeutic inclusiveness posed from the point of view of the individual analytic practitioner: Is psychoanalytic praxis both necessary and sufficient to deal with all the therapeutic dilemmas we encounter? This is an enormously complicated question. Just one facet of it is the basic bridge between psychoanalytic etiological theory and the determining theory of psychoanalytic change, that is, of what is mutative in the treatment process. Much of our etiological theory is developmental, and we

---

[1]When do family therapists refer clients to individual therapists? Probably most frequently when the client seems fragile and becomes unnerved by any shift in the relationship system or when lack of differentiation from the family of origin cannot be explored systemically (i.e., the parents will not come to treatment and the patient seems stuck). Some family therapists are particularly responsive to psychological-mindedness in clients and will not hesitate to recommend psychoanalytic treatment as a important therapeutic opportunity for the client. Others resist referring to individual therapists, preferring to work with individual problems as part of the family system.

assume that therapeutic engagement addresses, investigates, or reme-
diates developmental failure. Thus, analysts with an interpersonal
perspective assume that children learn to narrowly constrict their self
system via reflected appraisals and that the psychoanalytic relationship
calls for them to mitigate a patient's inhibiting anxiety while expanding
the scope of the self system. On the other hand, a classical analyst
whose basic focus is on neurosis will assume that the patient's libidinal
impulses have been repressed and will utilize techniques that call for
restoring these impulses to consciousness. Theories that make this
linkage seem intuitively to be psychoanalytic; theories that do not are
considered insubstantial.

Embedded in this relation between mutative processes and etiology
is the second question informing issues of referral: Are there aspects of
the human condition that cannot be explained by psychoanalytic theory? At first glance, it would seem not. Psychoanalysts have rushed
eagerly into interpretive literary criticism, historical explication, and
political theory, justifying these endeavors on the assumption that
dissociation and unconscious processing are ubiquitous aspects of
human experience. Then again, one could argue equally well that
linguistic patterning is likewise a ubiquitous aspect of psychological
functioning, and yet linguists have not been as eager to interpret vast
sectors of cultural life as we have. Psychoanalytic passion and excitement have fueled these intellectual enterprises—but have perhaps overextended them. In any event, in the shadow of this kind of expansive
cultural reach, there has been little questioning of the assumption that
all psychological problems can be sufficiently accounted for by psychoanalytic theory.

To be sure, there has long been a concern with patient suitability as a
criterion for beginning an analysis, but this concern, coming as it does
in the context of the modernist analytic belief in the absolute value of
self-exploration, tends to shift attention away from the limits of the
method in the direction of presumptive limitations in the patient. In
fact, psychoanalysts have been somewhat uncharitable toward individuals, both patients and therapists, who resort to approaches generally
regarded as mechanistic (behavioral therapy), narrow (cognitive therapy), or avoidant (psychopharmacology). We have too rarely inquired
how psychoanalytic theory might explain either the need for or the
usefulness of adjunctive approaches. I am not recommending submitting to the current political climate of psychotherapy bashing, in which
psychoanalysts are attacked for taking too long to help the patient, as
though restoring psychological well-being were as simple as lowering
an elevated white blood cell count with antibiotics. However, the cur-

rent unfriendly climate should not restrict our theoretical interest in the parameters of our work. Besides, in the last few decades we have become much more interested in stretching our parameters. Currently, we are oscillating between extending the vanishing point of traditional psychoanalytic vision and retaining a coherent and recognizable perspective.

Thus, one might wholeheartedly endorse a psychoanalytic basis for understanding human behavior and yet support referral to another modality because it is the most efficient approach to resolving a particular clinical problem. I recently worked with a talented young woman who had a lifelong phobia regarding elevators and police sirens. I had hoped that our initial psychodynamic exploration would alleviate her free-floating anxiety sufficiently to eliminate these phobic reactions. It did not. Her life continued to be constricted by her phobias, and her belief in therapy was compromised. It seemed best to refer her (she was not interested in simultaneous treatment) to a behaviorally oriented phobia specialist and to extend to her an open invitation to return when that treatment was completed. The ecological overview of systems theory encourages one to take this kind of perspective; it becomes a habit of mind to think of problems as existing on several layers, each with a different meaning system and a potentially different point for therapeutic entry.

To grant that behavior is externally shaped on an ongoing basis as well as inwardly motivated is to recognize that significant characterologic change can come about by processes other than intrapsychic exploration. But analysts might still question whether behavior change that does not come about from insight will be long-lasting. We have never really settled the circle or riddle of insight versus behavior change. Wachtel (1986) has organized some of the interesting aspects of this riddle in his "cyclical psychodynamics" formulation. For Wachtel, it is important for the therapist and patient to investigate how the patient creates a life context that maintains neurosis:

> The difficulties the patient finds himself in are not simply the product of early experiences, or defensive efforts which have achieved some sort of structuralization. The patient requires "accomplices" to maintain his neurosis. . . . Self-knowledge . . . includes understanding the impact that particular interactions have on one's own psychological state, and one's impact on others (which in turn feeds back, through their behavior in relation to oneself, to affect one's own sense of self, usually in a way that again keeps the entire pattern going) [pp. 62–63].

This circularity holds its own therapeutic promise. A serendipitous or therapeutically staged experience of a different way of being, of

thinking and feeling, with a significant other can have a profound effect
on an individual, sparking curiosity and self-exploration. Certainly, in
couples therapy one often sees a shift in relationship leading to a
cascade of new memories and questions about early childhood. Nevertheless, one must guard against always tipping the balance toward
placing the value on the intrapsychic aspect of change. Some patients
are satisfied with positive change and care little about its genesis
or generalization.

Psychoanalysts tend to feel more comfortable in referring patients to
concomitant couples therapy than to almost any other alternative modality. Some of this comfort no doubt derives from the possibility of
referring to other psychoanalysts working as couples therapists; the
referral carries an assumption of a common language and viewpoint.
This is no small matter, since major differences in technique, and
timing, and the meaning of therapeutic material can make for communication difficulties. Then, too, couples therapy seems to offer clinical
familiarity. Analysts who have an object relations perspective can link
their individual work to the concept of mutual projection processes as
they imagine these will emerge in couples therapy. Analysts will also
refer children to family therapy but here a somewhat more conservative
attitude obtains. In part this may be because there are fewer therapists
seeing whole families who have been psychoanalytically trained. Then,
too, psychodynamically oriented child therapists will sometimes include work with the whole family as part of their child treatment,
though some conservative analysts still feel that family inclusion ne-
glects or impinges on the sensitivities of children.

WHEN TO REFER?

Let us assume that there is an open referral policy between a psychoanalyst and a family therapist. I do not think there is any clinical
instance that would command universal agreement with regard to a
referral decision, but there are some rules of thumb. When a relatively
new, previously gratifying relationship between an analytic patient and
a spouse or lover goes sour, consultation with a couples or family
therapist may be in order. The clinician should be aware that there are
stages of the family life cycle that come with warning labels. An extensive research literature (Belsky, Lang, and Rovine, 1985) indicates that
the transition to parenthood, the second stage of the family life cycle, is
disequilibrating to young couples. On the other hand, the transition to
the empty nest, the sixth stage of the family life cycle, appears to be a

smoother one.[2] My own view is that any time distress between a couple first surfaces at one of the transitional points in the family life cycle, a family consultation can be useful.

There is a second (somewhat specific but clear) indicator that a family consultation would be useful: a number of family members in individual treatment signals that interpersonal, collective influences are being overlooked. I strongly believe that the individual treatments should not be suspended but that the shared emotional variance might usefully be explored. Parsimony is particularly disregarded when two children in a family are simultaneously referred to child therapy; from a systems perspective one would hypothesize that in this instance there is something dysfunctional in the life of the family and in the conduct of the parents.

A third fairly clear guideline for referral involves cultural considerations. There are cultural groups (e.g., the Japanese) for whom family loyalty and identification is paramount; if the issues can be clarified within the family arena and some form of harmony achieved, then individual dynamics become more available and legitimate for exploration. For example, Tamura and Lau (1992) note that "the preferred direction of change for Japanese families in therapy is toward a process of integration—how a person can be effectively integrated into the given system—rather than a process of differentiation" (p. 319).

On the other hand, there are some clear counterindications for referral to family therapy. However compelling the problem is on a systemic basis, it is foolish to wait around for a reluctant and despairing family to gather its collective motivation while a psychologically minded member is eager to begin individual therapy. I confess a bias with regard to treating children: I think a family consultation is always best as a first order of business, followed by play therapy with the child, as needed. My inclination is always to explore and perhaps strengthen parental competence first. Parents can offer a 24-hour-a-day mutative experience. Moreover, it is a good idea to investigate the contextual implications of a child's symptomatic behavior first. However, even a preference for family work can be taken too far. I once witnessed a "live" (behind a one-way mirror) consultation of a family with a depressed and very self-aware nine-year-old. The consultant was a highly skilled family therapist, but he could not motivate the family to consider how they might actually help this youngster feel better about himself. They would not accept the idea of family therapy. The recommendation

---

[2]For a feminist and social class perspective on the family life cycle see Gerson, Alpert, and Richardson (1984).

the consultant made was to wait (though not indefinitely) until they changed their mind. I wondered if they ever would. The whole family was depressed. Yet the parents might have joined their child in concomitant family treatment if their son had started individual treatment and benefited from it, thereby providing them with some hope for relief. We do not adequately understand existential and characterologic optimism in therapy, that is, what makes patients believe they can change and what makes people seek therapy. The variables are remarkably complex and include culture, character, traumatic experience — even, at times, a fortuitous good match between a skeptical client and a particular therapist.

There are other limiting factors in recommending (or continuing with) family treatment. Sometimes family treatment cannot proceed with *or* without a secret being shared. Usually this involves an affair or even, on occasion, the existence of a second family. Such secrets are considerably detrimental to therapeutic progress. Working to contextualize attributions and beliefs is impossible when the context is illusory. Similarly, if during the diagnostic process it is apparent that there are paranoid reactions that cannot be contained by family-wide interventions, the clinician may conclude that such reactions may make more trouble than the family therapy is worth. The dangers of an expansion or a widening of attributions outweighs its benefits.

Referral issues regarding adults are in some ways simpler to discuss than those regarding children. One reason to refer a patient in individual therapy to couples therapy is the exhaustion and confusion that result from trying to manage marital difficulties by "satellite communication." A case example that comes to mind involves an analytic supervisee who reported on a woman she was sure was borderline because of her involvement with and dependence on a volatile man who was likely a drug addict. The initial exploration of what the relationship meant to the patient had not been fruitful from the supervisee's perspective. In one session the patient brought in a Valentine's Day card bearing a somewhat threatening handwritten message as evidence of her lover's instability. The supervisee was tempted to bring the card to supervision but had refrained. It seemed to me that the analytic exploration had deviated into a kind of counterintelligence operation. I believed it simpler to have another therapist see the couple to help the woman sort out the actuality of her lover's volatility and for her individual therapist to explore the resonant meaning of this problematic relationship.

There are clinical situations where the issues of referral "out" versus persistence "within" are very murky. Several years ago a very talented young woman was referred to me who had an unusually traumatic family history. Her younger brother had committed suicide after seeming to recover from one of a series of psychotic episodes, often organized around bizarre accusations against my patient. She had been mildly to moderately depressed since early adolescence, had been anorectic in high school, and had recently been very involved with a New Age self-help movement. When she came to me, she had already started taking an antidepressant medication recommended by her internist. She was uncertain about which therapy—couples or individual therapy—to seek, though her initial speculation was that her problems could be resolved if her marriage improved. She felt her husband ignored her somewhat, much as her parents had, and she felt inferior to him because he was highly organized and professionally successful. The marriage felt "dead" to her. The couple had a baby boy who was 6 months old, and my patient felt that she was a barely adequate mother (her husband was not critical of her mothering). I strongly recommended individual twice-a-week therapy. The young woman's marital complaints were mild, and from a dynamic perspective I felt that her wish for couples therapy was a defense against her own deep feeling of worthlessness and a reflection of her belief that she could get help only if she had a man in tow whom she was helping. Our work together was relatively helpful to her. She stopped needing the medication and became somewhat more enlivened as a person and more committed to her profession. She began to form new relationships with her parents, asking them all sorts of thorny questions on return visits home. However, her marriage stayed pretty much stayed the same.

The issue of couples therapy came up again two years into the therapy, during a period when we differed in a fairly intense way about whether or not I had reached the end of my effectiveness for her. I viewed her discouragement as a transference reaction and was convinced that if I could maintain faith in myself, the patient's faith in herself could be revived. I viewed her wish for couples therapy as an escape from the jaws of my inevitable maternal failure, which would recapitulate her own mother's. The therapy continued. About a year later, however, she and her husband were going to be relocated out of the country; the decision threw her into a state of anxiety, and she asked if he could come in for a few sessions with her. I rarely see couples on that basis, but because of time and geographic constraints I agreed.

The experience was unsettling for me. The husband was a tightly wound individual, but he was particularly tense and concerned about his wife's low self-esteem and despair. He was eager to help her, and when he realized he might, they both brightened. I felt that I had been depriving my patient of a source of a greater sense of well-being.

During her analytic sessions we had been absorbed in historical data, transmuted through transference experience. Present time had been suspended, as it often is analytically, though usually necessarily and beneficially so. Putting aside the fact that remorse might be a counter-transference reaction, I could adopt (thus assuaging my discomfort) the customary rationale that the success of the couples consultation depended on my prior work with the patient. My hunch is that this is sophistry. I think I should have acceded to my patient's request for concomitant treatment earlier.

I had the opposite experience with another patient. This woman started working with me after two years of unsuccessful sex therapy with her totally sexually avoidant husband. Because our work did not relieve her marital dissatisfaction, I suggested after a while that she and her husband concomitantly see a male colleague of mine who was a couples therapist. After one year my patient and her husband divorced. She and I did not. In and out of various relationships, she eventually became intensely involved with a man who was both inconstant and exacting. He reminded both of us of her mother. She spent session after session complaining about his criticalness and his unreliability; I questioned this redundancy. Her dissatisfaction with this man seemed so clear that I was moved to ask what was at issue between us in her unrelenting complaints about him? What reaction from me was she expecting? Hoping for? She did not know. It seemed to me that complaining about a dissatisfying man was a way of staying bonded to me. She assumed that I required her to denigrate men; simultaneously, this man's presence in her life siphoned off the negative transference to me that this requirement evoked. Moreover, since my questions did little to clarify her dilemma, they themselves appeared to be a therapeutic reenactment of what she perceived to be her mother's utter lack of concern about her happiness. They also allowed her to feel toward me the defensive contempt with which she had dealt with her mother's neglect. One day she casually announced that she had put in a call to the couples therapist to inquire about his availability. This announcement surprised and, I must say, dismayed me. I felt even more impotent as a therapist with this patient, more imprisoned in a transference reenactment. After some time we were able to explicate this contretemps and the alternatives that were nearly foreclosed by it, namely, that she and I might really understand her dilemma, that we did not have to call in a male "expert," and that her attachments to men were worth exploring with seriousness and concern in terms of her own psyche.

There is no infallible clinical formula for deciding when to refer to an adjunctive modality, like couples therapy, and when to continue pursuing transference–countertransference explication. A similar issue arises when patients talk about their parenting difficulties. One can hear this material in several ways. A man I am currently working within individual therapy bemoans his lack of involvement with his son and is not in touch with his depth of resentment about his wife's assumed role as expert parent. He enjoys, in this way, the opportunity to identify with his incompetent father, and this allows him to overlook how much he resents his wife's superiority. This dynamic is gathering transferential intensity, inevitably so now that he has a female therapist. However, if I cannot usefully explore the quality of this patient's resentment and if his son develops psychological difficulties, I will suggest family therapy. If the dynamic remains unremitting, my patient could be saddled with the guilt of his son's troubled childhood. Time exacts real as well as symbolic costs.

Then, too, there is an unusually sticky dynamic that can be reflected in parenting styles that are clearly based on cross-generational dissociated identifications. I have worked with people who have been insightful and psychologically minded and who quite reasonably decry their parents' failing them in specific ways. Yet they get stuck in a tar pit of either an arbitrary reversal of the traumatic style or an oddly dissociated repetition of it in dealing with their own children. In some cases the material relating to parental style seems uniquely impervious to interpretation. It is as if having a cast of characters (i.e., their own children) available to reenact trauma compels the traumatic reenactment rather than destabilizes it. Approaching this somewhat rigid and perplexing dynamic from both a depth and interactional field perspective opens up more of the data.

SEQUENCING

Is it more useful for a patient to begin family treatment before exploring individual dynamics, or vice versa? A clear bias of this text is that it is almost always preferable to begin treatment with children from a family systems perspective. However, this preference does become entangled with the truly thorny theoretical issue of what internalization means developmentally. Needless to say, each psychoanalytic orientation has a different position paper on this issue. Classical theorists have long believed that basic character structure is inscribed at the end of the oedipal phase, though recently some classical theorists have begun to question the conceptual integrity of the concept of internalization.

Schafer (1983) has categorized it as but one of many examples of "literal corporealizations":

> From the standpoint of action language, these concepts implement somatic-mechanistic-anthropomorphic narrative strategies which, far from satisfactorily explaining things psychoanalytically, themselves require psychoanalytic explanation. A structure, a mechanism, a mental apparatus, a discharge of energy, an automatization, or an internalization: These and other such metapsychological terms evidence the importing of blatantly corporealized fantasy content into psychoanalytic theory [p. 243].

Object relations theorists, notably Fairbairnians, believe that fragmented representations jell even earlier and thereafter remain tantalizing or forbidding. More than the practitioners of any other orientation within psychoanalysis, interpersonal psychoanalysts have tended to ignore the concept of internalization. However, interpersonalists have a rather paradoxical way of eschewing internal personifications and yet working with stable resistances and character tendencies. Because of Sullivan's commitment to regard the self as fluid and constructed only in interpersonal interaction, interpersonalists have been left, according to D. B. Stern (1994), with the conceptual dilemma of explaining enduring characteristics (p. 267).[3] Nonetheless, from a psychoanalytic research perspective, D. N. Stern (1995), who has studied the interactions of mothers and children in terms of the development of the self, has come to question the heuristic value of the concept of internalization (p. 245).

Whatever its problematics, the concept of internalization can exert a decisive influence on treatment decision making. If one assumes that a structure has solidified, it seems warranted to suppose that the child will need individual work to help modify it, quite irrespective of what is done with regard to the family. However, against this point of view, one can note that clinical observation data indicate that symptomatology for children is fluid: a highly obsessional eight-year-old can grow astonishingly histrionic a year later. Symptoms in children seem to reflect anxiety more than stable structuralization. Furthermore, at the very foundation of the theory of child psychotherapy is Anna Freud's assumption that adults, whether parents, teachers, or therapists, are real

---

[3]An excellent discussion of this problem can be found in an article by D. B. Stern (1994) in which he proposes four solutions to the interpersonalist dilemma of explaining enduring characteristics, namely, regarding these as (1) models of internal object representation, (2) models of structure based in conceptions of the self, (3) models of structure based in schema theory, and (4) models derived from theories of language.

objects for children as much as transferential ones. Once we think of adult attachment figures as offering real relationship healing, we might well emphasize the parental relationship as a primary focus of therapy. It is possible for a child therapist to spend months and even years in unproductive symbolic play therapy around issues of impulse control when there is a considerable reality-based misalignment in parental limit setting in the home. I know of a case in which a child's preoccupation with death was being dealt with as a symbolic neurotic conflict. I also knew from the family treatment that his father was a diabetic who did not responsibly manage his condition. Ambulances would be summoned in the middle of the night to whisk the father to the emergency room when his insulin plummeted. Was the child's preoccupation with death neurotic? Or even symbolic?

In a similar case, a trainee therapist reported a stalemated treatment around an increasingly deteriorating "borderline" child. The child's fantasy life was becoming more and more perverse, and he was virtually out of control in the treatment room (making overly sexualized gestures and remarks to the therapist, breaking toys, etc.). The trainee was asked about the child's family life. In fact, his father was rarely at home; his mother accused him in front of the child of having another woman in his life. The boy slept in his parents' room and often in their bed. His daytime schedule was disorganized, and he was left to an incompetent housekeeper whom the mother had given up supervising. I thought it had been actually deleterious to initiate play therapy before addressing the family chaos. After all, the frame of play therapy, organized around eliciting fantasy, depends on real life having its rules and constraints. Real life was not safe for this boy, and dealing with it in play seemed to raise his anxiety rather than lower it. Play therapy was one more uncontained, impulse-driven milieu. However, once his family life was rendered adequately safe and predictable, this child would likely require individual therapy to help him symbolize his fears and confusion.

Then, too, children sometimes stand in for parental impulse difficulties. In one case a boy was referred because he deliberately destroyed a valued object displayed in a public place in his school. When he came for therapy with his parents, it was learned that his father "patrolled" outside his room each night, making sure that the boy completed his homework on a demanding and rigid schedule. Who was his father? A badly shaken, mildly alcoholic Vietnam veteran who had let his successful business go to pieces. Though ridiculed in the family, this man had found that he could feel somewhat self-regulating and somewhat in control if he monitored his son's behavior. It was necessary to have both parents and their son present to grasp this; in order to do so they needed to (1) witness the mother holding the father in rageful contempt; (2) witness the absence of any marital closeness; and (3) witness, most of all, the entire family colluding in allowing the father to use his son as a self-organizer by resorting to the mythologizing statement "Father wants his son to accomplish more in life than he has been able to do."

This case also illustrates a different kind of conundrum with regard to sequencing interventions. After initial consultation the family made a commitment to family therapy and to allowing their son to have his own therapist. Within short order, however, the son refused to attend individual treatment, stating, "My father's the one with the problems, not me." This can be a consequence of family therapy, as responsibility for personal problems is shifted to the family and sometimes to the parents. In general, the rejection of individual treatment is much more likely to occur with adolescents than with children or adults. Adolescents often do not want to be in treatment at all, are very sensitive to being blamed for family-wide difficulties, and resist the invitation to be self-revealing to an adult person.

Sometimes acting on a parental wish to initiate individual treatment for a child should be delayed. It is a rather unfortunate fault line of parenting that parents express concern for a child by detecting pathology in his or her behavior. For example, a single mother of an adopted foreign child was highly anxious about and unsupported in her efforts to be a good-enough mother; she almost perseveratively worried about undocumented abuse she suspected her daughter had suffered in her country of origin. This kind of parental anxiety is often fueled by someone else in the family, such as an overinvolved grandmother or an anxious sister-in-law. Such persons are generally off-limits to the child therapist but are often invited in by the contextually oriented family therapist.

The most pressing concern in working with children is to see that their difficulties are addressed, and the earlier the better. Thus, one must consider (1) the context of the child's difficulty; (2) what the parents will tolerate in terms of their own involvement; and (3) where parental optimism is fragile, if not absent. Some parents cannot enter family treatment until they feel their child's distress is being individually addressed; they have avoided their own difficulties so intensely that they are simply too frightened of the exposure. If their anxiety about the consequences of their avoidance is reduced (i.e., if their child's difficulties are ameliorated), they often chance it. But they will talk to their child's therapist about their concerns. However, a therapist who seriously considers systemic factors in relation to a child's problems works differently in parent guidance sessions, for example, emphasizing parental strengths as much as limitations. A well-designed research project (Szapocznki et al., 1989), which won an award by the American Family Therapy Academy a few years ago, compared the efficacy of structural family therapy to play therapy for Hispanic boys of latency age. Initially, the therapeutic modalities (i.e., family and individual therapy) were found to be equivalently and positively helpful for the children, but one year later the families of boys who had been in play therapy evidenced deterioration in their overall functioning. One inference that can be drawn from this result is that there can be systemic consequences to changing the status of the identified patient. Without someone to focus on and complain about, a family's general difficulties in living emerge.[4]

Sequencing is a issue in adult referrals as well, but because character is more stable in adults, the sequencing of referrals can move more flexibly in either direction. Some people become very interested in themselves when they face, with less selective inattention, the effect they are having on a significant other. On the other hand, there are individuals, particularly individuals who are loath to feel dependent, who have to feel recognized and supported therapeutically before they can risk a clear look at reflected appraisals. Still others, unfortunately, use a long period of "holding" or "therapeutic mirroring" to avoid facing their interpersonal style, thereby prolonging their deprivation and shame in their home environments.

---

[4]I'd like to briefly cover outcome research regarding family therapy, though this kind of research is highly complicated both theoretically and methodologically. In a major review article Piercy and Sprenkle (1990) summarize the benefits of family therapy based on accumulated research over four decades, and they draw particularly on a review by Gurman et al. (1986). The Gurman et al. review incorporates a distinction between systemic family therapy covered in this text and behavioral family therapy, which is part of the cognitive-behavioral paradigm.

1. Nonbehavioral marital and family therapies produce beneficial outcomes in about two-thirds of cases, and their effects are superior to no treatment.

2. When both spouses are involved in therapy conjointly for marital problems, there is a greater chance of positive outcome than when only one spouse is treated.

3. Positive results of both nonbehavioral and behavioral marital and family therapies typically occur in treatment of short duration, that is, from 1 to 20 sessions.

4. Family therapy is probably as effective and possibly more effective than many commonly offered individual treatments for problems attributed to family conflict (Gurman et al., 1986, p. 572).

SHARING INFORMATION

More than anything else, making useful referral decisions depends on
our remembering that our hunches and hypotheses about patients
emerge from the particular way we have been working with them. My
sense that a female patient dissociates from her competitive feelings
emerges from my particular treatment relationship with her. This dynamic may take another shape altogether in couples therapy, even with
another female therapist. And what applies to making a referral decision applies even more so to sharing information. Though I think
communication should always be an option between therapists working with the same person, a case can be made that the best policy when
adults are in both couples/family and psychoanalytic treatment is for
the therapists to say little to each other. I think that individual therapists
retain their balanced footing more securely in the transference–countertransference matrix when they do not hear a colleague's impressions
of their patient's spouse or lover. If they do take in this kind of extra-
mural information, they will rarely be free to share the impressions
fully; they thus risk mystifying the treatment by the withheld information. Certainly, individual therapists cannot assume that the observed
spouse is the same person they have been hearing about. The directionality for drawing valid inferences is actually the reverse: individual
therapists can more readily and safely assume that the same character
traits that evoke their therapeutic response to the patient are having an
even more powerful effect on a significant other in that patient's life!

We know that any clinical impression derived from a psychoanalytic
colleague may be transient or intermediate; that is, it is subject to the
particular transferential stage of the treatment. When I hear from an
analyst colleague that the husband in a couple I am seeing wishes in fact
to be hurtful toward his wife, what am I to make of this communication?
Perhaps it is true that he does seem ultradefensive and remarkably self-
absorbed but that she is unusually depriving. Perhaps his analyst is not
sufficiently cognizant of the wife's inattention. Maybe the hurtful material is an issue between analyst and analysand, perhaps a denial of
vulnerability to an uncaring woman. Such questions do not, in the
main, contribute much to professional collegiality.

Since one of the major efforts of couples work is to maintain a focus
on reciprocity, clinical data provided by an individual therapist, particularly when it is designed to evoke sympathy for one partner, can
distract the couple's therapist from a focus on reciprocity. I recently saw
a young couple who were very constricted in their emotional life. The
man was somewhat demanding of his partner's presence and sexual

participation; she, on the other hand, could rarely be affectionate to him and felt pushed and bullied by him. She could only see herself as "victimized" by his aggression and objectification of her. In describing her family history for the genogram she was able to present only the most roseate data about her parents and her childhood. She insisted that her parents "only got pleasure from their children's enjoyment of their own achievements," in spite of the fact that she and her brother had pursued a number of unusually demanding professional pursuits. It seemed possible that this young woman was denying her parents' pressuring and perhaps objectification of her. I had only a telephone conversation with her after her partner broke off their relationship. She felt "victimized" by the breakup and was angry that I saw both parties as sharing equally in its termination. At the same time, her individual therapist, with her permission, called to talk with me about the failure of the couples work to sustain the relationship. Her therapist, empathically connected to her and viewing her as somewhat developmentally arrested, said that she felt her patient had not really understood my efforts to probe and expand what victimization meant. Had our patient found a warm refuge in her individual therapist for her defensive resistance in exactly the arena where it could be opened up, that is, her shared responsibility? Unfortunately, analysts are pressured to assuage the wounds of patients who feel injured by couples therapists. In fact, a more useful position for analysts to take is that couples data have validity—at a different level of abstraction—and that they can help the patient puzzle over the possible relevance of such data. But this is easier said than done.

Clinicians do engage in these cross-conversations, but in doing so they often move outside their respective areas of expertise. Avrum Ben Avi, a senior interpersonal analyst, once commented on the experience of having a patient see him in a movie line when his (Ben Avi's) family was not behaving like a model of familial mental health. He made the point that psychoanalysts (and certainly the same applies to family therapists) are not experts in how to live but, rather, in how other people process their difficulties in living. The comparing of notes about patients' intimate relationships by clinicians in different treatment contexts can move discourse into whether "he and she are suited for each other," that is, beyond therapeutic parameters and into the sociology of romantic choice. Such an exchange calls for the talent of matchmakers rather than therapists.

Of course, there is always a Talmudic "on the other hand." One exception arises in shared cases involving relatively unpsychologically minded clients. In an earlier chapter I mentioned a couple whose main source of tension was the woman's pursuit of her less committed boyfriend. One of the reasons he was ambivalent was because of her singular interest in his degree of commitment, not in who he was as a person. This "loop" of her pursuit of commitment and his bristling resentment of it had been tightened to the breaking point; everything between them was routed through it. For example, when we momentarily succeeded in the therapy room in loosening this reciprocal loop and he dared to admit to deeply felt personal insecurities and self-doubts, she brought him right back to the issue of commitment and marriage. When I tactfully pointed to her self-absorption in her own agenda, she utterly failed to hear me. She and her therapist suggested that the therapists talk to each other. Her therapist found my observation about her patient's self-absorption initially a bit unfamiliar but then quite useful. One can assume that this characteristic would have emerged before long in this newly initiated individual therapy, but was there really an advantage in waiting past the point of imminent failure in the couple's relationship?

A second major exception to restricting information exchange arises when a couples therapist is working paradoxically. Psychoanalysts are often disquieted by reports about strategic interventions in family process. A couples therapist was working effectively, albeit strategically, with a couple who had never sexually consummated their ten-year marriage. She was called by the woman's individual therapist with a request to see the treatment consultation videotapes. Such was the degree of anxiety raised in the individual therapist by reports of this alien approach that the couples therapist, who was herself an analyst, felt as if the equivalent of an FBI investigation was in the offing—as indeed it was.

A colleague who is a supervisor of trainees doing individual therapy recently described to me his dismay in regard to a woman patient who was in concomitant couples therapy. The patient kept going back and forth on her decision to divorce a seemingly uncommitted spouse. The supervisor was dismayed by the concomitant couples work: "Do you believe that in what you call a 'live supervision' the supervisor of the couples therapist walked into the room and actually urged the husband to work harder at the marriage? Do you think that kind of advice giving is appropriate?" Unfortunately, my colleague had missed the paradoxical point. The supervisor of the couples therapist was trying to unfreeze the couple's paralysis regarding divorce. He knew that the history of this couple consisted of a very halfhearted commitment on the part of the husband. He likely believed that the clearest intervention was to highlight the husband's marital apathy. What better way than to urge him to act decisively? At least his wife would have the benefit of clearly seeing his lack of interest, and they both, of course, would benefit from the resolution of ambivalence. Cases such as this, where strategic interventions are being employed in the couples work while one or both partners are in individual therapy, can often benefit from the therapists' sharing information regarding the interventions. In the absence of learning the rationale for the paradoxical intervention, the wife's therapist and the supervisor of the individual work, my colleague, could easily have become hostile toward the work being done by the couples therapist, which might have introduced even more ambivalence into this couple's life!

The third reason to share information pertains to diagnostic syndromes that are worrisome to individual therapists. The more worrisome the diagnosis, the more determinedly an individual therapist is likely to seek to buttress the still fragile yearnings of the patient's self. Such determination is of course admirable and probably therapeutic in itself, but it can lead to worries about a colleague's interventions. For example, I considered it wise to speak to the individual therapist of the bulimic woman, Roberta, whom I introduced in the chapter on diagnosis. My family treatment involved a highly strategic intervention for chronic bulimia developed by Jay Haley, a treatment that involves the family shopping for food with the patient and being told by the patient exactly what was consumed before evacuation. This intervention is directed at exposing the artificial sense of control over family life that the patient has achieved via secrecy (i.e., she thinks she is in control but is really viewed as pitiful by them) as well as the obvious but denied invasion of boundaries (i.e., everyone talks about her bodily states, consumption, appearance, but this is actively denied because "it's her problem"). Roberta's individual therapist felt that the intervention ran exactly counter to what she and Roberta were struggling with, namely, Roberta's wish to distance herself from her parents and to mourn this loss. I felt that the individual therapy recognized what Roberta could imagine for herself but that the family therapy recognized why it was impossible for her to realize it. If we therapists had not communicated, we probably would have fought each other on behalf of the patient and our own egos. After hearing each other's point of view, we tried to account for each other's work. At a later point in the treatment I again talked with Roberta's individual therapist, this time about our patient's compulsive need to take a one-down position in her family; I thought the other therapist's view of Roberta as disabled and oppressed by her family reinforced this self-personification. This was harder to negotiate. Her individual therapist was not sympathetic to my belief that describing Roberta as oppressed by her parents fixed her in an under-dog position. In the family work it seemed palpably clear to me that this was the case; in addition, I felt concerned about the disrespect Roberta's behavior evoked in her parents and sister. The individual therapist wanted me to render Roberta's parents more sympathetic, and I wanted the individual therapist to help Roberta stop being her own worst enemy!

Before leaving the issue of sharing information, we should return to work with children. When children are in concomitant individual play therapy and family therapy, it is generally wise for the family therapist to stay in touch with the child therapist. The family configuration may shift rapidly and what the child therapist hears as confusion may be reality based. Moreover, if the family therapist is experimenting with intensive interventions, such as strategic approaches that involve the child, the child therapist can be very helpful in processing their mean-ing and supporting the child's anxiety about change. For the most part, the family therapist should be in charge of the parent counseling if children are participating in both forms of treatment. Otherwise, the child therapist usually siphons off the resistance to the family interven-tions, and no one benefits.

COMBINING TREATMENT APPROACHES

I would advocate a conservative approach about seeing significant others in consultation when working analytically. The analytic frame and the family context are easily blurred. Moreover, a diminution in dyadic intensity, the hallmark of analytic work, occurs when a signifi-cant other is invited into the analytic system. Similarly, patients can feel injured by the sudden sympathy their therapist shows for the new arrival. On the other hand, a therapist who is not sympathetic to the newly arrived member of the couple or family is both wasting the significant other's time and/or rendering that person justifiably cynical about the emotional traps lying in wait for the unwary in psycho-therapy. As for seeing both members of a couple simultaneously but psychoanalytically—I think it could be a tempting way to fill hours. Trained couples and family therapists are as negative about this kind of situation as analysts are about treating two or three people in the same nuclear family simultaneously.

It is difficult enough for therapists to try to keep levels of abstraction in place when working with patients who are being seen in more than one treatment modality. Family members sometimes try to discredit the authority of individual therapists and sometimes try to aggrandize it. This is a triangulating phenomenon that can be informative and that can help the couples therapist flesh out the systemic dynamics. Each therapist should probably stay neutral, or at most mildly curious about the other therapist's approach. Basically, neither has access to the other's work.

In a couples therapist's office the guerilla warfare of spouses who each cite their own individual therapist as an authority takes on an almost comic air. Why should patients ever tell their spouse what their analyst thinks about anyone, except as a strategic offensive? It is not so amusing hearing clients flout the boundaries of abstraction vis-à-vis treatment modalities in ways that are interpersonally hurtful. If a man who is struggling to become more honest tells his wife that he is glad she left for the weekend so that he could enjoy the children without her depressing effect, he should realize that he may be talking from his analysis but not to his analyst.

Therapeutic Interactions

It is a logical deduction of the position presented here that any change in a patient's experience should lead to a change in that person's relational style—if it can cross the threshold of redundant family patterns. If individual therapy is successful, why should we then have to focus directly on family relationships? The problem is that though relationships will change, we cannot predict the direction. System theorists in the old days of mechanistic metaphors talked about the possibility of "runaway systems"; for example, it was thought that raising the lid on the son's anger might lead to a rise in the father's attempts at suppression, which would feed the son's anger, and so on. The corollary of this is that some family therapists spend a fair amount of their time seeing one or another individual from a family to process family dynamics, even when other family members are within geographic range. Bowenians argue for this practice, firmly believing that if one works with the healthiest person in the family, the others will either fall into or out of line. They believe that at the very least the designated patient will achieve greater autonomy and differentiation. Other family therapists are less sanguine about the practice of helping individuals decode relationships in the family system.

Confidentiality is a key issue when combining forms of treatment and is generally handled differently in family and in individual therapy. If, as part of ongoing systemic work, I see one member of a family or couple on a one-session or short-term basis, I try to be clear about the parameters; confidentiality is not part of the treatment relationship as we know it analytically. I advise the individual that I cannot guarantee secrecy or privacy, but I assure him or her that I use discretion in disclosing the material we discuss together. It seems to me that the systems work has to be protected against secret alliances and collusion. I would rather not know about an extramarital affair than be bound in collusion with one member of a couple, thus skewing my relationship with both parties; the affair, as triangular escape valve, will be part of the systemic configuration in one way or another. Other family therapists disagree; they are wary of sacrificing the possibility of getting systemic information of any kind and are confident that coalitions and alliances can be dealt with.

Only rarely do I continue to see a family member individually as a second phase of treatment, and I do so only when the focus is fairly circumscribed and the work needing to be done calls for particular knowledge of the systemic dynamics. Thus, I saw a man who was stymied in his search for professional direction. He felt bitterly and ruminatively excluded from his wife's entrepreneurial success. His search had important individual and intrapsychic components, but his anxieties seemed to continually ricochet within the marital context—partly because of the subtle manner in which his wife fueled his embarrassment about his career paralysis (I had spent a great deal of time in the couples work decoding their competitiveness). The man was not very psychologically minded, and it seemed helpful to have the marital information available in working with him alone. Once or twice when patients have continued on in individual therapy, the shift from a more directive and playful stance to a more reserved, exploratory one has confused them. Patients who were not aware of the paradigm shift felt that I was depriving them or that I had become unconcerned about them when I shifted to an analytic stance. (There is considerably less risk with clients who are sophisticated about psychotherapy.)

Thus, I was able to work in an intensive, and I think useful, way with a woman who had a complete analysis before she began brief couples work with me around issues of shared parental responsibility and reliability. When I started to work with her individually afterward, there was little confusion on her part about what I was about. Later, this same patient was interested in a brief stint of couples work, and I referred her to a colleague. The synergistic effect of this experience was interesting. This later phase of couples work was stormy. The woman gained an understanding of her husband's periodic anxiety-producing flirtations as rooted in his own depressive tendencies. He, however, became offended by the challenge of the couples therapist and ended his participation in the therapy. The wife was deeply affected by her awareness that her husband acted out of desperation, not just disregard. She and I had previously looked at his flirtations from a multitude of perspectives (namely, her own history, impulses, and response to him), but our analytic work had not as deeply affected her. The understanding of her husband that this woman gained from the couples treatment enriched the work covered in her individual therapy. Over a period of a few months she found herself not only responding differently, more forgivingly, toward her father's serious lapses in sensitivity but also spontaneously thinking that her paternal grandmother had been a more attractive person than she had ever let herself know. Thus, she experienced a major shift in another relationship configuration, that is, in her relationship with the father she had previously rejected so firmly. Beyond this, this woman, whose professional principles had been, she believed, almost too rigid, found herself for the first time in her life comfortable with instrumental strategies in her professional work, with thinking of ends as justifying some bending of the means. Did this all stem from the couples treatment? It would be simplistic to think so. But I think that just as the infamous butterfly in China of chaos theory has powerful effects, so too does couples therapy sometimes create a certain storming of the psyche that transcends even what might have occurred previously in very determined analytic exploration.

There is no checklist anyone could draw up for a referral decision. The pragmatic question of when to make a referral is actually an instance of the very familiar and endlessly difficult job of tolerating ambiguity and uncertainty in clinical work. In the analytic situation we get to observe change at the deepest level that is articulate and narrative. In family work we get to observe change that is systemic, interactive, and behavioral, but we do not get to observe this change analytically (and therefore never know how deeply articulated it might become, nor how thoroughly integrated it might become in the patient's narrative). Conversely, we do not get to see how intrapsychic change manifests itself at home in interactive and systemic processes. Nor will we never know in individual cases (although controlled mix-and-match designs would give us some sense) whether such changes as are observed could have been achieved in the other modality. Or even how they would look if seen in the other modality! Basically, having a clearer sense of the process of both therapeutic approaches, however, makes planning and choosing clearer. One last example illustrating complexity rather than simplicity:

A woman I was seeing in analytically oriented psychotherapy asked for a referral to a couples therapist, which I was happy to provide. Though our work together had been somewhat successful, this woman's relationship with her husband was still fraught with bitter, sometimes violent arguments in which my patient screamed so shrilly she feared eviction from her apartment. No amount of interpretation about what appeared to be the dynamics behind these awful scenes (unbearable anger and humiliation, archaic loyalties and identifications, agitated dependency and vengefulness) seemed to make a difference in what happened between her and her husband. After the referral the patient described to me a couples session (the fourth or fifth) in which the family therapist, apparently in an effort to dramatize her autocratic, berating treatment of her husband had addressed her as "prime minister" and had asked her to stand on a chair in his office. The image and process captured the redundant, imbalanced, and absurd expression of power in this relationship where the husband played lamb and the wife played lion. The night after the session the wife had a dream in which her husband was swimming back and forth underwater in an effort to save a woman hanging limply onto him. Her husband had an oxygen mask; the woman had none. In order to stay underwater he had to cover or cup his ears (to avoid hearing her screams? her pain?), which prevented him from using the mask. In the dream the woman became desperate and screamed deafeningly.

Considered from the perspective of her dream, it seems clear that the patient's "prime minister" posture was at least partly compensatory for her more deeply rooted sense of deadness and extreme dependency. However, the dramatic expression of the compensatory dynamic, as orchestrated by the couples therapist's intervention, did have the extremely useful effect of allowing the deeper dynamic to emerge. It had not emerged clearly enough for us to explore transferentially and countertransferentially in the analytically oriented treatment, and the question remains as to why this was the case. Was this because I as her therapist could not tolerate a full-blown bullying transference? Or were her husband's dynamics so perfectly matched to her own defensive style that exploring only her dynamics (i.e., my therapeutic work with her) was insufficient to cross the threshold of redundancy? These are questions relevant to the constraints on transference interpretation that I have tried to raise in this text. I do not think that either therapeutic modality—the analytic or the family systems approach—is truer than the other. The analytic approach is perhaps more prismatic while the family systems approach is more focused, but an investigation and expansion at either level can be beneficial. Moreover, I am convinced that there are patients, such as this woman, who require both levels of intervention. I think my patient's dream clearly reflects her prevailing sense that both she and her husband were drowning in their shared difficulties in living, a crisis that requires the best set of therapeutics we have to offer.

chapter thirteen

Epilogue

At the end of this walk across the bridge between two therapeutic approaches, we return to the valley of cultural context. After all, whatever we try to do vis-à-vis each other reflects an organizing historical and cultural zeitgeist, which usually escapes identification until we can view it from afar. Where are we today in our organizing framework about self and relationship? And what are the implications of this framework for what we are trying to remedy therapeutically?

Gergen (1985) pointed out that the structure of relationships has become denser and the nature of the self more distributed because of the electronic revolution. In this age of electronic bonding, it is hard to know whether we are intensifying our connection to one another and thus moving toward an ever more context-dependent self-awareness or whether we are moving further into isolated autonomy as we type away at our computers, sporadically faxing and e-mailing our personal reflections to each other. It has become normative to have marriages located on separate coasts and in separate countries. The workplace has become atomized; the new work site is a series of desk stations leased and operated by totally unrelated companies. Are we in fact electronically weighting our self-awareness on fantasy remnants instead of ongoing reflected appraisals? Willi (1987) notes:

> Our culture is moving increasingly rapidly in the direction of the dissolution of circular regulations. This is not only evident in the dissolution of marriages and families, of associations and institutions, but also especially in the structuring of daily life. Whereas everyday life was previously full of interactions and circular regulations, it is now in the hands of the individual to carry out most tasks without having to relate to any other persons (in supermarkets, self-service gas stations, self-service restaurants, cash dispensers, or even dancing in a discotheque) . . . the question arises as to how people deal with this loss of shaping, circular regulations. The multiple circular regulations were not only a means of social control. They also furnished individuals with the opportunity to realize themselves, to sharpen their identity through feedback from their effects on people and

things. . . . It is possible that the loss of personal circularity in relation to social systems, and the increasing weakness of the family and working teams, will have destructive consequences. These may necessitate measures for the protection of the psychosocial ecology [Willi, 1987, p. 434].

When Sullivan first proposed his idea that a sense of unique individuality was damaging to human development, he raised the hackles of a psychoanalytic community that was committed to a modernist ethic of rich idiosyncratic subjectivity. However, more recently some clinicians have responded with a sense of historical perspective to this provocative notion:

The idea of a unique self arises basically as a defense against the terrible anxiety produced by one's inability to attain intimacy. It is a way of asserting one's difference, one's specialness, and therefore avoiding the emotions associated with the failure to achieve meaningful relationships. In a society where the cultural supports for ongoing familial and personal relationships are eroding away, the person must develop wholly new ways of establishing authentic contact and thereby the potential for consensual validation with others. If he fails to manage this on his own he is deprived of an enduring sense of meaning in his life. The assumption of uniqueness comes then as an explanation of such failure [Lionells, 1978, p. 152].

This is in fact a representation of the danger Willi postulated; that is, a sociocultural milieu in which the increasing difficulty of establishing regular and intense relationships will lead to defensive self-deception, leading to more problematic relationship formation, and on and on in a vitiating loop.

Ironically, it is likely that it was embeddedness in dense and cross-hatched relationship systems that enabled individuals to experience the acute pain of existential aloneness with courage:

I would guess that my generation, coming of age at the start of the 60s, when the national mood was one of intense political and moral crisis, is the last American generation to so contemplate inwardness as a romantic state of being; it is the last generation of literary-minded young men and women who interiorized the elegiac comedy of Beckett's characters, the radiant madness of Dostoyevsky's self-lacerated God-haunted seekers, the subtle ironies of Camus's prose [Joyce Carol Oates, 1993, p. 25].

A commonly voiced concern is that our postmodern cultural milieu currently precludes this kind of self-awareness. Interiority may simply be too terrifying in a vacuum of human connectedness.

There are implications for psychotherapy. It well may be that individuals—depending on their crises and their emotional complexions—may need a period of in-depth personal exploration *and* a period of relationship revitalization. Psychoanalysis has essentially constructed the former exploration for the culture at large, but I think as a professional community psychoanalysts have underestimated the importance of the latter. I pressed a wife of a couple I was working with recently to be open to hearing her husband's profound doubts and concerns about the meaning of his life. I pointed out that she was the only person he would expose these doubts to, since the rest of the world knew him as a doer and achiever. They were a psychoanalytically saturated couple, and she replied, "Why me? Isn't that what you have a therapist for?" Her husband looked chagrined. I said to her, "You might actually do a much better job than a therapist." I was not trying to be cleverly strategic or systemically inventive. At that moment I meant it.

References

Ackerman, N. W. (1966), *Treating the Troubled Family.* New York: Basic Books.

Albee, E. (1962), *Who's Afraid of Virginia Woolf?* New York: Dramatists Play Service.

Anderson, H. & Goolishian, H. A. (1988), Human systems as linguistic systems: Preliminary and evolving ideas about the implications for clinical theory. *Fam. Proc.,* 27(4):371–394.

Anderson, H. & Goolishian, H. A. (1990), Beyond cybernetics: Comments on Atkinson and Heath's "Further thoughts on second-order family therapy." *Fam. Ther.,* 29(2):157–163.

Andolfi, M. & Angelo, C. (1988), Toward constructing the therapeutic system. *J. Mar. Fam. Ther.,* 14(3):237–247.

Angyal, A. (1965), *Neurosis and Treatment: A Holistic Theory.* New York: Viking Press.

Aponte, H. J. (1992), Training the person of the therapist in structural family therapy. *J. Mar. Fam. Ther.,* 18(3):269–281.

Aron, L. (1991), The patient's experience of the analyst's subjectivity. *Psychoanal. Dial.,* 1(1):29–51.

Atwood, G. E. & Stolorow, R. D. (1984), *Structures of Subjectivity.* New York: Lawrence Erlbaum Associates.

Auerswald, E. H. (1987), Epistemological confusion in family therapy and research. *Fam. Proc.,* 26:317–330.

Bach, S. (1985), *Narcissistic States and the Therapeutic Process.* New York: Aronson.

Bakhtin, M. (1981), *The Dialogic Imagination.* Austin, TX: University of Texas Press.

Bateson, G. (1956), Information and codification: A philosophical approach. In: *Communication: The Social Matrix of Psychiatry,* ed. G. Bateson & J. Ruesch. New York: Norton, 1951, pp. 168–211.

—— (1958), *Naven* (rev. ed.). Stanford, CA: Stanford University Press.

—— (1972), *Steps to an Ecology of Mind.* New York: Ballantine Books.

—— Haley, J. & Weakland, J. (1956), Toward a theory of schizophrenia. *Behav. Sci.,* 1:251–264.

Beebe, B. & Lachmann, F. M. (1991), Reformulations of early development and transference: Implications for psychic structure formation. In: *Interface of Psychoanalysis and Psychology,* ed. J. W. Barron, M. N. Eagle & D. Wolitzsky. Washington, DC: American Psychological Association, 1992, pp. 133–153.

Belsky, J., Lang, M. E. & Rovine, M. (1985), Stability and change in marriage across the transition to parenthood: A second study. *J. Mar. Fam.,* 47:855–865.

Benjamin, J. (1988), *The Bonds of Love.* New York: Pantheon Books.

Bertalanffy, L. von (1968), *General System Theory.* New York: Braziller.

Bion, W. P (1962), *Learning from Experience.* New York: Basic Books.

Bloch, D. & Simon, R. (1982), *The Strength of Family Therapy.* New York: Brunner/Mazel.

Blum, H. P. (1992), Psychic change: The analytic relationship(s) and agents of change. *Internat. J. Psycho-Anal.,* 73:255–264.

Bollas, C. (1982), *The Shadow of the Object*. New York: Columbia University Press.

Bonamo, G. A. (1990), Repression, accessibility, and the translation of private experience. *Psychoanal. Psychol.*, 7(4):453–474.

Boszormenyi-Nagy, I. (1987), *Foundations of Contextual Therapy: Collected Papers of Ivan Boszormenyi-Nagy*. New York: Brunner/Mazel.

Bowen, M. (1978), *Family Therapy in Clinical Practice*. New York: Aronson.

Brighton-Cleghorn, J. (1987), Formulations of self and family systems. *Fam. Proc.*, 26:185–201.

Brodkin, A. M. (1980), Family therapy: The making of a mental health movement. *Amer. J. Orthopsychiat.*, 50(1):4–17.

Bromberg, P. (1979), Interpersonal psychoanalysis and regression. *Contemp. Psychoanal.*, 15:647–655.

Bronfenbrenner, U., Kessel, F., Kessen, W. & White, S. E. (1986), Toward a critical social history of developmental psychology: A propaedeutic discussion. *Amer. Psychol.*, 41(11):1218–1230.

Bruner, J. (1986), *Actual Minds, Possible Worlds*. Cambridge, MA: Harvard University Press.

—— (1990), *Acts of Meaning*. Cambridge, MA: Harvard University Press.

Burke, W. F. (1992), Countertransference disclosure and the asymmetry/mutuality dilemma. *Psychoanal. Dial.*, 2(2):241–271.

Carter, B. & McGoldrick, M. (1989), *The Changing Family Life Cycle* (2nd ed.). Needham Heights, MA: Allyn and Bacon.

Chasin, R., Roth, S. & Bograd, M. (1989), Action methods in systemic therapy: Dramatizing ideal futures and reformed pasts with couples. *Fam. Proc.*, 28(2):121–136.

Chrzanowski, G. (1978), Malevolent transformation and the negative therapeutic reaction. *Contemp. Psychoanal.*, 14:405–414.

Cohler, B. J. (1980), Adult developmental psychology and reconstruction in psychoanalysis. In: *The Course of Life: Psychoanalytic Contributions Toward Understanding Personality Development: Vol. 3. Adulthood and the Aging Process*, ed. S. J. Greenspan & G. H. Pollock. Washington, DC: National Institute of Mental Health, pp. 149–199.

Combrinck-Graham, L. (1985), A developmental model for family systems. *Fam. Proc.*, 24(2):139–150.

Csikszentmihalyi, M. & Bennett, S. (1971), An exploratory model of play. *Amer. Anthropol.*, 73:45–58.

Cushman, P. (1991), Ideology obscured: Political uses of the self in Daniel Stern's infant. *Amer. Psychol.*, 46:206–219.

Dicks, H. V. (1967), *Marital Tensions*. New York: Basic Books.

Duhl, B. S. (1983), *From the Inside Out and Other Metaphors*. New York: Brunner/Mazel.

Dyrud, J. (1990), Remembrance of things past and present. *Contemp. Psychoanal.*, 16(3):335–347.

Eagle, M. (1993), Enactments, transference, and symptomatic cure: A case history. *Psychoanal. Dial.*, 3(1):93–110.

Eagleton, T. (1983), *Literary Theory*. Oxford, UK: Basil Blackwell.

Ehrenberg, D. B. (1992), *The Intimate Edge*. New York: Norton.

Epston, D. (1994), Extending the conversation. *Fam. Ther. Netwrkr.*, 18(6):30–39.

—— & White, M. (1992), *Experience, Contradiction, Narrative and Imagination*. Adelaide, Australia: Dulwich Centre Publications.

Erikson, E. H. (1959), *Identity and the Life Cycle*. New York: Norton, 1980.

Erickson, G. D. (1988), Against the grain: Decentering family therapy. *J. Mar. Fam. Ther.*, 14:225–236.

Erickson, M. H. (1973), *Uncommon Therapy*. New York: Norton.

Fairbairn, W. R. D. (1952), *Psychoanalytic Studies of the Personality.* London: Routledge & Kegan Paul.

Falicov, C. J. (1978), *Family Transitions.* New York: Guilford Press.

Fish, V. (1993), Poststructuralism in family therapy: Interrogating the narrative/conversational mode. *J. Mar. Fam. Ther.,* 19:221–232.

Forrest, T. (1978), A synthesis of individual theory and therapy with family concepts. *Psychoanal. Rev.,* 65:499–521.

Framo, J. (1972), Symptoms from a family transactional viewpoint. In: *Progress in Group and Family Therapy,* ed. C. J. Sager & H. K. Singer. New York: Brunner/Mazel, pp. 251–308.

—— (1976), Family of origin as a therapeutic resource for adults in marital and family therapy: You can and should go home again. *Fam. Proc.,* 15:193–210.

Franz, C. E. & White, K. M. (1985), Individuation and attachment in personality development: Extending Erikson's theory. *J. Pers.,* 53(2):224–256.

Freud, S. (1910), The future prospects of psycho-analytic therapy. *Standard Edition,* 11:139–151. London: Hogarth Press, 1957.

—— (1913), Totem and taboo. *Standard Edition,* 13:1–161. London: Hogarth Press, 1955.

—— (1937), Constructions in analysis. *Standard Edition,* 23:255–269. London: Hogarth Press, 1964.

Friedman, E. H. (1984), The play's the thing. *Fam. Ther. Netwrkr.,* 10:24–29.

Friedman, L. (1988), *The Anatomy of Psychotherapy.* Hillsdale, NJ: The Analytic Press.

Geertz, C. (1986), Making experiences, authoring selves. In: *The Anthropology of Experience,* ed. V. Turner & E. Bruner. Urbana-Champaigne, IL: University of Illinois Press, pp. 373–380.

Genijovich, E. (1995), Empowering an impossible blended family: Searching for hidden treasures in troubled families. Presented at New York University Psychology Clinic, New York City, March 7.

Gergen, K. J. (1982), *Toward Transformation in Social Knowledge.* New York: Springer-Verlag.

—— (1985), The social constructionist movement in modern psychology. *Amer. Psychol.,* 40:266–295.

—— (1991), *The Saturated Self.* New York: Basic Books.

Gerson, M. J. (1980), The lure of motherhood. *Psychol. Women Quart.,* 5(2):207–218.

—— (1986), The prospect of parenthood for women and men. *Psychol. Women Quart.,* 10(1):49–62.

—— (1988), Sullivan and family therapy: An unconsummated affair. *Contemp. Psychoanal.,* 24:669–724.

—— (1989), Tomorrow's fathers: The participation of fatherhood. In: *Fathers and Their Families,* ed. S. H. Cath, A. Gurwitt & L. Gunsberg. Hillsdale, NJ: The Analytic Press, pp. 127–144.

—— (1993), Sullivan's self-in-development. *Contemp. Psychoanal.,* 29(2):197–218.

—— Alpert, J. & Richardson, M. S. (1984), Mothering: The view from psychological research. *Signs: J. Women Cult. Soc.,* 9(31):434–453.

Ghent, E. (1989), Credo: The dialectics of one-person and two-person psychologies. *Contemp. Psychoanal.,* 25(2):169–211.

—— (1992), Paradox and process. *Psychoanal. Dial.,* 2(2):135–160.

Gill, M. M. (1993), Comments on Morris Eagle's "Enactments, transference, and symptomatic cure: A case history." *Psychoanal. Dial.,* 3(1):111–122.

—— (1994), *Psychoanalysis in Transition.* Hillsdale, NJ: The Analytic Press.

—— & Hoffman, I. Z. (1982), *Analysis of Transference II.* New York: International Universities Press.

Gleick, J. (1988), *Chaos: Making a New Science.* New York: Penguin Books.

Goldberg, A. (1986), The wishy-washy personality (reply to discussion by P. Bromberg, pp. 387–388). *Contemp. Psychoanal.*, 22:357–374.

Goldenberg, I. & Goldenberg, H. (1991), *Family Therapy.* Pacific Grove, CA: Brooks/Cole.

Goldner, V. (1985), Feminism and family therapy. *Fam. Proc.*, 24(1):31–48.

—— (1988), Generation and gender: Normative and covert hierarchies. *Fam. Proc.*, 27(1):17–32.

Goodrich, T. J., Rampage, C., Ellman, B. & Halstead, K. (1988), *Feminist Family Therapy.* New York: Norton.

Green, A. (1978), Potential space in psychoanalysis: the object in the setting. In: *Between Reality and Fantasy,* ed. S. A. Gralnick, L. Barkin & S. Muensterberger. New York: Jason Aronson, pp. 169–189.

Greenberg, J. R. (1986), Theoretical models and the analyst's neutrality. *Contemp. Psychoanal.*, 22(1):87–106.

—— (1995), Words and acts: The round robin. *Newsletter of Sect. I, Div. of Psychoanal. (39),* *Amer. Psychol. Assoc.*, April 11(1):12–13.

Grotstein, J. S. (1994), Projective identification reappraised. *Contemp. Psychoanal.*, 30(4): 708–746.

Guerin, P. J., ed. (1978), *Family Therapy.* New York: Gardner Press.

Gurman, A., Kniskern, D. P. & Pinsof, W. M. (1986), Research on the process and outcome of marital and family therapy. In: *Handbook of Psychotherapy and Behavior Change* (3rd ed.), ed. S. Garfield & A. Bergin. New York: Wiley, pp. 565–624.

Haley, J. (1963), Transference revisited. *J. Nerv. Ment. Dis.*, 137:363–371.

—— (1976), *Problem-Solving Therapy.* San Francisco: Jossey-Bass.

—— (1980), *Leaving Home.* New York: McGraw-Hill.

Hare-Mustin, R. (1989), The problem of gender family therapy theory. In: *Women in Families,* ed. M. McGoldrick, C. Anderson & F. Walsh. New York: Norton, pp. 61–77.

Harris, A. (1994), Gender practices and speech practices: Towards a model of dialogical and relational selves. Presented at Division of Psychoanalysis (39), American Psychological Association, Baltimore, April 14.

Havens, L. (1986), *Making Contact.* Cambridge, MA: Harvard University Press.

Henry, W. P., Schact, T. E. & Strupp, H. H. (1986), Structural analysis of social behavior: Application to a study of interpersonal process in differential psychotherapeutic outcome. *J. Consult. Clin. Psychol.*, 54:27–31.

Hermans, J. M., Kempen, J. J. G. & Van Loon, R. J. P. (1992), The dialogical self: Beyond individualism and rationalism. *Amer. Psychol.*, 47:23–33.

Hirsch, I. & Roth, J. (1995), Changing conceptions of the unconscious. *Contemp. Psychoanal.*, 31(2):263–276.

Hoffman, I. Z. (1983), The patient as interpreter of the analyst's experience. *Contemp. Psychoanal.*, 19(3):389–422.

—— (1991), Discussion: Toward a social-constructivist view of the psychoanalytic situation. *Psychoanal. Dial.*, 1:74–105.

Hoffman, L. (1981), *Foundations of Family Therapy.* New York: Basic Books.

—— (1985), Beyond power and control: Toward a "second order" family systems therapy. *Fam. Sys. Med.*, 3:381–396.

—— (1990), Constructing realities: An art of lenses. *Fam. Proc.*, 29:1–12.

Holt, R. R. (1985), The current status of psychoanalytic theory. *Psychoanal. Psych.*, 2:289–316.

Horner, T. M. (1991), Staying the course. *Readings: J. Reviews & Commentary Ment. Hlth.*, 6(1):12–17. American Orthopsychiatric Association.

Huizinga, J. (1944), *Homo Ludens.* Boston: Beacon Press, 1955.

Imber-Black, E. (1991), A family-larger-system perspective. *Fam. Sys. Med.*, 9:371–395.
—— Roberts, J. & Whiting, R., eds. (1988), *Rituals in Families and Family Therapy.* New York: Norton.
Jackson, D. D. (1965a), Family rules: Mental quid pro quo. *Arch. Gen. Psychiat.*, 12: 589–594.
—— (1965b), The study of the family. *Fam. Proc.*, 4:1–20.
Jacoby, R. (1983), *The Repression of Psychoanalysis.* New York: Basic Books.
James, W. (1890), *The Principles of Psychology, Vol. 1.* Cambridge, MA: Harvard University Press, 1981.
Jantsch, E. (1975), *Design for Evolution.* New York: Braziller.
Kaufman, E. & Kaufman, P. N., eds. (1981), *Family Therapy of Drug and Alcohol Abuse.* New York: Gardner Press.
Kaye, K. (1987), Draft of family and self. In: *The Psychology of Education in Early Infancy,* ed. V. Ugazio. Milan, Italy: Franco Angeli Libri (in Italian).
Keeney, B. P. & Silverstein, O. (1986), *The Therapeutic Voice of Olga Silverstein.* New York: Guilford Press.
Kernberg, O. (1975), *Borderline Conditions and Pathological Narcissism.* New York: Aronson.
Kerr, M. E. & Bowen, M. (1988), *Family Evaluation.* New York: Norton.
Kobak, R. R. & Waters, D. B. (1984), Family therapy as a rite of passage: Play's the thing. *Fam. Proc.*, 23:89–100.
Kohut, H. (1977), *The Restoration of the Self.* New York: International Universities Press.
Korzibsky, A. (1954), *Time-Binding.* Lakeville, CT: Institute of General Semantics.
Laplanche, J. & Pontalis, J. B. (1973), *The Language of Psychoanalysis.* New York: Norton.
Lasch, C. (1977), *Haven in a Heartless World.* New York: Basic Books.
Lesser, R. (1978), Sibling transference and countertransference. *J. Amer. Acad. Psychoanal.*, 6:37–49.
Levenson, E. A. (1972), *The Fallacy of Understanding.* New York: Basic Books.
—— (1983), *The Ambiguity of Change.* New York: Basic Books.
—— (1988), The pursuit of the particular. *Contemp. Psychoanal.*, 24(1):1–16.
—— (1989), Whatever happened to the cat? Interpersonal perspective on the self. *Contemp. Psychoanal.*, 25:537–553.
—— (1991), Back to the future: The new psychoanalytic revisionism. Presented at the Institute for Contemporary Psychoanalysis, New York City, April 19.
—— (1992), Mistakes, errors and oversights. *Contemp. Psychoanal.*, 28:555–571.
—— (1993), Shoot the messenger: Interpersonal aspects of the analyst's interpretation. *Contemp. Psychoanal.*, 29(3):382–396.
Levenson, T. (1994), How not to make a Stradivarius. *Amer. Scholar*, 63:351–378.
Lichtenberg, J. & Galler, F. (1987), The fundamental rule: A study of current usage. *J. Amer. Psychoanal. Assn.*, 35:47–76.
Lidz, T. (1976), *The Person.* New York: Basic Books.
Lionells, M. (1978), A reply to Klenbort's "Another look at Sullivan's concept of individuality." *Contemp. Psychoanal.*, 14(1):149–152.
London, N. J. (1981), The play element of regression in the psychoanalytic process. *Psychoanal. Inq.*, 1:7–27.
Luepnitz, D. (1988), *The Family Interpreted.* New York: Basic Books.
Madanes, C. (1980), Protection, paradox and pretending. *Fam. Proc.*, 19(1):3–12.
—— (1981), *Strategic Family Therapy.* San Francisco: Jossey-Bass.
—— (1984), *Behind the One-Way Mirror.* San Francisco: Jossey-Bass.
Marlin, E. (1989), *Genograms.* Chicago: Contemporary Books.
Masson, J. M. (1984), *The Assault on Truth.* New York: Farrar, Straus & Giroux.

McGee, C. (1993, Nov. 19), The many faces of every family are found in one. *The New York Times*, p. 6.

McGoldrick, M. (1981), Family therapy with Irish-Americans. *Fam. Proc.*, 20(2):223–240.

Minuchin, P. (1985), Families and individual development: Provocations from the field of family therapy. *Child Dev.*, 56:289–302.

Minuchin, S. (1965), Conflict-resolution family therapy. *Psychiatry*, 28:278–286.

—— (1974), *Families and Family Therapy*. Cambridge, MA: Harvard University Press.

—— (1985), My many voices. Presented at Evolution of Psychotherapy (conference sponsored by the Milton H. Erickson Foundation), Phoenix, December 12.

—— (1989), Family therapy development: A parable. In: *Family Transition*, ed. C. J. Falicov. New York: Guilford Press, pp. ix–xii.

—— (1991), The seductions of constructivism. *Fam. Ther. Ntwrkr.*, 15(5):47–50.

—— & Fishman, H. C. (1981), *Family Therapy Techniques*. Cambridge, MA: Harvard University Press.

—— Montalvo, B., Guerney, B., Rosman, B. & Schumer, F. (1967), *Families of the Slums*. New York: Basic Books.

—— & Nichols, M. P. (1993), *Family Healing*. New York: Free Press.

—— Rosman, B. L. & Baker, L. (1978), *Psychosomatic Families*. Cambridge, MA: Harvard University Press.

Mitchell, S. A. (1984), Object relations theories and the developmental tilt. *Contemp. Psychoanal.*, 20(4):473–499.

—— (1988), *Relational Concepts in Psychoanalysis*. Cambridge, MA: Harvard University Press.

—— (1993), *Hope and Dread in Psychoanalysis*. New York: Basic Books.

—— & Greenberg, J. R. (1983), *Object Relations in Psychoanalytic Theory*. Cambridge, MA: Harvard University Press.

Neill, J. R. & Kniskern, D. P., eds. (1982), *From Psyche to System: The Evolving Therapy of Carl Whitaker*. New York: Guilford Press.

Newton, P. M. (1989), Free association and the division of labor in psychoanalytic treatment. *Psychoanal. Psychol.*, 6(1):31–46.

Nichols, M. P. & Schwartz, R. C. (1994), *Family Therapy* (3rd ed.). Needham Heights, MA: Allyn and Bacon.

Oates, J. C. (1993, July 25), Despair: The one unforgiveable sin. *The New York Times*, Book Review section, pp. 3–25.

Ogden, T. (1979), On projective identification. *Internat. J. Psycho-Anal.*, 60:357–383.

O'Hanlon, B. (1994), The third wave. *Fam. Ther. Netwrkr.*, 18(6):18–29.

Papp, P. (1982), Staging reciprocal metaphors in a couples group. *Fam. Proc.*, 21(4):453–468.

Pendergast, E. G. & Sherman, C. O. (1977), A guide to the genogram family systems training. *The Family*, 5(1):3–14.

Penn, P. (1985), Feed forward: Future questions, future maps. *Fam. Proc.*, 24(3):299–310.

Piercy, F. P. & Sprenkle, D. H. (1990), Marriage and family therapy: A decade review. *J. Mar. Fam.*, 52(4):1116–1126.

Pizer, S. A. (in press), Negotiating potential space: Illusion, play, metaphor and the subjunctive. *Psychoanal. Dial.*

Racker, H. (1968), *Transference and Countertransference*. New York: International Universities Press.

Real, T. (1990), The therapeutic use of self in constructionist systemic therapy. *Fam. Proc.*, 29(3):255–272.

Roberto, L. (1986), Bulimia: The transgenerational view. *J. Mar. Fam. Ther.*, 12(3):231–240.

Roberts, J. (1988), Setting the frame: Definition, functions, and typology of rituals. In: *Rituals in Families and Family Therapy,* ed. E. Imber-Black, J. Roberts & R. Whiting. New York: Norton, pp. 3–46.

Rorty, A. (1976), A literary postscript: Characters, persons, selves, individuals. In: *The Identities of Persons,* ed. A. O. Rorty. Berkeley, CA: University of California Press, p. *xx.*

Rorty, R. (1989), *Contingency, Irony and Solidarity.* New York: Cambridge University Press.

Ruland, R. & Bradbury, M. (1991), *From Puritanism to Post-Modernism.* New York: Viking Press.

Sacks, O. (1985), The president's speech. *NY Rev. Books,* 32(13):29.

Sander, F. (1979), *Individual and Family Therapy.* New York: Aronson.

Sandler, J. (1976), Countertransference and role-responsiveness. *Internat. Rev. Psycho-Anal.,* 3:43–47.

Satir, V. (1967), *Conjoint Family Therapy.* Palo Alto, CA: Science and Behavior Books.

—— (1972), *Peoplemaking.* Palo Alto, CA: Science and Behavior Books.

Schafer, R. (1981), Narration in the psychoanalytic dialogue. In: *On Narrative,* ed. W. J. T. Mitchell. Chicago: University of Chicago Press, pp. 25–50.

—— (1983), *The Analytic Attitude.* New York: Basic Books.

—— (1992), *Retelling a Life.* New York: Basic Books.

Scharff, D. & Scharff, J. (1987), *Object Relations Family Therapy.* New York: Aronson.

Schechner, R. (1986), Magnitudes of performance. In: *The Anthropology of Experience,* ed. V. W. Turner & E. M. Bruner. Urbana-Champaigne, IL: University of Illinois Press, pp. 344–372.

Schecter, D. (1983), Notes on the development of creativity. *Contemp. Psychoanal.,* 19: 193–199.

Schimek, J. G. (1983), The construction of the transference. *Psychoanal. Contemp. Thought,* 6(3):435–456.

Selvini Palazzoli, M. (1974), *Self-Starvation.* London: Human Context Books (Chaucer Publ.).

—— Cecchin, G., Prata, G. & Boscolo, L. (1978), *Paradox and Counterparadox.* New York: Aronson.

Siegel, L. I. (1987), Sullivan's contribution to child psychiatry. *Contemp. Psychoanal.,* 23:278–298.

Simon, R. (1985a), Take it or leave it: An interview with Carl Whitaker. *Fam. Ther. Netwrkr.,* 9(5):27–37;70–74.

—— (1985b), An interview with Humberto Maturana. *Fam. Ther. Netwrkr.,* 93:37–43.

Singer, E. (1969), *Key Concepts in Psychotherapy* (2nd ed.). New York: Basic Books.

Skynner, A. C. R. (1976), *Systems of Family and Marital Psychotherapy.* New York: Brunner/Mazel.

Spence, D. P. (1982), *Narrative Truth and Historical Truth.* New York: Norton.

Sroufe, L. A. and Fleeson, J. (1988), The coherence of family relationships. In: *Relationships Within Families,* ed. R. A. Hinde & S. Stevenson-Hinde. Oxford, UK: Clarendon Press, pp. 27–47.

Stanton, A. & Schwartz, M. (1954), *The Mental Hospital.* New York: Basic Books.

Stegner, C. (1989), The classic and the romantic vision in psychoanalysis. *Internat. J. Psycho-Anal.,* 70:593–610.

Steinglass, P., Bennett, L. A., Wolin, S. J. & Reiss, D. (1987), *The Alcoholic Family.* New York: Basic Books.

Stern, D. B. (1994), Conceptions of structure in interpersonal theory. *Contemp. Psychoanal.,* 30(2):255–300.

Stern, D. N. (1985), *The Interpersonal World of the Infant*. New York: Basic Books.

—— (1995), *The Motherhood Constellation*. New York: Basic Books.

Stern, P. N. (1978), Stepfather families: Integration around child discipline. *Issues Ment. Health Nurs.*, 1:50–56.

Stierlin, H. (1977), *Psychoanalysis and Family Therapy*. New York: Aronson.

Strachey, J. (1934), The nature of the therapeutic action of psychoanalysis. *Internat. J. Psycho-Anal.*, 15:127–159.

Sullivan, H. S. (1940), *Clinical Studies of Psychiatry*. New York: Norton, 1956.

—— (1950), The illusion of personal individuality. In: *The Fusion of Psychiatry and Social Science*. New York: Norton, 1964, pp. 198–226.

—— (1953), *The Interpersonal Theory of Psychiatry*. New York: Norton.

Sulloway, R. J. (1983), *Freud, Biologist of the Mind*. New York: Basic Books.

Szapocznik, J., Murray, E., Scopetta, M., Hervis, O., Rio, A., Cohen, R., Rivas-Vazquez, A., Posada, V. & Kurtines, W. (1989), Structural family versus psychodynamic child therapy for problematic Hispanic boys. *J. Consult. Clin. Psychol.*, 57(5):571–578.

Tamura, T. & Lau, A. (1992), Connectedness versus separateness: Applicability of family therapy to Japanese families. *Fam. Proc.*, 31(4):319–340.

Tansey, M. J. & Burke, W. F. (1989), *Understanding Countertransference*. Hillsdale, NJ: The Analytic Press.

Turner, V. (1977), Frame, flow and reflection: Ritual and drama as public liminality. In: *Performance in Postmodern Culture: Theories of Contemporary Culture, Vol. 1*, ed. M. Benamou. Madison, WI: Center for Twentieth Century Studies, pp. 33–58.

—— (1982), *From Ritual to Theatre*. New York: Performing Arts Journal publications.

—— (1986), Dewey, Dilthey, and drama. In: *The Anthropology of Experience*, ed. V. Turner & E. Bruner. Urbana-Champaign, IL: University of Illinois Press, pp. 33–44.

Van Gennep, A. (1909), *The Rites of Passage*. London: Routledge & Kegan Paul.

Visher, J. S. & Visher, E. B. (1984), Stepfamilies and stepparenting. In: *Normal Family Processes*, ed. F. Walsh. New York: Guilford Press, pp. 331–353.

Wachtel, E. F. (1982), The family psyche over three generations: The genogram revisited. *J. Mar. Fam. Ther.*, 8:335–343.

Wachtel, P. L. (1977), *Psychoanalysis and Behavior Therapy*. New York: Basic Books.

—— (1986), On the limits of therapeutic neutrality. From Neutrality to Personal Revelation: Patterns of Influence in the Analytic Relationship (symposium). *Contemp. Psychoanal.*, 22(1):60–70.

—— & Wachtel, E. F. (1986), *Family Dynamics in Individual Psychotherapy*. New York: Guilford Press.

Walters, M., Carter, B., Papp, P. & Silverstein, O. (1988), *The Invisible Web*. New York: Guilford Press.

Wamboldt, F. S. & Reiss, D. (1989), Defining a family heritage and a relationship identity: Two central tasks in the making of marriage. *Fam. Proc.*, 28(3):317–336.

Waters, D. (1994), Prisoners of our metaphors. *Fam. Ther. Netwrkr.*, 18(6):73–76.

Watzlawick, P. (1978), *The Language of Change*. New York: Basic Books.

—— Beavin, J. H. & Jackson, D. D. (1967), *Pragmatics of Human Communication*. New York: Norton.

—— Weakland, J. H. & Fisch, R. (1974), *Change: Principles of Problem Formation and Problem Resolution*. New York: Norton.

Weiner, N. (1948), *Cybernetics or Control and Communication in the Animal and the Machine*. Cambridge, MA: Technology Press.

Weiss, J. & Sampson, H. (1994), The analyst's task. *Contemp. Psychoanal.*, 30(2):236–254.

Wheelis, A. (1950), The place of action in personality change. *Psychiatry*, 13:135–148.

Whitaker, C. (1975), Psychotherapy of the absurd: With a special emphasis on the psychotherapy of aggression. *Fam. Proc.*, 14(1):1–16.

—— (1976a), A family is a four-dimensional relationship. In: *Family Therapy*, ed. P. J. Guerin. New York: Gardner Press, pp. 182–192.

—— (1976a), The hindrance of theory in clinical work. In: *Family Therapy*, ed. P. J. Guerin. New York: Gardner Press, pp. 154–164.

White, M. & Epston, D. (1990), *Narrative Means to Therapeutic Ends.* New York: Norton.

Whitehead, A. N. & Russell, B. (1910–1913), *Principia Mathematica.* New York: Cambridge University Press.

Willi, J. (1987), Some principles of an ecological model of the person as a consequence of the therapeutic experience with systems. *Fam. Proc.*, 26:429–435.

Wilson, M. N. (1989), Child development in the context of the black extended family. *Amer. Psychol.*, 44(2):380–385.

Winnicott, D. W. (1971), *Playing and Reality.* New York: Tavistock.

—— (1975), *Through Pediatrics to Psychoanalysis.* New York: Basic Books.

Wittgenstein, L. (1958), *Philosophical Investigations* (2nd ed.), trans. G. E. M. Anscomb. New York: Macmillan.

Wrightsman, L. S. (1988), *Personality Development in Adulthood.* Newbury Park, CA: Sage.

Wynne, L. C. & Wynne, A. R. (1986), The quest for intimacy. *J. Mar. Fam. Ther.*, 12(4):383–394.

Yalom, I. D. (1975), *The Theory and Practice of Group Psychotherapy* (2nd ed.). New York: Basic Books.

Youniss, J. (1980), *Parents and Peers in Social Development.* Chicago: University of Chicago Press.

Index

A

Ackerman, N. W., 43n, 132, 134, *257*
Affect, 42, 68
Albee, Edward, *Who's Afraid of Virginia Woolf?*, 195–196, *257*
Alpert, J., 163, *259*
Analytic relationship. *see* Therapeutic relationship
Anderson, H., 39, 40, 214, *257*
Andolfi, M., *257*
 on family enactments, 211
Angelo, C., *257*
 on family enactments, 211
Angyal, A., *257*
 on health and neurosis, 103
Anxiety, 137, 144, 202. *see also* Figure/ ground connection
 family-of-origin theory and, 29, 30, 31
Aponte, H. J., 208, *257*
Aron, L., 203, 223, *257*
Assessment. *see* Family assessment
Attachment theorists, 138
Atwood, G. E., 161, *257*
Auerswald, E. H., *257*
 on physics, 47
Authoritativeness vs. authoritarianism
 family therapy orientations and, 220–221
 social systemic view and, 222–223
 strategic therapy and, 224–225
Autopoesis
 "New science" perspectives and, 50–51
 self organization and, 51–52

B

Bach, S., 11, *257*
Baker, L., 140, *262*
Bakhtin, M., 64, *257*
Bateson, G., 11, 26, 70, 133, 197, 216, *257*
 on analytic play, 217
 "cybernetic epistemology" and, 23–24
Beavin, J. H., 24, 88, 89, 180, *264*
Beebe, B., 74, *257*
Belsky, J., 232, *257*
Benjamin, J., 74, *257*
Bennett, L. A., 144n, *263*
Bennett, S., 217, *258*
Bertalanffy, L. von, 21–23, 52, *257*
Bion, W. P., 161, *257*
Bloch, D., 132, *257*
Blum, H. P., 197, *257*
Bograd, M., 184, *258*
Bollas, C., *258*
 on the "unthought known," 185
Bonamo, G. A., 185, *258*
Boscolo, L., 37, *263*
Boszormenyi-Nagy, I., 42, *258*
Boundaries, family patterning and, 100–101
Bowen, M., 25, 26, 28–30, 39, 75, 221, 222, *258*, *261*
 orientation of. *see* Family-of-origin theory
Bradbury, M., 7, *263*
Brighton-Cleghorn, J., 42, *258*
Brodkin, A. M., *258*
 on "remodernization" trend, 85
Bromberg, P., 107, *258*

Bronfenbrenner, U., 117, *258*
Bruner, J., 40, 70, 186, *258*
  on character, 81
  on self, concept of, 62
Burke, W. F., 194, 222, *258*, *264*

C

Carter, B., 25, 111, 112t, 113, *258*, *264*
Cecchin, G., 37, *262*
Chaos theory. *see* "New Science"
    perspectives
Character, 82, 103, 125
  Bruner on, 81
Chasin, R., 184, *258*
Child referrals, 237, 246. *see also*
    Referrals
  parental relationship and, 239–241
  sequencing and. *see* Internalization
Child therapy, 122–123
Chrzanowski, G., 122, *258*
Circular questioning, 38
Circularity, 122–126
  family systems perspective and,
    124–125
  parent–child relationship and, 122,
    123–125
Classical theory, 41, 46, 80, 134, 199,
    200, 237
  developmental theory and, 106, 107
  interpersonal perspectives and,
    46–47
Cohen, R., 241, *264*
Cohler, B. J., 107, 108, *258*
Combrinck-Graham, L., 111, *258*
Communication, 23, 89, 226. *see also*
    Relationship systems
  digital vs. analogic, 93–94, 98, 180
  paradoxical, 35–36
  schizophrenic, 24, 133
  strategic family therapy and, 35–36
Complementarity, 73
Confidentiality, 247
Constructivism, 5, 51, 62, 162, 197. *see*
    also Social constructionism

Countertransference, 2, 42, 194. *see*
    also Therapeutic relationship;
    Transference
  couples therapy and, 200
  figure/ground connection and, 195,
    213
  influence, self-to-self creation, 65
  "outsider" experience, 199–202
  reaction, Friedman on, 194–195
  tracking of, 202–203
    case example, 203–207
Couples therapy, 13, 15, 71, 184, 197
  countertransference and, 200
  cultural contextualization and, 78
  exclusion and, 201–202
  marriage and, 83, 195, 196
  referrals and, 232, 234
    case examples, 234–239, 250–251
  sharing information and, 242, 245
  therapeutic relationship and,
    201–202
Csikszentmihalyi, M., 217, *258*
Cultural contextualization, 79. *see also*
    Culture
  couples therapy and, 78
  family therapists and, 77, 80
  parenthood and, 78, 80
Culture, 2, 6, 7, 125, 142, 233. *see also*
    Rituals
  American, therapeutic movements
    and, 20–21
  Willi on, 253–254
Cybernetics, 23–24, 36, 53

D

Development. *see* Family systems
    model of development
Diagnosis. *see also* Family
    assessment; Psychoanalytic
    treatment
  diagnostic attributions,
    relationship patterns and,
    136–138
  family health and, 158–159
  identified patient and, 132–133, 135

strategic orientation
  family assessment and, 148–150
  symmetry vs. complementarity,
    142–143
  symptomatology and, 144–145
structural perspective,
    enmeshment and, 140–142
symptomalogy and, 132, 144–145,
    151
  family metaphor and, 133–135
  symptom uses, developmental
    assessment and, 138–140
Dickinson, E., *The heart has narrow
    banks*, 171
Dicks, H. V., *258*
  on tenacity in relationships, 71
Dramatic techniques
  enactment and, 184–185
  role play and, 183–184
  schema of representation and,
    185–186
  sculpting and, case example,
    186–191
Dreams, 7, 205, 206
Duhl, B. S., 98, *258*
Duhl, F., 98
Dyrud, J., *258*
  on the illusory other, 74

E

Eagle, M., 185, *258*
Eagleton, T., *258*
  on metaphor, 172
Eating disorders, case example,
    150–151, 245
Ehrenberg, D. B., 216, 218, *258*
Ellman, B., 25, *260*
Empathy, 161, 199
Enactments, 102, 132, 184–185, 208,
    211, 219. *see also* Family
    therapists
  case example, 208–210
Enmeshment, 140–142, 150
Epston, D., 39, 40, 214, *258*, *265*
Erickson, G. D., 23, *258*

Erickson, M. H., 36, *258*
Erikson, E. H., 107, *258*
Existential family therapy, 159
  hypothetical clinical application of,
    35
  Whitaker's orientation, 33–35
Experiential family therapy, 25, 39.
    see also Existential family
    therapy
Extended family systems theory, 25.
    see also Bowen; Family-of-
    origin system

F

Fairbairn, W. R. D., 71, 73, *259*
Falicov, C. J., 138, *259*
  on symptomatology, 113
Families and Family Therapy
    (Minuchin), 140
Family assessment, 145. *see also*
    Family *related topics*
  first interview, 146–151
    case example, 150–155
  the genogram and, 155–158
  the second session, 151–155
Family health, diagnosis and, 158–159
Family life cycle, 105, 158
  case example, 115–117
  differentiation and, case example of
    adolescent, 115–117
  stage theory and, 110–112t, 113
    normative expectations and,
    114–115
  transitional points, referrals and,
    232–233
Family-of-origin theory (Bowenian
    orientation), 28–30, 39, 177n,
    211, 213
  anxiety and, 29, 30, 31
  constructs of, psychodynamic
    theory and, 28
  genograms and, 28–29
  hypothetical clinical application of,
    30–31
  psychoanalysts and, 28, 29

Family patterning, 98–99
  boundaries and, 100–101
  case example, 87, 91–92
  family therapists and, 87–89, 92
  interactional view, 88–89
  psychoanalysis and, 101–104
Family rules
  family roles and, 25, 70
  Jackson on, 69–70
  relationship contextualization and,
    68–72
Family sculpting, punctuation and, 98
  case example, 99, 186–191 *see also*
    Dramatic techniques
Family structure, 1, 118, 120, 158
  authority and, 120–121
  extended family support, case
    example, 119–120
  Haley on, 109
  multigenerational, 28–29
  sibling relationships and, 121–122
  structural model and, 32–33,
    118–119
Family systems model of
    development, 9. *see also*
    Circularity; Family life cycle;
    Family systems theory;
    Psychoanalytic developmental
    theory
  case example of Little Hans,
    108–110
  compared to psychoanalytic,
    105–106
  personal history in, 126–130
Family systems theory, 7, 21–24, 100.
    see also Authoritativeness;
    Experiential family therapy;
    Extended family systems
    therapy; Family systems
    model of development; Family
    therapists; Narrative
    movement; Strategic family
    therapy; Structural family
    therapy; Systems theory
  patriarchy and, 25, 26

psychoanalytic perspectives and.
    see Figure/ground connection
  systems theory and, 21–24, 42
Family therapists, 68, 118, 139, 217. *see
    also* Family patterning; Family
    therapy
  clinical practice and, 16–17
  compared to psychoanalysts, 80,
    105, 227
    authoritativeness and, 221–222
    contertransference, 195–196,
      199–202, 211–213
    developmental theory, 105–106,
      126–130
    intervention versus
      interpretation, 161–164
    nested contexts and, 67–68
    playfulness, 218–220
    referral policy and, 232–233
    self concepts and, 62–63, 81
    transgenerational exploration
      and, 74–75
  cultural contextualization and, 77,
    80
  family therapy enactments and,
    208, 210–213
    case example, 208–209
  Haley on, 134
  psychoanalytically oriented, 41–43
  thematic discontinuity and, 60–61
  therapeutic authenticity and,
    225–227
Family therapy. *see also* Family
    systems theory; Interventions;
    Nested contexts; "New
    Science" perspectives;
    Psychoanalysis
  case example: the Gibsons, 27–28,
    30–31, 33, 35, 38–39, 50
  case example of role reversal, 56–57
  criticisms of, 84–85
  founding theorists of, 24–26
  movement, 8, 19–21
  outcome research regarding, 241n
  systems theory and, 49–50

theory, 21, 24, conceptual
   struggles, 45–46, 47
Willi on, 10
Feedback loops, 89, 95
   punctuation and, 90, 91
Feminism, 1, 25, 84
   case example, 56–57
Figure/ground relationship of
   psychoanalysis and family
   therapy, 11–12
   case example, 8–10
   countertransference and, 195, 213
   personified self and, anxiety and,
      14–15, 41
   transference and, 12–13, 195, 213
Fisch, R., 37, *264*
Fish, V., 51, *259*
Fleeson, J., 138, *263*
Forrest, T., 41, *259*
Forster, E. M., 184
Frame of therapy, 11–12, 197
   in relation to context, 67–68
Framo, J., 75, *259*
Freud, S., 11, 46, 105, 192, *259*
   on Little Hans, 108
   transference and, 193–194
Friedman, E. H., 185, *259*
Friedman, L., 193, *259*
   on countertransference reaction,
      194–195

G

Galler, F., 223, *261*
Galveston Family Institute, 39
Geertz, C., 6, *259*
Genijovich, E., 158n, *259*
Gender issues, 84
Genograms, 164–165f
   family assessment and, 155–158
   family-of-origin theory and,
      28–29
Gergen, K. J., 67, 140, 253, *259*
   on social interchange, 54–55
Gerson, M. J., 41, 43, 166, *259*
Ghent, E., 195, 222n, *259*

Gill, M. M., 162, 194, 202, *259*
Glaser, S., 184
Gleick, J., *260*
   on chaos theory, 48
Goldberg, A., 106, *260*
Goldenberg, H., 5, *260*
Goldenberg, I., 95, *260*
Goldner, V., 84, *260*
Goodrich, T. J., 25, *260*
Goolishian, H. A., 39, 40, 214,
   257
Green, A., 200, *260*
Greenberg, J. R., 58, 162, *260, 262*
Grotstein, J. S., 210, *260*
Group therapy, 19–20, 42
Guerney, B., 31, *262*
Gurman, A., 241n, *260*

H

Haley, J., 25, 26, 39, 222, *260*. *see also*
   Strategic family therapy
   on family structure, 109
   on the family therapist, 134
Halstead, K., 25, *260*
Hare-Mustin, R., 25, *260*
Harris, A., 63, *260*
Havens, L., *260*
   on clinical concern, 17
Henry, W. P., 197, *260*
Hermans, J. M., 64, *260*
Hervis, O., 241, *264*
Hirsch, I., 163n, *260*
Hoffman, I. Z., 53n, 161, 202, 223,
   259, 260
Hoffman, L., 32, 51, 53–54, *260*
Holt, R. R., 24, *260*
Horner, T. M., 105, *260*
Huizinga, J., 220, *260*

I

Identified patient, 132
Imber-Black, E., 52, 179, *261*
   on larger systems, 52–53
Individuation, 115

Internalization
  sequencing and, 237–238
  treatment and, 238–239, 240–241
Interpersonal perspectives, 14, 41, 73,
    80, 200, 224
  classical theory and, 46–47
  developmental perspective of,
    106–107
Interpretation, 161–163
Interventions. *see also* Dramatic
    techniques; Psychoanalytic
    treatment; Punctuation;
    Reframing; Rituals; Family
    sculpting; Task assignment;
    Metaphor
  extended case example, 164–167,
    169, 173–176, 182
  interpretations and, 161–163
    analytic perspective and, 177–178
  psychoanalytic treatment and,
    191–192
  reframing, 181–183
Intimate relationships, 1, 10, 12, 15,
    42

J

Jackson, D. D., 24, 35, 69–70, 88, 89,
    180, 226, *261*, *264*
  on family rules, 70
Jacoby, R., 20, *261*
James, W., 64, 128, *261*
Jantsch, E., 49, *261*
Joyce, J., *Portrait of the Artist*, 7

K

Kantor, D., 98
Kaufman, E., 144n, *261*
Kaufman, P. N., 144n, *261*
Kaye, K., 121, *261*
Keeney, B. P., 102, *261*
Kempen, J., 64, *260*
Kernberg, O., 101, *261*
Kerr, M. E., 177n, *261*
Kessel, F., 117, *258*

Kessen, W., *258*
  on developmental psychology, 117
Kniskern, D. P., 33, 241n, *260*, *262*
Kobak, R. R., 191, *261*
Kohut, H., 82n, 199, *261*
  self psychology and, 14, 25, 80, 131
Korzibsky, A., 5, *261*
Kurtines, W., 241, *264*

L

Lachmann, F. M., 74, *257*
Lang, M. E., 232, *257*
Laplanche, J., 162, *261*
Lasch, C., 84, *261*
Lau, A., 233, *264*
Lesser, R., 121, *261*
Leupnitz, D., 25, *261*
Levenson, E. A., 11, 13, 46, 90, 107,
    161, *261*
  on the patient, 135–136
  on psychoanalytic frame for
    therapy, 197
Levenson, T., *261*
  on cellos, 48–49
Lichtenberg, J., 223, *261*
Lidz, T., 43n, *261*
Liminality, 166–167, 191
Lionells, M., *261*
  on a "unique self," 254
London, N. J., *261*
  on transference play, 219

M

McGee, C., 184, *262*
McGoldrick, M., 111, 112t, 113, *258*,
    262
Madanes, C., 26, *261*
  on power negotiations, 143
Marlin, E., 155, *261*
Marriage, 196. *see also* Couples
    therapy
  as a rule-governed system, 70–71
  transitional difficulties in, 139–140
Masson, J. M., 77, *261*

Maturana, H., 54
  autopoesis and, 50–51
Mead, M., 23
Memory, 68, 107–108
  storage and retrieval of, 107–108
Mental Research Institute (MRI), 25
Metaphor, 92, 171–173
Milan group, 37–38
  on task prescription, 170
Miller, M., 35
Minuchin, P., 138, 262
Minuchin, S., 8, 25, 26, 31–33, 39, 45,
    47, 51, 57, 75, 100, 132, 140–142,
    168, 184, 221, 262
  on complementarity, 73
  on fluctuation, family level of
    functioning and, 49
  orientation of. *see* Structural family
    therapy
  on relativism, 54
  on systems thinking, 24
  on therapeutic relationship,
    221–222
  on therapist's message, 170
Mitchell, S. A., 63, 162, 163n, 216, 262
Montalvo, B., 31, 262
Murray, E., 241, 264

N

Narrative perspective on character,
    81–83
Narrative movement, 39
  "externalization" and, 40
  hypnotic induction and, 40–41
  key figures in, 39
Neill, J. R., 33, 262
Nested contexts. *see also* Cultural
    contextualization; Narrative
    distinctions; Relationship
    contextualization
  family therapy and, 72, 79, 82,
    83–85
Neutrality. *see* Psychoanalytic
    treatment

"New science" perspectives. *see also*
    Autopoesis
  chaos theory, 48–49, 55
  order out of fluctuation and, 49–50
  physics and, Auerswald on, 47
Newton, P. M., 223, 262
  on systemic context of analyst, 223
Nichols, M. P., 5, 31, 262

O

Oates, J. C., 262
  on the 60s generation, 254
Object relations theory, 15, 46, 63, 71,
    200, 238
  developmental perspective of, 106,
    107
  disowned parts of self, 71–72
  systems theory and, 42–43
Ogden, T., 72, 262
O'Hanlon, B., 41, 262
Outcome research, 241n

P

Palazzoli, M., 26, 37, 170, 263
  on rituals, 179
Palo Alto Institute, 26, 35
Papp, P., 25, 98, 172, 262, 264
Paradoxical communication, 35–36
Parental relationship, 121. *see also*
    Circularity; Parenthood
  child referrals and, 239–241
Parenthood, 42, 120, 196, 232. *see also*
    Interventions; Parenting
  cultural contextualization and, 78,
    80
  transition to, 232
Parenting, 2, 124–125, 207, 237
Pathology, 10, 20, 131, 142
Patient–therapist interaction. *see also*
    Therapeutic relationship
  psychoanalysis and, 11–12
  psychotherapy, therapeutic
    outcome and, 196–197
  as a transference construction, 15

Penn, P., 38n, *262*
Personified self, 12, 14–15
    case example, 72. *see also* Figure/
        ground connection
Piercy, F. P., 241n, *262*
Pinsof, W., 241n, *260*
Pizer, S. A., *262*
    on metaphor, 172
Playfulness, 220–221. *see also*
        Psychoanalytic developmental
        model
Playing and Reality (Winnicott), 216
Pontalis, J. B., 162, *261*
Portrait of the Artist (Joyce), 7
Posada, V., 241, *264*
Pragmatism, American, 7
Prata, G., 37, *263*
Prigogine, I., 49
Primary process, 34–35
Projection, 15, 135
Projective identification, 12, 72n
Psychoanalysis, 7, 45, 63, 161, 197,
        212, 221, 255. *see also*
        Psychoanalysts;
        Psychoanalytic *related topics*
    "Americanization" of, 20–21
    family patterning and, 101–104
    patient–therapist interaction and,
        11–12
Psychoanalysts, family therapy and,
        5–6, 7–8, 192. *see also* Family
        therapists
    context of therapy, 67–68
    family-of-origin theory and, 28,
        29
    family patterning and, 87–88
    family systems approach and, 2–3,
        8, 39, 43n, 227
        developmental theory and, 115,
            120, 124–125
        playfulness and, 215–216
        therapeutic relationship and, 193,
            197–198, 200, 201, 213–214
Psychoanalytic developmental
        theory, 106–108, 121–122. *see*
        also Family systems
        developmental theory;
        Psychoanalysts
    developmental unfolding,
        playfulness and, 215–217
    early formation theory and, 107–108
    family systems developmental
        model and, 105–110
        classical theory and, 106, 107
        early formation theory and, 105,
            106, 107–109
        playfulness and, 217–219
        normative end points and, 117–118
Psychoanalytic theory, 62, 163n, 195.
        see also Classical theory;
        Intersubjective perspectives;
        Object relations theory; Self
        psychology
    development of, conceptual
        struggles and, 46–47
    link to systems theory, 15–16
Psychoanalytic treatment, family
        therapy and, 214. *see also*
        Therapeutic relationship
    child therapy and, 122–123
    countertransference and, 194–195
    cultural context and, 253–255
    diagnosis and, 131–132, 138, 143–144
    interpretation and, 161, 162–163
    interventions and, 161, 181, 191–192
    metaphoric language and, 172–173
    neutrality and, 58–60, 198–199
    redundancy vs. immediacy and,
        60–62
    referrals and. *see* Referrals
    working through and, 42, 61–62
Psychoanalytically oriented family
        therapists, 41–43
Psychosomatics, 140–141
Punctuation
    case example of, 91–92, 96–98
    communication and. *see*
        Relationship systems
    eliciting a central metaphor, 92–97
    family sculpting and, 98–99

feedback loops and, 90, 91
repunctuation, bypassing insight
and, 94–95

R

Racker, H., 162, *262*
Rampage, C., 25, *260*
Real, T., *262*
 on efficacy, 214
Referrals, 13, 241. *see also* Child
 referrals
 across treatment paradigms, 1–2,
 229–231, 236–237, 249
 case example, 250–251
 insight vs. behavior change and,
 231–232
 psychoanalytic theory and,
 230–231
 combining treatment approaches
 for, 246–247
 therapeutic interactions and,
 247–249
 couples therapy and, 232, 234
 family life cycle and, 232–233
 information and, sharing vs.
 restricting, 242–246
 "out" vs. persistence "within," case
 examples, 234–236
Reframing, 181–183
Reiss, D., 144n, 221, *263, 264*
Relationship contextualization. *see
 also* Relationship *related topics*
 complementarity and, 73–74
 family rules and, 68–72
 family therapists and, 67, 68, 75
 transgenerational contextualization
 and, 74–77
Relationship patterns
 diagnostic attributions and, 136–138
 dissociated, 211–212
 object relations theory and, 71–72
Relationships, 7, 42. *see also* Intimate
 relationships; Therapeutic
 relationship

Relationship systems,
 communication and, 88–89,
 93–94
Representational modes, 185–186
Resistance, 12, 103, 135, 174
Richardson, M., 163, *259*
Rio, A., 264, *264*
Rituals, 6, 181
 case example, 179–180
 cultural, therapy process and,
 178–179
 in psychoanalytic treatment, 181,
 191–192
Rivas-Vazquez, A., 241, *264*
Roberto, L., 151, *262*
Roberts, J., 179, *261, 263*
Role play, 183–184
Rorty, A., 81, 82, *263*
Rorty, R., 7, *263*
Rosman, B., 140, *262*
Roth, J., 163n, *260*
Roth, S., 184, *258*
Rovine, M., 232, *257*
Ruland, R., 7, *263*
Russell, B., 36, *265*

S

Sacks, O., 93, 94, *263*
Sampson, H., 73, *264*
Sander, F., 196, *263*
Sandler, J., 74, *263*
Satir, V., 25, 26, 35, *263*
Schact, T. E., 197, *260*
Schafer, R., 40, *263*
 on "literal corporealizations,"
 238
Scharff, D., 42, *263*
Scharff, J., 42, *263*
Schechner, R., *263*
 on performance, 183
Schecter, D., 107, *263*
Schimek, J. G., 194, *263*
Schizophrenic communication, 24,
 133
Schumer, F., 31, *262*

Schwartz, M., 19, *263*
Schwartz, R., 5, *262*
Sculpting, *see* Family sculpting
Scopetta, M., 241, *264*
Self, 7, 10, 67, 70n, 71, 106, 254. *see also* Family therapists; Personified self
    cohesion, 63, 135
    concept of distributive, 62–64
    differentiation, 28, 29, 30
    multiple versus singular, 63–64
    organization, autopoesis and, 51–52
        external versus internal, 64–65
    personal history, 127–130
Self psychology, 42, 58, 63, 136
    developmental perspective of, 106, 107
    Kohut and, 14, 25, 80, 131
Sequencing. *see* Internalization
Siegel, L. I., 41, *263*
Silverstein, O., 102, 225, *261*, *264*
Simon, R., 132, *257*, *263*
    on disintegration of family systems, 50
    on Whitaker, 35
Singer, E., 220, *263*
Skynner, A. C. R., 41, *263*
Social constructionism, 53–55, 221
Spence, D. P., 102, 162, 218, *263*
    on interpretation, 90
Sprenkle, D., 241n, *262*
Sroufe, L. A., 138, *263*
Stanton, A., 19, *263*
State theory. *see* Family assessment
Stegner, C., 199, *263*
Steinglass, P., 144n, *263*
Stern, D. B., 54n, *263*
Stern, D. N., 63, 93, 238, *263*, *264*
Stern, P. N., 140, *264*
Stierlin, H., 42, *264*
Stolorow, R. D., 161, *257*
Strachey, J., 162, *264*

Strategic family therapy (Haley's orientation), 25, 26, 35–38, 53, 159. *see also* Diagnosis
    authoritativeness and, 224–225
    circular questioning approach of Milan school, 37–38
    communication and, 35–36
    hypothetical clinical application, 38–39
        "second/first order change" and, 36–37
Structural family therapy (Minuchin's orientation), 25, 31–33, 39, 159, 184, 211. *see also* Family structure
    diagnosis and, 140–142
    family subsystems and, 31, 32
    hypothetical clinical application of, 33
Strupp, H. H., 197, *260*
Sullivan, H. S., 12, 14, 32, 46, 63, 125, 163n, 221, *264*
    on inner psychological life, 14–15
    on malevolent transformation, 122
Sulloway, R. J., 107, *264*
Symptomatology, family functioning and, 113, 133–135, 144, 158. *see also* Diagnosis Systems theory. *see also* Family systems theory
    context sensitivity and, 84
    family therapy and, 49–50
    larger-system perspective and, 52–53
    object relations theory and, 42–43
    problems of power, 53–55
Szapocznik, J., 241, *264*

T

Tamura, T., 233, *264*
Tansey, M. J., 194, *264*
Task assignment, 167–168
    case example, 169–176
        analytic perspective, 177–178
    intensity of therapist's message and, 169–170

metaphoric language and, 171-173
Milan group style of, 170-171
Therapeutic movements, American
culture and, 20-21
Therapeutic relationship, 7, 68, 77,
196-198, 223. *see also*
Patient-therapist interaction;
Transference and
countertransference
asymmetry vs. mutuality and,
222-223
authoritative versus authoritarian,
220-225
couples therapy and, 201-202
family systems vs. psychoanalytic
approach, 197, 223
circle of intimacy and, 199-200
issue of power, 53-55
neutrality and, 198-199
playfulness, 218-220
transference/countertransference
and, 193-196, 200-201
Transference, 2, 10, 15, 28, 60, 77, 87,
101, 193-194, 219. *see also*
Countertransference; Figure/
ground connection
contextual, transgenerational
phenomena and, 42-43
countertransference exploration,
237
countertransference matrix, 68,
69
Freud and, 193-194
interpretation, constraints on, 250
issues, exploration of, 178
message, dreams and, 206
play, London on, 219
Transgenerational phenomena
contextual transference and, 42-43
irrational role assignment, 125
relationship contextualization and,
74-77
Whitaker on, 75
Triangulation, 15, 76, 135
clinical situation and, 29-30

Turner, V., 191, 217, *264*
on liminality, 166-167
on rituals, 180

U

Unconscious, 7, 12, 163n, 193, 422

V

Van Gennep, A., 191, *264*
Van Loon, R. J. P., 64, *260*
Varela, F., 54
autopoesis and, 50-51
Visher, E. B., 140, *264*
Visher, J. S., 140, *264*

W

Wachtel, E. F., 155, *264*
on neurosis, 231
Wachtel, P. L., *264*
on neurosis, 231
Walters, M., 25, *264*
Wamboldt, F. S., 221, *264*
Waters, D. B., 191, *261*, *264*
Watzlawick, P., 24, 35, 37, 88, 147,
180, *264*
on communication, 89
on rituals, 179
Weakland, J. H., 26, 35, 37, *264*
Weiner, N., 23, *264*
Weiss, J., 73, *264*
Wheelis, A., *264*
on thought and action, 171
Whitaker, C., 20, 25, 26, 33-35, 39,
159, 221, *265*
on transgenerational exploration,
75
orientation of, *see* Existential family
therapy and, 33-35
White, K. M., 107, *259*
White, M. E., 39, 40, 214, *258*, *265*
White, S. E., 117, *258*
Whitehead, A., 36, *265*
on progress, 5

Whiting, R., 179, *261*
Who's Afraid of Virginia Woolf? (Albee),
      195–196
Willi, J., 11, *265*
   on culture, 253–254
   on family therapy, 10
Wilson, M. N., 119, *265*
Winnicott, D. W., 10, 42, 63, 161, 162,
      199, *265*
   Playing and Reality, 216
Wittgenstein, L., *265*

Wolin, S., 144n, *263*
Working through. *see* Psychoanalytic
      therapy
Wrightsman, L. S., 105–106, *265*
Wynne, A. R., 83, *265*
Wynne, L. C., 83, *265*

Y

Yalom, I. D., 20, *265*
Youniss, J., 221, *265*